The Territorial Battalions

A PICTORIAL HISTORY
1859–1985

by

Ray Westlake

HIPPOCRENE BOOKS INC
New York

SPELLMOUNT LTD
Tunbridge Wells, Kent

To Johanne

In the Spellmount Military list:

The Uniforms of the British Yeomanry Forces 1794–1914 Series:
The Sussex Yeomanry
The North Somerset Yeomanry
The Yorkshire Hussars
Westmorland and Cumberland Yeomanry
3rd County of London (Sharpshooters)
Duke of Lancasters Own Yeomanry
Yorkshire Dragoons
Lovat Scouts

The Yeomanry Regiments – A Pictorial history
Over the Rhine – The Last Days of War in Europe
Riflemen Form
History of the Cambridge University OTC
Yeoman Service

In the Nautical list:
Sea of Memories

First published in the UK 1986 by
Spellmount Ltd
12 Dene Way, Speldhurst
Tunbridge Wells, Kent TN3 0NX
ISBN 0–946771–68–5

First published in USA 1986 by
Hippocrene Books Inc,
171 Madison Avenue,
New York, NY 10016
ISBN 0–87052–309–0

British Library Cataloguing in Publication Data
Westlake, Ray
   The Territorial battalions : a pictorial history.
   — (Militaria pictorial history)
   1. Great Britain. *Army, Territorial and Army*
Volunteer Reserve — History
   I. Title   II. Series
   355.3′7′0941   UA661

Designed by Words & Images, Speldhurst, Tunbridge Wells, Kent.
Typeset by Metra Graphic, Southborough, Tunbridge Wells, Kent.
Printed in Great Britain by Adlard and Son Ltd, Dorking, Surrey.

Contents

Foreword

This interesting, well documented and illustrated book gives an admirable overall history of the Territorial Army and some of the teeth arm units who form it.

The section dealing with the Post-War Re-organisations covers in outline some of the recent changes but the events of the period from 1965 were so dramatic that they are well worth recording. As I was the Director of the TA at the time I was, so to speak, at the receiving end.

In 1965 the Labour Government of the day demanded considerable savings in the defence budget. To meet this the relevant military authorities at the time produced a plan for a saving of £20 million which would not affect the Regular Army. The onus was to fall on the TA. In all fairness it must be admitted that quite a number of units were well below strength and well above average age. Sergeants messes were full. War service medal ribbons gleamed.

A plan was concocted, virtually in secret, without the knowledge of either the TA Council or even the GOCs of the Home Commands of the United Kingdom.

Furthermore its details were not announced until the day before the House of Commons rose for the Summer recess. It had been reckoned that the scheme might cause a ten day furore and then evaporate. How wrong they were.

In effect it virtually decimated the TA, renamed it the Territorial and Auxiliary Voluntary Reserve, and divided it into various categories.

What hurt was the disbandment of large numbers of teeth arm units, Regiments with long and distinguished service records.

The result was an outcry in the press and the start of a brilliant campaign led by Bernard Duke of Norfolk, President of TA Council and supported by all the County Associations. One of the many features of the battle was a letter in *The Times* decrying the plan and signed by six Field Marshals.

The climax came in December when it was debated in the House of Commons and the Labour Government of the day squeezed home with a majority of one.

The Government reacted quickly and set up a Committee under the Under Secretary of State for War consisting of the military authorities and members of the TA Council.

Out of this was born what was known as TAVR III which in effect was the resuscitation of 87 teeth arm units of Yeomanry, Artillery and Infantry in the form of home defence battalions. They were armed with rifles and the odd machine gun, a few civilian type wireless sets and about three or four Land Rovers.

Despite this, the morale was such that units carried on cheerfully, went to camp, and above all retained their old cap badges.

Two years later in 1968 the same Government reneged and disbanded TAVR III.

Fortunately two years later there was a change of Government with a Prime Minister who had commanded a Gunner Regiment in the war, and the TAVR came into its own again.

Over the years it has improved, grown in strength and been given up-to-date equipment. The old name TA has been restored. As a fighting force it has an active role in the order of battle in BAOR and is now probably better manned and equipped and more efficient than ever before in its history.

I believe these facts are worth remembering and in what better setting than this splendid history.

Major General Sir James d'Avigdor-Goldsmid

Introduction

It would not be possible within these pages, to make an attempt at any form of complete written record of the Territorial infantry. Each individual battalion has given sufficient service to justify a volume to itself. What has been endeavoured, however, is to show the history of the part-time infantrymen in pictures. I hope that the fine uniforms and enthusiasm of the early volunteer, together with the camouflage and high standard of efficiency of the soldier of the modern-day Territorial Army is apparent.

The book has been arranged according to the old 'County' regiments that would be well known to most readers even though some have not existed as such for over 20 years. The regiments appear according to their order of precedence. Each regimental section contains a record of the lineage and a brief account of the war service for every battalion that constituted part of the Territorial Army.

Generally the book is only concerned with units while serving in an infantry role and therefore included as part of the 'corps' or 'family' of a regular regiment. On the occasion where infantry battalions were converted to other arms, their subsequent records have not been included and are considered outside the scope of this work.

It is hoped that readers will gain from this book some understanding of the service provided by part-time soldiers over the past 125 years. It is also hoped that an interest in this aspect of military history has been kindled and that further studies have been encouraged.

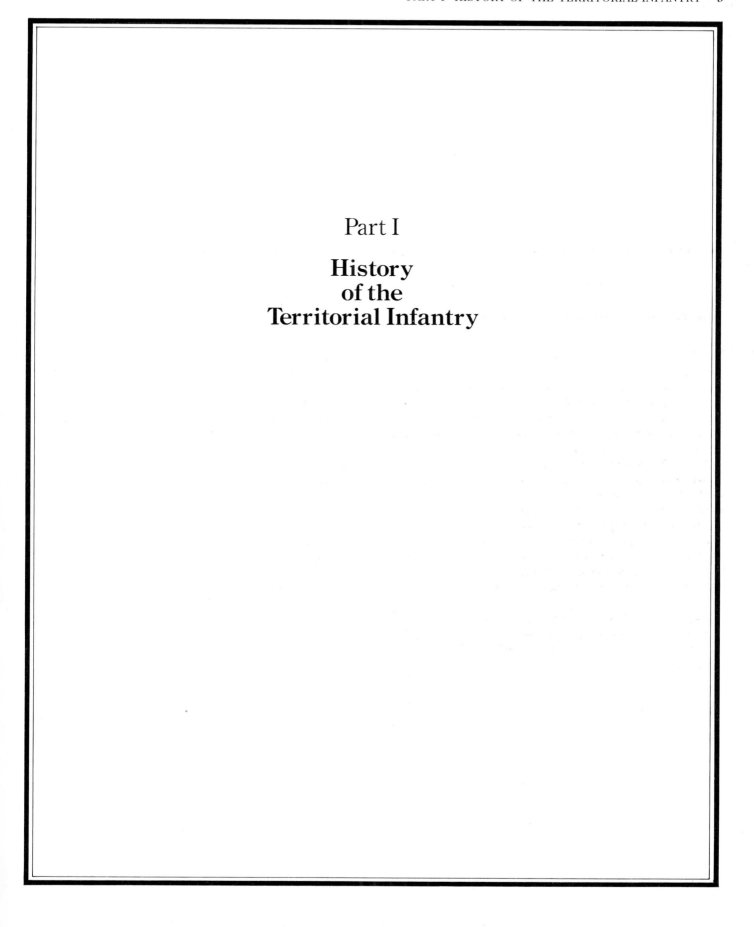

Part I

History
of the
Territorial Infantry

1 The Volunteer Force

The history of the territorial infantry officially dates from 1859, when in that year the Volunteer Force was created under the provisions of an act passed in 1804. The 'Volunteer Act' had been introduced to provide the large number of non-regular troops that were required due to the declaration of war by France in 1793. As a home defence force, the 'Volunteers' were armed and trained, ready for any attack on Britain by the enemy.

Although a full-scale assault was always thought to be imminent, and there were some 150,000 men of the French Army mustered at Boulogne during 1804, no invasion ever took place. The Volunteers were subsequently stood down after Waterloo.

In the following years of peace, the British Government, as far as the volunteer infantryman was concerned, required no defence force. His mounted counterpart in the Yeomanry Cavalry, however, was allowed to continue service, and was to do good work as an aid to the authorities in times of civil unrest.

In a large number of cases, former volunteer units retained their arms and subsequently organised themselves into 'Rifle Clubs'. Such bodies were completely unofficial, and although receiving no assistance from the Government, trained on military lines and kept up a good standard of musketry.

After the regular Army, there existed a second force for the defence of the realm – the Militia. The history of this force is quite separate and is not part of the succession of the volunteer movement and the Territorial Army. Briefly, it dates back to Tudor times and was a form of part-time conscripted service, each county being expected to fill a quota determined by the government. On occasions it was embodied for long periods. It was, in many respects, the inadequacies of the Militia system that prompted the volunteer movement in the 1790s and the mid-nineteenth century.

By 1847, a number of politicians were of the opinion that Britain's home defences needed to be reviewed. The Duke of Wellington was as concerned as most and did not share the general opinion of the Government that the United Kingdom was in fact, safe from attack. 'It is wrong,' he commented, 'to sit back in a false sense of security', and urged that a substantial defence force be immediately set up.

Stirred by the Duke's opinions, fresh attempts were made to organise a force of volunteer riflemen. These were turned down by the Government who thought that an organisation of any size, and containing 'amateur soldiers', would be of

The Victoria Rifles. Coloured aquatint by J. Harris after Orlando Norie, published in 1859. The uniforms of this corps were green with black facings, black belts with silver badges.

Above
The 1st Norfolk Rifle Volunteers in camp at Gunton Park, 1864. From an oil painting by Claude Lorraine Nurset. **National Army Museum**

Below
Captain Williams of the 19th Middlesex Rifle Volunteer Corps, c1862. The 19th wore grey uniforms at this time.

little military value and would possibly interfere with the recruiting of the Regular Army. Further opposition came from influential quarters who were not in favour of the proposed intention of including the commercial, artisan, or working classes in an armed force: previous volunteering had been confined to those that could maintain the expense of uniforms, arms and ammunition.

A typical example of this attitude is illustrated in a letter from Lord Hardwicke, in which he suggests that, 'a man who has no property to lose could hardly be relied upon to fight, if a weapon was given to such a man,' he went on, 'his natural tendency would be to acquire a property which he had not.'

In 1852, however, the services of a corps of riflemen at Exeter were offered to the Government. The unit was accepted and the following year Her Majesty Queen Victoria signed commissions appointing the officers of the Exeter and South Devon Rifle Corps, later the 1st Devonshire Rifle Volunteers and the senior battalion of volunteer infantry. Following the example of Exeter, the Royal Victoria Rifle Club, was also given the authority to form a corps in London.

It was not until 1859 that the Government eventually gave way and permitted the large scale formation of volunteer rifle corps throughout the country. This change in policy had come about due to the current menacing attitude towards Britain by the French, who believed that the British Government was in league with Italy, the instigators of a recent attempt on the life of Emperor Napoleon III.

With a large number of the regular army committed abroad, and the daily threats of invasion appearing in the French press, the British public was greatly alarmed about the security of Britain. Throughout the country, numerous meetings were set up to debate the problem and to take the names of those that were willing to enrol in rifle corps. There was no shortage of volunteers and by 9 May, when the famous poem by Lord Tennyson was published in *The Times*, many thousands were ready to take up arms.

> There is a sound of thunder afar,
> Storm in the South that darkens the day,
> Storm of battle and thunder of war,
> Well, if it do not roll our way,
> Storm! storm! Rifleman form!
> Ready, be ready to meet the storm!
> Rifleman, rifleman, rifleman form!

Christ Church Company, Oxford University Rifle Volunteers, in quad, 28 May 1864.
National Army Museum

On 12 May 1859, sanction to form a volunteer force, in the form of a circular addressed to the Lord Lieutenants of Counties, was issued. Each county was asked to submit any plans that it may have regarding the formation of corps under the Volunteer Act of 1804. The main points of the Act were summarised in the circular as follows: that the officers' commissions should be signed by the Lord Lieutenant; that volunteers could be called out in the case of actual invasion, or rebellion; while under arms members of a corps would be subject to military law and while on active service no member could quit his unit. He could, however, at other times leave after giving 14 days notice.

The next circular concerning the formation of volunteer corps was issued on 25 May. In the main, this document made clear the views of the Government regarding the corps. Requirements as to the standards of drill and discipline were set out and the establishment of ranges for each corps was advised. It was also suggested in the circular that rifle volunteers should be organised into companies or sub-divisions.

The third War Office circular of 1859 was issued on 13 July and again made clear the Government's requirements regarding arms and training. Accompanying the circular was a memorandum which, among other things, fixed the 'establishment' (the numerical strength) of each rifle corps. A company was to consist of not less than sixty or more than one hundred effectives. These were to be officered by one captain, one lieutenant and one ensign. Sub-divisions were to have thirty 'effective' riflemen with one lieutenant and one ensign. Where several companies were raised in the same locality, a battalion could be formed. Then the requirements were for eight companies or a total strength of not less than five hundred. In addition to its company officers, a battalion could have a lieutenant-colonel, a major and the services of an adjutant.

Lieutenant C. S. Alderson of the 5th Yorkshire West Riding Rifle Volunteer Corps, c1876. The 5th had their headquarters in Wakefield and bore on their badges a fleur de lys from the town Arms. **York Castle Museum**

It was in the memorandum of 13 July that the subject of precedence was settled. Each arm of the Volunteer Force was to rank more or less on the lines of the regular forces. At the time of the memorandum, Rifles were to rank after Artillery volunteers as these were the only arms then in existence. Within a short time, however, others were created and the precedence list of volunteers read as follows: Light Horse, Artillery, Engineers, Mounted Rifles and Rifles.

The precedence of a corps within its county was indicated by the number allotted to it by the Secretary of State for War. The procedure was that when the Lord Lieutenant received an application for the formation of a corps, he would note its date and forward the offer of service on to the War Office. When the Secretary of State for War had satisfied himself that the proposed corps had fulfilled the necessary conditions, he would allot the corps its number according to the date entered on the application by the Lord Lieutenant. The corps was then informed of its acceptance for service by the Queen. It is the date of the letter bearing this information that is considered to be the official formation date of a corps. As a rule these dates coincide with the precedence number assigned. However, on occasion a number was allotted but due to some special circumstances where reference had to be made to the corps, owing to some informality in its offer of service, the acceptance date was held up. Very soon after the acceptance of the corps and the assignment of its number, the gazetting of the officers was proceeded with.

Very few letters accepting the services of corps have survived and therefore the official date of formation is not known. However, as the date borne on the commission of the corps' first officer varies in the majority of cases by only a matter of weeks, these are now generally accepted.

Above left
2nd South Middlesex Rifle Volunteer Corps, c1870. Dark grey uniforms with scarlet collar, cuffs and piping were worn. The shako has a star pattern badge bearing the Arms of Middlesex, a red band and pom-pom. **Major R. McDuell**

Above right
11th Middlesex Rifle Volunteer Corps. This corps was formed in the Parish of St George, Westminster and wore a cap badge of St George and the Dragon, 1870s. **National Army Museum**

Below left
Kent Rifle Volunteers, Musician.

Below right
The London Scottish. The uniform of the London Scottish is Elcho grey, named after the corp's first Commanding Officer, Lord Elcho, with blue collar, cuffs and piping. The doublet is edged with silver lace and has two thistle badges on the collar, 1890s.

Below left
Cover of a song-sheet published in 1860
showing an early uniform of the 79th
Lanarkshire Rifle Volunteer Corps.
Below right
Robert Pudimore and his son, Robert James
Pudimore both of the 15th (Bourne)
Lincolnshire Rifle Volunteer Corps c1870.
E. Dickinson

County precedence was settled according to the date on which the first company in the county was formed. The eventual order of seniority is still acknowledged today and is as follows:

1. Devonshire
2. Middlesex
3. Lancashire
4. Surrey
5. Pembrokeshire
6. Derbyshire
7. Oxfordshire
8. Cheshire
9. Wiltshire
10. Sussex
11. Edinburgh (City)
12. Essex
13. Northumberland
14. Renfrewshire
15. Northamptonshire
16. Dorsetshire
17. Norfolk
18. Staffordshire
19. Berkshire
20. Gloucestershire
21. Brecknockshire
22. Suffolk
23. Stirlingshire
24. Bucks
25. Lanarkshire
26. Kent
27. Glamorgan
28. Nottinghamshire
29. Merionethshire
30. Yorkshire (W. Rid.)
31. Leicestershire
32. Mid-Lothian

33. Aberdeenshire
34. Roxburgh
35. Cinque Ports
36. Monmouthshire
37. Cornwall
38. Ross-shire
39. Worcestershire
40. Inverness-shire
41. Warwickshire
42. Lincolnshire
43. Denbighshire
44. Hampshire
45. Somersetshire
46. Forfar
47. Cambridgeshire
48. Shropshire
49. London
50. Yorkshire (E. Rid.)
51. Hertfordshire
52. Perthshire
53. Berwickshire
54. Sutherland
55. Kincardineshire
56. Haverfordwest
57. Haddington
58. Isle of Wight
59. Ayrshire
60. Dumfries
61. Elgin
62. Argyll
63. Cardigan
64. Durham

65. Wigtown
66. Buteshire
67. Yorkshire (N. Rid.)
68. Cumberland
69. Herefordshire
70. Dumbartonshire
71. Huntingdon
72. Carnarvonshire
73. Montgomeryshire
74. Orkney
75. Carmarthen
76. Caithness
77. Kirkcudbright
78. Westmorland
79. Fifeshire
80. Bedfordshire
81. Newcastle-on-Tyne
82. Linlithgowshire
83. Selkirkshire
84. Banffshire
85. Radnorshire
86. Flintshire
87. Berwick-on-Tweed
88. Clackmannan
89. Tower Hamlets
90. Nairn
91. Peeblesshire
92. Isle of Man
93. Kinross-shire
94. Anglesey
95. Shetland

Facing page:
Left
Two Highland volunteers, the figure on the left being of the 105th Lanarkshire Rifle Volunteer Corps, c1876. **J. B. McKay**
Right
36th Middlesex Rifle Volunteer Corps.
Below
29th Middlesex Rifle Volunteer Corps, c1876. The 29th wore green uniforms with black facings. **Major R. McDuell**

This page:
Right
Sergeants of the 2nd Bucks Rifle Volunteers. The 2nd Bucks was formed from members of Eton College and wore grey uniforms with light blue facings, 1870s. **J. G. Woodroff**
Below
Cadet of the 38th Middlesex (Artists) Rifle Volunteer Corps. The subject of the photograph is a member of the fife and drum corps, 1870s.

By the beginning of 1860 it was realised by the War Office that due to the unforeseen number of independent companies formed, some kind of higher organisation was necessary. In a circular issued to Lord Lieutenants of counties dated 24 March, suggestions for companies to merge either as consolidated or administrative battalions were put forward.

A consolidated battalion, the circular explained, 'applies to a battalion whose constituent companies are drawn from the same town or city'. When such a battalion was formed the corps involved were to lose their original numbers and continue service either as numbered or lettered companies. It was also laid down that after consolidation the new corps would thereafter be known by the number previously held by its senior company. An example of this procedure was in Lanarkshire, when at the beginning of 1860 several corps formed in Glasgow, the 19th, 23rd, 24th, 28th, 36th and 41st, were united under the title of – 19th Lanarkshire Rifle Volunteer Corps.

The administrative battalion was usually formed from corps situated in rural areas. In this case each battalion was designated, i.e. 1st Administrative Battalion of Shropshire Rifle Volunteers, and was allotted its own staff and headquarters. The corps included in an admin battalion, unlike those that were consolidated, remained distinct and financially independent units and were permitted to retain their county numbers. The object of the formation of an administrative battalion, according to a memorandum dated 4 September 1860, '. . . is to unite the different corps composing it under one common head, to secure uniformity of drill among them, and to afford them the advantage of the instruction and assistance of an adjutant; but it is not intended to interfere with financial arrangements of the separate corps, or with the operation of the respective rules, or to compel them to meet together for battalion drill in ordinary times, except with their own consent'.

HER MAJESTY'S
REVIEW AT WINDSOR.

ON Saturday next, the 20th of June, 1868, to enable those Officers of the Post Office who are Volunteers to attend the Review, Letters will be delivered in London as follows, viz.:—

At	7.30 a.m.	At	4.10 p.m.
,,	9.30 ,,	,,	6.10 ,,
,,	12.10 p.m.	,,	7.30 ,,
,,	2.10 ,,		

On the same day Letters will be collected from the Receiving Offices and Pillar Boxes

At	4. 0 a.m.		At	4. 0 a.m.	
,,	8.30 ,,		,,	8.30 ,,	
,,	11. 0 ,,	In the	,,	10.45 ,,	
,,	1. 0 p.m.	Eastern	,,	12.45 p.m.	
,,	3. 0 ,,	Central and	,,	2.45 ,,	In the
,,	4. 0 ,,	Western	,,	4.45 ,,	other
,,	5. 0 ,,	Central	,,	5.30 ,,	Districts.
,,	5.30 ,,	Districts.	,,	6. 0 ,,	
,,	6. 0 ,,		,,	9. 0 ,,	
,,	9. 0 ,,				

By Command of the Postmaster General.

[401]

Printed by W. P. Griffith, 5, Langley Street, Long Acre, W.C.

Facing page:
Above left
39th Middlesex Rifle Volunteer Corps, 1877. A green uniform with scarlet collar and cuffs is being worn.
Above right
Notice showing amended delivery and collection times in London, allowing members of the Post Office who are volunteers, to attend a Review by the Queen at Windsor on 20 June 1868. **B. Boon**
Below left
Captain Edmund Hemingway of the 43rd Yorkshire West Riding Rifle Volunteer Corps. The 43rd was a member of the 3rd Admin Battalion of Yorkshire West Riding Rifle Volunteers and wore the battalion's uniform consisting of scarlet tunic with blue collar and cuffs, white piping and silver lace. The headdress is grey and the trousers blue with a red stripe, c1876. **York Castle Museum**
Below right
Lieutenant F. Crook, 29th Yorkshire West Riding Rifle Volunteer Corps, c1875. The scarlet tunic has a blue collar edged with silver lace. The cuffs are also blue and have silver cord Austrian knots. **York Castle Museum**

This page:
Above
Rifle Volunteers at the Wimbledon Ranges during the 1870s. **National Army Museum**
Below
An officer of the 1st Lincolnshire Rifle Volunteer Corps c1867. **E. Dickinson**

In counties where there were insufficient corps to constitute a battalion, these companies were permitted to join that of one of its neighbours. Single corps, where situated in a border area, were occasionally included in a battalion from outside of its county. Admin battalions were also permitted to consolidate if and when they chose.

Corps were designated, i.e. 1st Essex RVC, and in the first regulations published for volunteers in 1861, special titles in addition to numbers were permitted.

By General Regulations and Instructions of 2 July 1873, the United Kingdom was divided into seventy infantry sub-districts. Each was designated as a 'Sub-District Brigade' and to it were allotted for recruiting purposes, two line battalions and the Militia and volunteers of a certain area. This was the first sign of a closer association of the volunteers with the regular forces.

A committee was set up in 1878 (under the presidency of Viscount Bury, Parliamentary Under Secretary of State), to look into the organisation of the Volunteer Force. The recommendations did not include any material changes in its composition, but the consolidation of the existing administrative battalions was recommended.

This page:
Above
Drums and Bugles, 2nd Volunteer Battalion, Royal Fusiliers. Each man wears a 'drum' badge on the right arm. The buglers also play the fife which is carried in the long white pouch worn on the waist belt when not in use, 1890s.
Below
Members of the 1st Volunteer Battalion, Hampshire Regiment resting while on manoeuvres, c1895.

Facing page:
Above
Silver and gilt helmet plate of an officer of the 3rd London Rifle Volunteer Corps, 1880–c1902.
Below
Shooting Team, 2nd Kent (East Kent) Rifle Volunteer Corps, c1880s.

During 1880 these recommendations of the committee were carried out and all remaining admin battalions were consolidated. By the practice laid down in 1860, the corps contained within each battalion lost their independent status and became lettered companies of the new corps. The new corps also, at first, took on the number of its senior corps, but in counties that had more than one unit, this created a series of numbers with many unallotted. By June 1880, a general re-numbering within each county had begun and corps were numbered from one onwards. Only Suffolk, which in 1880 had its corps organised into two battalions, chose to retain the original numbers, 1st and 6th, adopted at the beginning of the year.

The 1881 reorganisations of the army that formed the old sub-districts into territorial regiments are well known. In general the regular infantry lost their old regimental numbers and were from then on to be known by the county titles that are familiar today. The volunteer corps, who were now to constitute 'volunteer battalions' of the new regiments, were to be numbered in a separate sequence, apart from the regulars and militia. This change in designation was carried out over a period of time, each battalion being notified in General, later Army, Orders. It was the 1st, 2nd and 3rd Somersetshire Rifle Volunteer Corps who were the first to adopt the new style, when under General Order 261 of October 1882, they assumed the titles of – 1st, 2nd and 3rd Volunteer Battalions, The Prince Albert's (Somerset Light Infantry).

The following is a list of line regiments together with the various rifle volunteer corps that provided volunteer battalions.

Royal Scots:	1st, 2nd Edinburgh, 1st, 2nd Midlothian, 1st Haddington, 1st Linlithgow, 1st Berwick.
Queen's:	2nd, 4th, 6th, 8th Surrey.
Buffs:	2nd, 5th Kent.
King's Own:	10th Lancashire.
Northumberland Fus:	1st, 2nd Northumberland, 1st Newcastle.
Royal Warwickshire:	1st, 2nd Warwick.
Royal Fusiliers:	5th, 9th, 10th, 11th, 22nd, 23rd Middlesex, 1st Tower Hamlets.
King's Liverpool:	1st, 5th, 13th, 15th, 18th, 19th Lancashire, 1st Isle of Man.
Norfolk:	1st, 2nd, 3rd, 4th Norfolk.
Lincolnshire:	1st, 2nd Lincoln.
Devonshire:	1st, 2nd, 3rd, 4th, 5th Devon.
Suffolk:	1st, 6th Suffolk, 1st, 2nd Cambridge.
Somerset LI:	1st, 2nd, 3rd Somerset.
West Yorks:	1st, 3rd, 7th Yorks West Riding.
East Yorks:	1st, 2nd Yorks East Riding.
Bedfordshire:	1st, 2nd Herts, 1st Bedford.
Leicestershire:	1st Leicester.
Yorkshire:	1st, 2nd Yorks North Riding.
Lancashire Fus:	8th, 12th, 17th Lancashire.
Royal Scots Fus:	The Galloway, 1st, 2nd Ayrshire, 1st Dumfries, 1st Roxburg and Selkirk.
Cheshire:	1st, 2nd, 3rd, 4th, 5th Cheshire.
Royal Welsh Fus:	1st Denbigh, 1st Flint and Carnarvon.
South Wales Borderers:	1st, 2nd, 3rd Monmouth, 1st Brecknock.
King's Own Scottish Borderers:	1st Roxburgh and Selkirk, 1st Berwick, 1st Dumfries, The Galloway.
Cameronians:	1st, 2nd, 3rd, 4th, 7th Lanark.
Gloucestershire:	1st, 2nd Gloucester.
Worcestershire:	1st, 2nd Worcester.
East Lancs:	2nd, 3rd Lancashire.
East Surrey:	1st, 3rd, 5th, 7th Surrey.
Duke of Cornwall's:	1st, 2nd Cornwall.
Duke of Wellington's:	4th, 6th, 9th Yorks West Riding.
Border:	1st Cumberland, 1st Westmorland.
Royal Sussex:	1st, 2nd Sussex, 1st Cinque Ports.
Hampshire:	1st, 2nd, 3rd, 4th Hants, 1st Isle of Wight.
South Staffs:	1st, 3rd, 4th Stafford.
Dorsetshire:	1st Dorset.
South Lancs:	9th, 21st Lancashire.
Welsh:	1st Pembroke, 1st, 2nd, 3rd Glamorgan.
Black Watch:	1st Fife, 1st, 2nd, 3rd Forfar, 1st, 2nd Perth.
Oxfordshire LI:	1st, 2nd Oxford, 1st, 2nd Bucks.
Essex:	1st, 2nd, 3rd, 4th Essex.
Sherwood Foresters:	1st, 2nd Derby, 1st, 2nd Notts.
North Lancs:	11th, 14th Lancashire.
Northamptonshire:	1st Northampton.
Royal Berks:	1st Berks.
Royal West Kent:	1st, 3rd, 4th Kent.
Yorkshire LI:	5th Yorks West Riding.
Shropshire LI:	1st, 2nd Shropshire, 1st Hereford.
Middlesex:	3rd, 8th, 11th, 17th Middlesex.
King's Royal Rifle Corps:	1st, 2nd, 4th, 5th, 6th, 9th, 10th, 11th, 12th, 13th, 21st, 22nd, 25th, 26th, 27th Middlesex, 1st, 2nd, 3rd, 4th London.
Wiltshire:	1st, 2nd Wilts.
Manchester:	4th, 6th, 7th, 16th, 17th, 20th, 22nd Lancashire.
North Staffs:	2nd, 5th Staffords.
York and Lancaster:	2nd, 8th Yorks West Riding.
Durham LI:	1st, 2nd, 3rd, 4th, 5th Durham.
Highland LI:	5th, 6th, 8th, 9th, 10th Lanark.
Seaforth Highlanders:	1st, Elgin, 1st Inverness, 1st Ross, 1st Sutherland.
Gordon Highlanders:	1st, 2nd, 3rd, 4th Aberdeen, 1st Banff, 1st Kincardine and Aberdeen.
Cameron Highlanders:	1st Inverness.
Argyll and Sutherland:	1st Argyll, 1st Clackmannan, 1st Dumbarton, 1st, 2nd, 3rd Renfrew, 1st Stirling.
Rifle Brigade:	7th, 14th, 15th, 16th, 18th, 19th, 20th, 21st, 24th, 26th Middlesex, 1st, 2nd Tower Hamlets.

Private of the 7th (Clackmannan and Kinross) Volunteer Battalion, The Argyll and Sutherland Highlanders. The uniform worn here includes a scarlet doublet with yellow collar and cuffs, and trews of 42nd pattern tartan, c1890.

Member of the 3rd Volunteer Battalion Cheshire Regiment, 1901. An old badge of the Cheshire Regiment – an Acorn, is worn on the white collar.

By no means all corps assumed the new designations and several, whilst taking their place in their regiment's volunteer listing, chose to retain their rifle volunteer titles. These, however, were required to change, i.e. from 1st Dunbartonshire Rifle Volunteer Corps, to 1st Dunbartonshire Volunteer Rifle Corps in 1891.

The organisation of the volunteer infantry into brigades commenced in 1888. Nineteen were created under Army Order 314 of July which were followed by a further twelve in September (Army Order 408). The number of battalions forming each brigade varied from just three in one case, to seventeen in another. In 1890 additional brigades were formed and the battalions distributed on a more even basis. The next change affecting the volunteer infantry brigades occurred in 1906 when under Army Order 130 the total was brought up to forty-four.

13ᵗʰ Mˣ (Queen's Westminster) R.V. – Bugler.

This page:
Above
1st Volunteer Battalion, Royal Fusiliers with transport, c1905. **5th (V) Bn, Royal Regiment of Fusiliers**
Below
Bugler of the 13th Middlesex (Queen's Westminster) Rifle Volunteer Corps. The Westminsters wore a grey uniform with scarlet collar and cuffs, 1890s.

Facing page:
Above left
Post card sent by a member of the 1st Volunteer Battalion, Worcestershire Regiment while at camp in Porthcawl during August 1907.
Above right
Colonel W. C. Horsley, Lieutenant Colonel Commandant of the Artists Rifles, 1907. The Colonel wears the Volunteer Decoration. **J. G. Woodroff**
Below
Queen's Westminsters shooting team at Bisley, 1907.

VOLUNTEERING

A little "butt" practice.

This page:
Above – 26th Middlesex (Cyclist) Rifle Volunteer Corps. Note the special fitting for carrying the rifle on the cycle.
Below left – 2nd Middlesex (South) Rifle Volunteer Corps. The collar badges worn are the crest and motto of Viscount Ranelagh who commanded the Corps from its formation until 1885.
Below right – Medical Detachment, 3rd London Rifle Volunteer Corps, 1907.

Facing page:
Above – 1st Cadet Battalion, Royal Fusiliers at its Hampstead headquarters, 1903.
Below – Harrow School Volunteers skirmishing at Chorley Wood, c1906.

1st CADET BATTALION. THE ROYAL FUSILIERS.

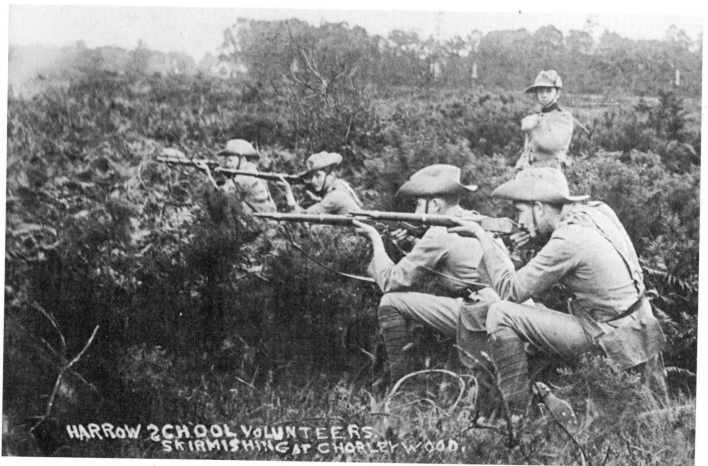

HARROW SCHOOL VOLUNTEERS.
SKIRMISHING AT CHORLEY WOOD.

Above
Group of volunteer sergeants attending a musketry course. The seated figure in the centre is a member of the School of Musketry, 1880s.
Right
4th Volunteer Battalion, The Queen's (Royal West Surrey Regiment). Worn with the green uniform is valise equipment that includes water-bottle, mess-tin, haversack and two ammunition pouches, 1890s.

2 The Boer War 1899–1902

Although it was the South Africa War of 1899–1902 that gave the volunteers as a whole their first opportunity of active service overseas, two earlier campaigns used non-regulars in the field. In 1882, two officers and 100 men from the 24th Middlesex Rifle Volunteer Corps, sailed for Egypt where they were to undertake work as an Army Post Office Corps. The 24th was in fact recruited from the Post Office in London, and its members all postal workers were well suited for the requirements of the Expeditionary Force. The 24th were later awarded the rare battle honour, 'Egypt 1882'.

Following the success of the Post Office Corps in Egypt, it was decided that a section devoted to Telegraph duties also be formed from the ranks of the 24th Middlesex. This was styled as the Field Telegraph Corps and in 1885 served along with a postal detachment at Suakin in the Sudan. Also present in the Sudan were members of two northern Volunteer Engineer Corps who were to do good work on a railway constructed between Suakin and Khartum.

With a threat of war in 1899 in South Africa, the volunteers once again offered their services. Lt. Col. Eustage Balfour, of the London Scottish, is on record as being the first to come forward, and recommended that a special service company be formed by his unit to be used in the event of war.

Even after 11 October 1899, when war was eventually declared in South Africa, the War Office still declined the offers of assistance from the volunteers.

Above
Colonel W. H. Mackinnon, Colonel-Commandant of the City Imperial Volunteers, 1900.
Right
Group of volunteers at Ladysmith, 1900.

'The cost of transporting them,' it was maintained, 'would be as much as that for regular troops, their eventual effect being nowhere near as efficient.'

It would seem that the turning point in the Government's attitude to the use of volunteers in South Africa occurred during December 1899. In that month the Army had experienced three major defeats within six days, 'the Black Week', resulting in serious public concern in Britain and a demand for changes in military command and tactics.

On 20 December, the formal offer by the Lord Mayor of London, Sir Alfred Newton, to raise and equip 1,000 men from within the City of London, was accepted by the War Office. This force, which was funded to a large extent by City banks, livery companies and West-end firms, became known as The City Imperial Volunteers. It eventually went overseas consisting of one infantry battalion, two mounted infantry companies and one battery of Vickers-Maxim quick-firing guns.

The CIV was made up by existing volunteer regiments from the London area, each being invited to supply a small contingent, proportionate to its strength at the time. Volunteers to join were so many and competition so keen, that a high standard of fitness and efficiency was laid down. In one company alone there were some 30 senior NCOs serving in its ranks as privates.

The infantry of the CIV sailed for South Africa in three contingents, leaving Southampton between 13 and 27 January. It arrived during February and after a period of preliminary training was posted to the 21st Brigade under General Bruce Hamilton. As part of the brigade, and serving alongside men of the Royal Sussex Regiment, the Sherwood Foresters and the Cameron Highlanders, the CIV joined the mobile column under Lord Roberts prior to its start on the long

Above left
The Oswestry members of the 1st Volunteer Service Company, King's Shropshire Light Infantry on 13 February 1900. **G. Archer Parfitt**
Above right
Members of the CIV on board the SS 'Briton' en route for South Africa, 1900.
Below left
Queen's Westminster's Detachment, City Imperial Volunteers, 1900.
Below right
Volunteers from Brighton and Hove photographed on their return from South Africa, 10 June 1901.

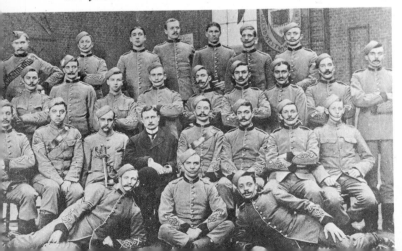

Bugler A. D. Pink of the CIV Mounted Infantry Detachment, 1900.

march to Pretoria. While on the march the volunteers were to receive their baptism of fire, taking part in the action at the Zand River and in the Battle of Johannesburg.

With the success at Johannesburg, Lord Roberts was then able to enter Pretoria. After a few days' rest the CIV moved out to attack General Botha who was then in command of the hills just outside of the city. The battalion played a big part in the battle of Diamond Hill in which two volunteers were killed and some twenty more wounded. The battalion was later to encounter Christian de Wet at Freederickstadt. It pursued him over a distance of 224 miles in 14 days but lost the guerrilla leader who escaped through the Magalisberg range of mountains.

The battalion eventually left South Africa in October 1900, arriving at Southampton on the 27th. Upon reaching London, the volunteers were welcomed by a great crowd which accompanied them on their march through the capital. The return of the CIV was to resemble a great state occasion, the streets being lined by the volunteer battalions from which the unit had been formed, and the day ending in a great banquet at the Guildhall.

While the CIV was being organised, a Special Army Order dated 2 January 1900 authorised the raising of a number of volunteer service companies by county regiments. Each was to contain 116 men between the ages of 20 and 35, they were required to be first class shots, physically fit, of good character, passed as 'efficient' for the last two years and preferably unmarried.

In order to overcome the legal restrictions of the Volunteer Act, the volunteers were required to enlist into the regular army, the service period being one year. The number of companies formed were to be one for each regular battalion then serving in South Africa. The several volunteer battalions of a regiment were to raise the company which, upon arrival in South Africa, would be attached to its affiliated regiment and under the orders of its commanding officer.

Having reached South Africa, the volunteer service companies joined their regiments and throughout the year served alongside their comrades in the regular forces. The history of their service is that of their parent regiments.

With their service completed, the first series of volunteer companies were ordered home. Their places was taken by a newly-formed group which had been raised under an Army Order issued in January 1901. These in turn came home after seeing a great deal of action and were again replaced by a fresh draft in 1902.

With the ending of the Boer War the volunteers returned to their normal duties and training, much having been learned from their experiences on active service. In 1905 the battle honour 'South Africa', together with the years during which companies had been provided, was granted to volunteer battalions in commemoration of their services during the Boer War. However, since all volunteer battalions were still technically Rifle Corps, they possessed no colours on which to bear the new honour. It was recorded below the title of the battalion in the *Army List*, and on many occasions included in the blank spaces and empty scrolls that were a feature of the volunteers version of the regulars' badges.

3 Formation of the Territorial Force 1908

By 1907 the volunteer infantry was made up of 221 battalions. Each regular regiment in England, Scotland and Wales contained a number of volunteer units that ranged in number from only one of the Dorsets to the eleven of the King's Royal Rifle Corps. There were no volunteers in Ireland at this time.

In addition to these battalions there were also in existence some eight cadet battalions, and almost 200 cadet units, usually at company strength. Cadet formations were affiliated to volunteer battalions, whose responsibility it was to provide suitable training, and prepare the boys for possible enrolment into the Volunteer Force when they became of age.

10th (County of London) Battalion, The London Regiment (Paddington Rifles), Longmoor Camp, August 1910.

Left
5th Battalion, Argyll and Sutherland Highlanders, 1910.
Right
Recruiting poster, 25th (County of London) Cyclist Battalion, The London Regiment, c1912.

Under the Army reforms, introduced by the Secretary of State for War – Richard Haldane in 1907 – the existing Yeomanry and Volunteer Forces were to be combined under a new organisation to be known as The Territorial Force. In his Territorial and Reserve Forces Bill, Mr Haldane set up an establishment of 14 Divisions, each including three Infantry brigades of four battalions. Further infantry battalions were attached to divisions as Army Troops and as part of a coastal defence system.

The transfer of the volunteers to the new force was, for the infantry at any rate, a fairly straightforward matter. The vast majority of battalions simply continued service under a new designation and with the regiment to which they were previously attached. Whereas before, the volunteer battalions of a regiment were numbered in a separate sequence, the territorial scheme included its infantry battalions in one series of numbers. The regulars would usually be the 1st and 2nd Battalions, followed by the Militia (now Special Reserve) as 3rd and then the territorials in their turn.

When the Territorial Force came into being on 1 April 1908 the above plans were quickly put into effect. As already mentioned, a large proportion of the volunteer infantry changed to the new system with little or no disturbance. In several cases, however, volunteer units were required to reorganise to such an extent that their members chose not to continue service and subsequently to resign. In one case, that of the 1st Volunteer Battalion, Royal Sussex Regiment, the whole battalion stood down at the news of their proposed conversion to an artillery unit.

Two further innovations of the 1908 reforms, concerning the non-regular forces, were the establishment of several new regiments made up entirely of territorials, and the creation of the Officers' Training Corps.

The new regiments were created under the titles of – Monmouthshire, Cambridgeshire, Hertfordshire, Herefordshire and lastly, from the Greater London area, the London Regiment.

The formation of the Officers' Training Corps saw the old Inns of Court Volunteers reorganised into a unit for the training of officers both for the Territorial Force and Special Reserve. Also under the title of Officers' Training Corps, contingents were formed from the university battalions at Oxford and Cambridge, and other university companies. Junior contingents were created from the former public school cadet corps of the Volunteer Force.

Artists Rifles at camp, 1913.

As with the volunteer system, territorials could not be ordered overseas and were intended for use as a home defence force. However, provisions in the form of an 'Imperial Service' section were made to enable a man to volunteer for service abroad if required. Upon joining the Imperial Service Section, a territorial was permitted to wear above the right breast a badge consisting of tablet inscribed 'Imperial Service' surmounted by a crown. An additional distinction of the section was that any unit of the Territorial Force, having achieved 90% of its strength as overseas service volunteers, could place below its title in the *Army List* the words 'Imperial Service'. Very few formations were ever to reach this target, those of the infantry being the 6th Battalion, East Surrey Regiment and the 7th and 8th Middlesex.

Another aspect of the Territorial Force that gave its members the opportunity of additional service was the 'Special Service Section'. Members were distinguished by an arm badge consisting of three 'S's enclosed within a circle and surmounted by a crown. They were expected to turn out in cases of national emergency, for the purposes of defence within the United Kingdom even when the Territorial Force had not been embodied as a whole.

4th and 5th Battalions, Royal Scots. Painted by R. Caton Woodville, c1910.

5th Battalion, Royal Sussex Regiment. This photograph shows the Colour Party that received the battalion's first set of Colours from the King in June 1909 at Windsor.

5th Battn Royal Sussex Regt Colour Party, Windsor Castle.

Collotype No 51.x

Facing page:
Above
Pipers of the Liverpool Scottish, c1909.
Below
25th (County of London) Cyclist Battalion,
The London Regiment, at Church Parade,
Lewes Camp, 1909.

This page:
Above
Sergeant of the 5th Battalion, King's Liverpool
Regiment, c1909.
Below
25th (County of London) Cyclist Battalion,
The London Regiment at the Royal Naval and
Military Tournament.

Royal Naval and Military Tournament – Olympia.
Cyclist Display – 25th (County of London) Cyclist Batt.n

Drummers of the Artists Rifles, c1913.

4 The First World War 1914–18

Mobilisation of the regular and territorial troops was ordered on 3 August 1914. Despite the Imperial Service provision, there were severe restrictions, written into the constitution of the Territorial Force, to the sending of territorial units overseas. It was some time before they were relaxed and, in any event, the home defence task could not be left unfulfilled. The Secretary of State for War, Lord Kitchener, seeing the requirement for a very large number of new battalions, set about raising and training them under Regular Army auspices. The natural antagonism between professional and amateur traditions was understandably not far beneath the surface.

There were numerous battalions raised in the First World War and the Second World War which were accorded county regimental titles. Many of them, however, had no formal Territorial Force or Territorial Army antecedents, and thus have histories and traditions of their own beyond the scope of this work.

Thus in August 1914, the Territorial Force was at once sent to its wartime home defence stations. The next move was to replace the regulars, then serving overseas and now needed to reinforce the British Expeditionary Force in France and Belgium. Many battalions of the Territorial Force were now available for this purpose and the Government dispatched battalions to Egypt, India and the Mediterranean. Members of the 1st Battalion, London Regiment, as an example, were on duty guarding the railway between London and Newhaven in August 1914. By the middle of the following month they found themselves as part of the garrison in Malta.

It was also in September 1914 that the first territorials crossed to France, the

Cooks of the 3/23rd (County of London) Battalion, The London Regiment at Winchester 1916.

London Scottish being the first infantry battalion to land and subsequently see action at Messines on 30 October. This was the first major action of the war in which territorials were involved and heavy casualties were suffered, the London Scottish losing over 600 men that day.

The wartime organisation of the territorial infantry saw the formation of both second and third line battalions, the latter providing trained reinforcements for the front line formations. With this arrangement the original battalion was renumbered as e.g. 1st/4th Gordon Highlanders. The second line unit became 2nd/4th followed by the third as 3rd/4th Battalion.

In 1916 all third line units were redesignated as reserve battalions, e.g. 4th Reserve Battalion Gordon Highlanders. A further change took place in September of the same year which saw the reserve battalions of a regiment merged, usually as one.

Turning to the higher organisation of the territorial infantry during the First World War, each regional division received its new number in May 1915. The second line battalions were organised into second line divisions and received their numbers in August 1915.

Pre war division	First line number	Second line number
East Anglia	54th	69th
Highland	51st	64th
Home Counties	44th	67th
East Lancashire	42nd	66th
West Lancashire	55th	57th
1st London	56th	58th
2nd London	47th	60th
Lowland	52nd	65th
North Midland	46th	59th
South Midland	48th	61st
Northumbrian	50th	63rd
West Riding	49th	62nd
Welsh	53rd	68th
Wessex	43rd	45th

Band of the South Midland Infantry Brigade, c1915. At this time the Brigade consisted of the 5th Gloucestershire Regiment, 4th Royal Berkshire Regiment, The Buckinghamshire and 4th Battalions of the Oxfordshire and Buckinghamshire Light Infantry.

The new numbers were designated according to the order in which the Division went overseas. The 63rd, 64th, 65th, 67th, 68th and 69th, however, did not leave the United Kingdom.

Additional divisions to be formed during the war were – 71st, 72nd and 73rd, which were raised for home defence in November 1916, the 74th, formed in Egypt in March 1917 from dismounted Yeomanry regiments, and the 75th, also formed in Egypt during 1917. The components of the 74th Division were all redesignated as numbered battalions of infantry regiments.

By no means all territorial troops were included in the battalions that volunteered to serve overseas. At first any man that was unfit or unwilling to go abroad was included in the third line of his battalion. Later, in 1915, these personnel were withdrawn and formed into formations known as Provisional Battalions (TF). By 1916 all Provisional Battalions had been organised into ten Provisional Brigades. In November 1916 these battalions of the 6th, 8th and 9th Brigades were used to make up the three Home Service Divisions, 71st, 72nd and 73rd. In January 1917 Provisional Battalions became numbered territorial battalions of infantry regiments.

Members of 5th Battalion The Queen's (Royal West Surrey Regiment) with captured equipment, Ramadi, Mesopotamia, 1917.
Imperial War Museum

The service records of the First World War Territorial Divisions cover the entire conflict on all fronts. Those divisions that found themselves in Egypt, in 1915, were to do good work as part of the Suez Canal Defence Force before moving on to Gallipoli in May. Upon reaching the peninsula, men from such Lancashire towns as Bury, Rochdale and Salford, were to serve and die alongside other volunteers from Sydney, Melbourne and Brisbane, the famous Anzac soldiers.

The intensity of the fighting can be judged, for example, when in December 1915 the 53rd (Welsh) Division was withdrawn from Gallipoli. It had been reduced to just 162 officers and 2,428 other ranks. The wartime establishment was over 17,000 men.

Having returned to Egypt from Gallipoli, the 52nd (Lowland) Division later fought as part of No 3 Section, Canal Defences, in the Battle of Romani, where some 8,000 Turks were either killed or taken prisoner.

From Egypt a number of territorial divisions moved to Palestine in 1917. There they were to play major roles in the great battles of Gaza, Nabi Samweil, Jerusalem and Jaffa. Finally they were moved to the Western Front for the last months of the war.

Many territorial divisions spent their war service on the Western Front, seeing action throughout France and Belgium and later in the Italian Campaign. It was the 46th (North Midland) Division that gained the distinction of being the first complete territorial division to reach France, and indeed to arrive in any theatre of

1/25th (County of London) Cyclist Battalion, The London Regiment in India during the First World War.

war. With Divisional Headquarters originally at Lichfield, the twelve infantry battalions came from – Walsall, Wolverhampton, Burton, Handley, Leicester, Loughborough, Lincoln, Grimsby, Newark, Nottingham, Derby and Chesterfield. Having accepted the liability of foreign service, the division moved to France and between the 30 and 31 July one brigade was present at the 'liquid fire' attack at Hooge. The 46th later fought at Gommecourt and at the Hindenburg Line.

A number of territorial divisions fought in the Somme offensive of 1916, when on the 1 July a great British assault was launched against the German lines. The outcome of this attack resulted in some 60,000 men being killed, wounded or taken prisoner before nightfall. Almost half of the attacking force was lost that day, and some old territorial battalions were reduced in strength to just a handful of men.

The campaigns and battles that involved territorial battalions on the Western Front were many. London workers in the General Post Office, the Post Office Rifles, served with distinction at Vimy Ridge, Yorkshiremen of the 49th Division suffered the agonies of the first phosgene gas attack in December 1915, while territorials of the 6th Northumberland Fusiliers were to see the first tanks going into action at Flers-Courcelette on 15 September 1916, little knowing that future members of their battalion would serve in such machines during the next war.

For a number of territorial battalions, the First World War was spent in India. One division, the 44th (Home Counties), arrived at Bombay in early December 1914, and having reverted to peacetime conditions, posted its various infantry battalions to Lucknow, Cawnpore, Fyzabad, Mhow, Kamptee, Jubbulpore, Jhansi, Dinapore and Fort William. Two battalions were also sent to Burma where they were stationed at Rangoon and Maymyo.

Facing Page:
Above
1/9th Battalion, The Middlesex Regiment, en route for Amballa, 1917.
Below
Members of the Post Office Rifles with captured German mortar near Malard Wood, France, August 1918. **B. Boon**

While stationed in India, several territorial units were sent to Aden, Singapore, Hong Kong and other places, usually on garrison duty. A detachment of the 1/4th King's Shropshire Light Infantry served in the Anderman Islands during December 1914 and were later used to disarm a native battalion which was on the verge of mutiny.

In 1915, a number of territorial battalions were sent to Mesopotamia, where they replaced the casualties incurred by the British serving in that theatre of the war.

A small force that included territorials were also sent out to North Russia in 1918. Included in the expedition were the 1/9th Hampshire Regiment who, upon reaching home in December 1919, had completed a world tour of over 50,000 miles.

Above
2/8th Battalion, Middlesex Regiment, Gibraltar, June 1915. **Imperial War Museum**
Below left
Members of the 6th Battalion Seaforth Highlanders inspecting a German dug out after the capture of Greenland Hill by the 51st (Highland) Division, 29 August 1918.
Imperial War Museum
Below right
4th Battalion The East Lancashire Regiment in the trenches, France, September 1917. A periscope consisting of a mirror attached to a bayonet is being used to observe the enemy.
Imperial War Museum

London Territorials passing a ruined house on the La Bassee Road, 1914–18. **D. Barnes**

The 1st (City of London) Battalion, The London Regiment (Royal Fusiliers) passing through Trafalgar Square during the First World War Victory Parade. **5th (V) Bn, Royal Regiment of Fusiliers**

5 The Territorial Army 1920–39

The Territorial Force was in effect disbanded after the First World War. But this was purely a formality and in 1920 it was reconstituted. The Territorial Force was renamed Territorial Army with effect from 1 October 1921, and during the next months its allocation and organisation were set out.

The original fourteen divisions were to remain and be known under the numbers and titles that they received during the war. The same arrangement requiring three brigades to a division and four battalions to a brigade was retained, thus requiring a total of 168 infantry battalions. As the new plans did not include the infantry as Army Troops or as part of the Coastal Defence System, the pre-war number of battalions, of which there were 208, had to be reduced.

A number of battalions were not reformed in 1920, some were converted and transferred to other arms, as gunners or signallers but in the main the additional battalions were amalgamated in pairs. In some cases two battalions of a regiment would merge and simply adopt the number of the senior unit, an example of this

Above
Recruiting poster for the Territorial Army,
c1930.
Right
TA recruit taking instruction on the Vickers
machine gun. **5th (V) Bn, Royal Regiment**
of Fusiliers

Queen Mary presenting new Colours to the 4th Battalion, Queen's Royal Regiment (West Surrey), Croydon, 7 May 1938.

was the pairing of the 7th Battalion London Regiment with the 8th Battalion (Post Office Rifles) to form the 7th Battalion (Post Office Rifles). On other occasions two numbers would be incorporated, as in the case of the 7th/9th Battalion, Royal Scots.

One small but significant change in the history of the Territorial Army had occurred back in 1917. Ever since the linking of the volunteer battalions with regiments of the regular army in 1881, any honours displayed by the regulars on their badges were forbidden to the volunteers. Scrolls on badges that were inscribed with battle honours were either left blank or completely omitted until the Boer War provided the volunteers with their own distinctions. In Army Order 298 of 22 September 1917, the following instruction was issued – 'In consideration of the services of the Territorial Force during the war, His Majesty The King has been pleased to approve of units of the Territorial Force being permitted to wear on their badges the mottoes and honours worn on the badges of the corps, regiments or departments of which they are part.' However, the letter 'T' was still to be worn by officers on the collar, and by other ranks incorporated into the designation worn on the shoulder straps.

With the growing reality of mass attacks from the air in any future war, a number of infantry battalions of the 56th and 47th London Divisions, were converted to an anti-aircraft role in 1935. Formed on 15 December, the 1st Anti-Aircraft Division (Territorial Army) was to absorb seven of the old London Regiments and one battalion of the Essex. The units transferred either to the Royal Artillery or Royal Engineers and were trained in the use of anti-aircraft guns or searchlights. By 1940, however, all battalions had been incorporated into the Royal Artillery. The infantry battalions assumed their new roles, but being proud

Recruiting display, 2nd City of London Regiment, c1936. **5th (V) Bn, Royal Regiment of Fusiliers**

A territorial taking instruction on the Bren gun at the Small Arms School, c1939 **5th (V) Royal Regiment of Fusiliers**

of their infantry traditions and service, deeply resented the change. In effect, however, the old identities were never completely lost, as whatever their operational role they still considered themselves to be part of their old regiments.

With the subsequent formation of additional anti-aircraft divisions more infantry battalions were converted. Others were later transferred as battalions of the Royal Tank Corps, when in 1938 a major reorganisation of the Territorial Army saw each division reduced from twelve to nine battalions.

On 15 March 1939, the German Army marched into Czechoslovakia. With the international situation having deteriorated to this extent, the Government announced its plan to double the strength of the Territorial Army. A new infantry battalion was to be styled 'duplicate' and could be raised either by posting half the serving members of the 'original' battalion to the new unit and then completing the establishment of both with new recruits, or to set up a small cadre of officers and NCOs from an existing battalion and then build from that.

The numbering of 'duplicate' battalions usually followed after those already in existence. On some occasions, however, where a number had been left vacant due to a former battalion's conversion, this position was filled. Where two battalions had been merged in 1920 under a dual number, they were sometimes separated and the old individual numbers revived. By far the most frequent method of designating new units was to style them in the same way as those second line battalions formed in the First World War, e.g. 2/4th, 2/5th etc.

Above left
Men of the 2/7th Battalion, Middlesex
Regiment relaxing on a Bren carrier near
Anzio in 1943. **Imperial War Museum**
Above right
Private List of the 2/7th Battalion, Middlesex
Regiment sharing tea with an American
soldier in Italy 1943. **Imperial War**
Museum
Centre
Bren carrier, 5th Battalion, King's Own
Scottish Borderers, Waldefeucht in 1945.
King's Own Scottish Borderers
Museum
Below
Machine guns of the 1/7th Battalion,
Middlesex Regiment in action in Sicily, 1943.
Imperial War Museum

6 The Second World War 1939–45

Mobilised on 3 September 1939, a number of territorial divisions joined the British Expeditionary Force in France. They were subsequently involved in the fighting throughout May, and suffered heavy casualties during the retreat to Dunkirk. Having reached the coast, several units found themselves trapped outside the Dunkirk perimeter and were forced to fight their way down the coast to Brest. On the way, the 1st Queen Victoria's Rifles played a large part in the fierce fighting around Calais and were to serve with distinction alongside the regulars of the King's Royal Rifle Corps. South of the Somme, the 51st (Highland) Division became trapped at St. Valery and after an heroic stand was forced to surrender.

Territorials were later to serve in all theatres of war, particularly in North Africa, Libya, Burma, Malaya, Sicily, Italy and North West Europe. Other battalions fulfilled the important duties of home defence.

In 1939 some infantry regiments were joined by 'Home Defence' battalions. These had been formed from the existing National Defence Companies and consisted of men below the standard of fitness required for overseas service. Home Defence battalions assumed the next highest number available and undertook the protection of important areas and later the training of the Home Guard. These duties were later handed over to the Home Guard itself, and in 1941 all home defence units were allotted men suitable for field training and subsequently redesignated as the 30th battalions of their regiments.

Bren gunner, 4th Battalion, King's Own Scottish Borderers on the Maas in 1945.
King's Own Scottish Borderers Museum

7. Post-War Reorganisations

After the Second World War, changes in the strength, organisation and role of the territorial infantry were many. In 1947 vast reductions in the number of battalions occurred when most of the war-raised 'duplicate' units were either disbanded or merged back into their parent battalions. Also at this time, a good number were converted into regiments of the Royal Artillery. 1947 also saw the formation, for the first time, of infantry territorials in Ireland, the Royal Inniskilling Fusiliers, Royal Ulster Rifles and Royal Irish Fusiliers all receiving one battalion each. With the formation during the Second World War of the Parachute Regiment, and its inclusion as a regiment of the line, nine TA battalions were introduced in 1947. Four were formed by the conversion of existing battalions, while the remainder were new units. Another wartime organisation, the Special Air Service, also formed a territorial component in 1947.

This page:
4th Battalion, The Border Regiment leaving Carlisle Castle. **Border Regiment Museum**

Facing Page:
Above left
Members of the 7th Battalion, Argyll and Sutherland Highlanders on a battlefield tour in Germany, 1949. **Argyll and Sutherland Highlanders Museum**
Above right
Members of the 4th Battalion, Somerset Light Infantry at a camp briefing in 1957. The officer

During the years of National Service, the Territorial Army provided the continuation training for National Servicemen and Reservists, and thus for the first time in its history contained a non-volunteer element.

Further changes in organisation occurred in 1951, 1956 and 1961, but by far the greatest and most far-reaching was in 1967 upon the formation of the Territorial and Army Volunteer Reserve (T&AVR). At first the new system was divided into four categories, T&AVR I and II, which were to be styled as 'Volunteers', the first official use of the term since 1908, T&AVR III, which was to continue as 'Territorials' and T&AVR IV which included other categories of reserves such as University OTCs and bands. Each category had its own special terms of service and commitments.

HRH The Duke of Edinburgh, Honorary Colonel of the Liverpool Scottish, inspecting the Pipes and Drums of the regiment, Castlemartin Camp, 1960. **Liverpool Scottish Regimental Museum**

C (City of London) Company, 5th (V) Battalion, Royal Regiment of Fusiliers at the Lord Mayor's Show. **5th (V) Bn, Royal Regiment of Fusiliers**

Colour presented to the TAVR by the Greater London Council on 3 March 1979.
R. J. Marrion

The 4th Battalion, Somerset Light Infantry working with members of the Auxiliary Fire Service during a Civil Defence exercise.
Somerset Light Infantry Museum

Members of the 5th (Volunteer) Battalion, Royal Regiment of Fusiliers on the ranges, 1970s. **5th (V) Bn, Royal Regiment of Fusiliers**

Pipers of The London Irish, North Irish Militia, 1980s. **R. J. Marrion**

Above right
Colour Party The City of London Battalion,
Royal Fusiliers. **5th (V) Bn, Royal Regiment of Fusiliers**

Below left
Drum-Major of the 5th (Volunteer) Battalion,
The Queen's Regiment, 1980s.
R. J. Marrion

Below right
London Territorials taking part in the
'Courage Trophy' at the Duke of York's
Headquarters, Chelsea, 1970s.

Two members of the 4th Battalion, King's Own Border Regiment on exercise, 1982.
King's Own Border Regiment Museum

Four members of the 4th Battalion, King's Own Border Regiment on exercise, in 1982.
King's Own Border Regiment Museum

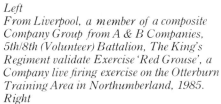

Left
From Liverpool, a member of a composite Company Group from A & B Companies, 5th/8th (Volunteer) Battalion, The King's Regiment validate Exercise 'Red Grouse', a Company live firing exercise on the Otterburn Training Area in Northumberland, 1985.
Right
A Royal Navy Helicopter from Yeovilton lifts 105mm Light Guns of 100 (Northumbrian) Field Regiment RA (V) on Exercise 'Northern Outlaw' on the Otterburn Training Area, in support of Territorials, 1985.
Major C. Vere

By 1969 all 'Territorial' battalions of T&AVR III had either been disbanded or reduced to a cadre of just eight men. However, a later change in Government policy saw these cadres expanded and formed into additional volunteer battalions.

Although the re-introduction of the term 'Volunteer' was a welcome one, only one unit, the 3rd Volunteer Battalion, Royal Welsh Fusiliers, now uses it in conjunction with a regimental title that would have been familiar to the old volunteers of 1881 to 1908. Very few infantry regiments of today, still bear the old and much-loved county titles either in the Regular Army or Territorial Army.

In 1979 the title 'Territorial Army and Volunteer Reserve' was dropped and replaced by the former name, the 'Territorial Army'.

TA infantry units of today are generally styled as volunteer battalions, e.g., 5th Volunteer Battalion, Royal Regiment of Fusiliers. New regiments of territorials have been formed – the 51st Highland, 52nd Lowland, Mercian and Yorkshire Volunteers, all containing more than one battalion, and one unit which is known as the Wessex Regiment.

The present day territorial infantry battalions have an important role in the defence of Britain and the Western Alliance, and are at a state of readiness to carry out their task never before achieved in peacetime. This reflects the greater and more immediate dangers of our modern world. Some of the battalions have a NATO role as part of the TA reinforcement plan to 1st (British) Corps in West Germany; others have a home service role and are being joined by new infantry units of the Home Defence Force.

The tradition of voluntary military service continues unabated in the Territorial Army. It is an honourable one and embodies all that is best in the British character.

Above left
Lt John Storr – off to Exercise Lionheart '84 – he serves with 1/51st Highland Volunteers and is an engineer by profession. He was working in the Oman, but flew back to UK to join his Battalion en route for Germany.
Roger Goodwin

Above right
1st Battalion, The Mercian Volunteers at annual Camp in Germany.
Stockport Express

Left
The Colour Party of 5th (Volunteer) Battalion, The Royal Regiment of Fusiliers. Drawn from members of their 'D' (Lancashire) Company from Bury & Rochdale, the parade in Salford exercised their Freedom of the City of Salford during a re-dedication of colours that had been laid up from the First World War from the 15th, 16th, 19th & 20th Battalions of The Lancashire Fusiliers (The Salford Pals). The parade, on 3rd November 1985 was the first time that the 'freedom rights' had been exercised since its grant in 1980. The Mayor of Salford, Councillor Fred Brockbank took the salute.
Major C. Vere

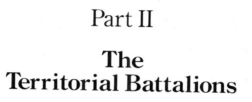

Part II

The Territorial Battalions

Lance Corporal of the 9th (Highlanders) Battalion, The Royal Scots, 1916.

Metal shoulder insignia worn by 4th Battalion, Royal Scots. This title is made from brass and finished in black.

The Royal Scots (The Royal Regiment)

4th Battalion (Queen's Edinburgh)

The 1st Edinburgh (City) Rifle Volunteer Corps was formed in 1859 by the merger of several rifle corps already existing within the city. By the end of 1860 the corps consisted of twenty-two companies, each showing in its title an indication as to the trade or profession of its members – e.g. No 1 (Advocates), No 3 (Writers to the Signet), No 5 (Solicitors), No 7 (Bankers) etc.

One rifle corps to be formed in the Edinburgh area, which at first remained outside of the 1st, was a company raised by employees of Messrs W. D. Young, the ironworks at Fountainbridge. This corps was numbered as 2nd Edinburgh, and was to join up with the 1st Corps in 1867. By this time the 1st Edinburgh was known as the Queen's City of Edinburgh Rifle Volunteer Brigade, and had been organised into two separate battalions.

The Edinburghs joined the Royal Scots in 1881, but although serving as 1st, 2nd and 3rd Volunteer Battalions, did not make any change in designation. During the Boer War the Queen's Edinburghs contributed 117 men to the service companies formed for duty with the Royal Scots in South Africa. Three such companies were sent out, the Edinburghs providing personnel for each.

When the Territorial Force was formed in 1908, the Edinburgh Brigade was large enough to provide two battalions, the 4th and 5th (Queen's Edinburgh Rifles).

The 1/4th left Liverpool for Gallipoli in May 1915 and later saw service in Egypt, Palestine and on the Western Front. The 2/4th went to Ireland in January 1917 and was later absorbed into other battalions of the 195th Brigade. A 3/4th Battalion was also formed which absorbed the reserve battalions of the 5th, 6th, 7th, 8th and 9th Royal Scots to form the 4th (Reserve) Bn.

In 1921 a reduction was made in the infantry battalions attached to the Royal Scots, resulting in an amalgamation between the 4th and 5th. The new formation was designated, 4th/5th Battalion (Queen's Edinburgh), The Royal Scots, a title which was maintained until 1938 when a change in organisation saw '52 Search-light Regiment' added. Two years later the battalion transferred to the Royal Artillery.

5th Battalion (Queen's Edinburgh)

As previously mentioned, the 5th Royal Scots was formed in 1908 from the Queen's Edinburgh Rifle Volunteer Brigade (see 4th Bn R Scots). The year 1914 saw the 5th with the Lothian Brigade on coastal defence work, and in 1915 the battalion became part of the 29th Division with whom it saw service at Gallipoli, Egypt and on the Western Front. While in France the battalion transferred to the 32nd Division and amalgamated with the 1/6th Royal Scots to form the 5th/6th Battalion.

After the war the 5th and 6th assumed the former titles. However in 1921 the 5th was linked with the 4th and this time provided the 4th/5th Bn Royal Scots.

Second and third line units were formed by the 5th Battalion during the First World War. The 2/5th, formed in September 1914, was absorbed into the 2/4th, while the 3/5th, formed in 1915, joined the 4th (Reserve) Battalion.

6th Battalion

When the 1st Edinburgh (City) Rifle Volunteer Corps was formed in 1859, its No 16 Company was raised by total abstainers and members of the British Temperance League.

In 1867 the founder of the company, John Hope, decided that a much larger corps of volunteers, all 'teetotallers', could be found. He subsequently raised the 3rd Edinburgh (City) Rifle Volunteer Corps, using the No 16 Company of the 1st as a nucleus.

The 3rd was renumbered as 2nd in the volunteer reorganisations of 1880, and in 1888 became known as the 4th Volunteer Battalion of the Royal Scots. The battalion contributed volunteers to each of the three service companies that were sent out to serve with regular troops in South Africa.

As the 1/6th Bn, and part of the Lothian Brigade, the unit embarked at Devonport for Alexandria in September 1915. It served with the Western Frontier Force between November 1915 and February 1916 and then with the 32nd Division on the Western Front. While in France the battalion amalgamated, until the end of the war, with the 1/5th Royal Scots. Lt. David McGregor, of the 6th, and also 29th Bn Machine Gun Corps, gained a posthumous Victoria Cross for his part in an action near Hoogemolen, Belgium on 22 October 1918.

When the Territorial Force was reorganised in 1920 the 6th Royal Scots was one of the infantry battalions chosen to convert to an artillery role. It was subsequently amalgamated with the 8th Royal Scots to form 57th (Lowland) Medium Brigade, Royal Garrison Artillery.

Second and third line units were formed by the 6th during the First World War.

Members of the 4th Battalion, Royal Scots. Khaki service dress is worn, the NCOs having black chevrons. Note the broken shoulder title of the man second from the right.

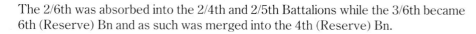

The 2/6th was absorbed into the 2/4th and 2/5th Battalions while the 3/6th became 6th (Reserve) Bn and as such was merged into the 4th (Reserve) Bn.

7th Battalion

On 6 December 1859 four companies of rifle volunteers were raised at Leith and formed into the 1st Midlothian Corps. The strength was increased to nine companies in 1863 when the 4th Midlothian RVC was absorbed at Corstorphine. The corps became the 5th Volunteer Battalion, Royal Scots in 1888 and during the Boer War contributed 290 members to various units serving at the front in South Africa.

On 22 May 1915 a great disaster befell the battalion in a train crash which was to go on record as the worst railway accident in Great Britain. On that day Battalion HQ with A and D Companies were travelling to Liverpool when near Gretna they hit a local train. The London to Glasgow express was due, but before signals could be changed and men cleared from the scene, that train ploughed into the wreckage, killing some 227 officers and men and injuring 246 others.

In the First World War, the battalion as the 1/7th Royal Scots, joined the 52nd (Lowland) Division and subsequently saw service at Gallipoli, Egypt, Palestine and on the Western Front. The battalion also formed second and third line units for service in the war. The 2/7th was raised in 1914 and served with the 65th Division in Ireland until disbandment in 1918. The 3/7th was formed at Peebles in 1915 and as 7th (Reserve) Battalion was absorbed into the 4th (Reserve) Battalion the following year.

When the Territorial Force was reorganised after the First World War, the 7th was amalgamated with the 9th (Highlanders) Battalion to form the 7th/9th Royal Scots. The additional title 'Highlanders' being assumed in 1924.

With the outbreak of war in 1939 the 7th/9th formed a duplicate battalion at Kinghorn, designated as 8th (Lothians and Peeblesshire). The original unit was to receive training in both mountain warfare and airlanding operations, but was never used in these roles. The 7th/9th served with the 52nd (Lowland) Infantry Division, in France 1940 and in NW Europe during 1944.

In 1944 the battalion was reduced to a cadre and later placed in suspended animation. It was, however, reconstituted in 1947, and in 1961 amalgamated with its war time duplicate unit, the 8th Bn, to form the 8th/9th Royal Scots.

Officer, Queen's Edinburgh Rifle Volunteer Brigade, c1875. The dark grey uniform is trimmed with black lace and the black busby bears the badge of a bugle horn.

Sir Robert Cranston, Kt, KCVO, VD, Lieutenant Colonel Commandant, Queen's Rifle Volunteer Brigade, 1903–06.

8th Battalion

The 8th Battalion Royal Scots was formed in 1908 by the amalgamation of two of the regiment's former volunteer battalions, the 6th and 7th. The senior battalion was recruited in both Midlothian and Peeblesshire and consisted of several rifle companies that had been raised within the areas since 1859.

The 7th Volunteer Battalion was from Haddington where in 1860 an admin battalion consisting of the 1st to 7th Rifle Corps was formed. This was consolidated as the 1st Haddingtonshire Rifle Volunteer Corps in 1880 and in 1888 redesignated as the 7th Volunteer Battalion Royal Scots.

Both battalions contributed men for service with regular troops during the war in South Africa. In 1914 the 8th battalion was serving with the Lothian Brigade on coastal defence duties. On 5 November the battalion went to France where it joined the 7th Division at Merris. In August 1915 the battalion was transferred to the 51st (Highland) Division for service as pioneers. The 2/8th Battalion was formed in September 1914 and served with the 65th Division throughout the war. Disbandment took place in Ireland in 1917. The 3/8th, which became the 8th (Reserve) Bn, was absorbed into the 4th (Reserve) Bn in 1916.

When the Territorial Force was reorganised after the First World War, the battalion was amalgamated with the 6th Royal Scots to form 57th (Lowland) Medium Brigade Royal Garrison Artillery.

8th (Lothians and Peeblesshire) Battalion

The battalion was formed in August 1939 as a duplicate of the 7th/9th (Highlanders) Battalion. After joining the 44th Infantry Brigade the battalion saw action during 1944 at The Odon, Caen, Mont Pincon and the Nederrijn, and in 1945 in the Rhineland.

With the reorganisations of the Territorial Army in 1947 it was usual for the duplicate unit to be merged with its parent battalion. However the 8th Royal Scots continued as such and in 1961 amalgamated with the 7th/9th to form the 8th/9th Battalion. The battalion now forms part of the 2nd Bn 52nd Lowland Volunteers.

9th (Highlanders) Battalion

The 9th Volunteer Battalion Royal Scots was one of the several formed as a result of the war in South Africa, and was recruited from Highlanders then resident in the City of Edinburgh. At first the unit was known as, the 'Highland' Battalion of the Queen's Edinburgh Rifle Volunteer Brigade. However on the 24 July 1900 it was recognised as an independent formation and soon designated as 9th (Highlanders) Volunteer Battalion, the Royal Scots. A number of officers and men from the 9th served with the volunteer service companies of the Royal Scots in South Africa.

In 1908 the 9th retained its number upon transfer to the Territorial Force. After war was declared in 1914 the battalion went to France to join the 27th Division. It subsequently saw action on the Western Front with the 51st (Highland) Division and took part in the Somme battles at High Wood and Beaumont Hamel, the Battle for Arras and the actions in the Ypres sector at Pilckem and Menin Road Ridges.

The 2/9th Battalion served as part of the 65th Division in Ireland and was disbanded in 1918 having been known for a short time as No 20 Battalion, 65th Division. The 3/9th became the 9th (Reserve) Battalion and was absorbed into the 4th (Reserve) Bn Royal Scots in 1917. The 9th was amalgamated with the 7th Battalion Royal Scots in 1920 to form the 7th/9th Battalion.

Party from the 9th (Highlanders) Battalion, Royal Scots at camp in 1909. The uniforms worn include a scarlet doublet, with blue collar and cuffs, and kilts of Hunting Stuart tartan.

10th (Cyclist) Battalion

In 1862 the rifle corps then in existence within the County of Linlithgowshire were organised as the 1st Admin Battalion of Linlithgowshire Rifle Volunteers. The headquarters of the battalion was at Linlithgow and in 1880 the 1st Linlithgowshire Rifle Volunteer Corps was formed by consolidation. Redesignation as the 8th Volunteer Battalion, Royal Scots took place in 1888. About 40 members of the battalion went to South Africa in 1900.

The 8th Volunteer Battalion became the 10th (Cyclist) Battalion (TF) in 1908 and in 1914 took up coastal defence duty at North Berwick. As part of the coastal defence system it was considered that the battalions role was too important to send it overseas. Of the original members, however, over 90% saw action with other units. The battalion moved to Ireland in April, 1918. When the Territorial Force was reorganised after the war the 10th was not re-formed as a battalion. Its members transferred to artillery and engineer units.

Formed in September 1914, the 2/10th Battalion served on coastal defences at Berwick and Coldingham. In June 1918 the battalion was sent to Ireland, where it was reorganised and trained as an infantry unit. By mid-October the 2/10th had returned to England and, while at Aldershot, prepared to take part in an expedition to Russia. Arriving at Archangel on the 25 August the battalion was led through the town by a band of American Marines. It subsequently took part in actions against the Bolsheviks and returned home in June 1919.

A third line depot was formed during the war which was sometimes known as the 3/10th Battalion. This was disbanded in March 1916 with its personnel going to the 1/10th and 2/10th Battalions.

10th (Home Defence) Battalion

See 30th Battalion

11th (Home Defence) Battalion

It was formed in September 1936 as 72 Group National Defence Companies, redesignated as 11th (Home Defence) Battalion, Royal Scots in November 1939 and absorbed into the 10th (HD) Battalion the following year.

30th Battalion

The battalion was formed as 66 Group National Defence Companies in September 1936 and redesignated 10th (Home Defence) Battalion, Royal Scots in 1939. It was later redesignated the 30th Battalion in 1941 and disbanded in June 1943.

The Queen's Royal Regiment (West Surrey)

4th Battalion

The battalion was formed in 1859 as the 2nd Surrey Rifle Volunteer Corps, its members being drawn from the Croydon, Crystal Palace and Caterham areas. Redesignation as the 1st Volunteer Battalion, Queen's Regiment was in 1883 and in 1900 a number of volunteers served with the regular 2nd Battalion in South Africa. As the 1/4th Queen's and part of the 44th (Home Counties) Division, the battalion sailed for India in October 1914. Before returning home it sent a draft to Mesopotamia, where it saw action, and in 1919 took part in the Third Afghan War.

Of the three additional battalions formed by the 4th for war service, the 2/4th saw action with the 53rd (Welsh) Division at Gallipoli, Egypt and Palestine. It later joined the 34th Division and fought in France and Belgium. The 3/4th also went to France, while the 4/4th, later, 4th (Reserve) Battalion remained at home with the Home Counties Reserve Brigade.

In 1938 the battalion was converted to an anti-aircraft role and in 1940 transferred to the Royal Artillery as 63rd Searchlight Regiment. After several changes in role and designation the battalion became infantry again in 1961. It was amalgamated with the 5th and 6th Battalions, Queen's to form the 3rd Battalion, The Queen's Royal Surrey Regiment. The battalion now forms part of the 5th and 6th/7th Volunteer Battalions, The Queen's Regiment.

5th Battalion

The 5th Queen's began as a battalion in 1860 with the formation at Dorking of the 3rd Admin Battalion of Surrey Rifle Volunteers. The senior company of the battalion was the 5th Surrey at Reigate, which had been formed in 1859 and was now linked with others from Guildford, Dorking, Godstone and Farnham.

The 3rd Admin Battalion was consolidated as the 4th Surrey Rifle Volunteer Corps in 1880, redesignated as the 2nd Volunteer Battalion, Queen's in 1883 and became the 5th Battalion (TF) in 1908. Members of the battalion served during the Boer War.

In October 1914 the 1/5th embarked for India with the 44th (Home Counties) Division. It later served with the 15th Indian Division in Mesopotamia. The 2/5th Battalion was formed in September 1914 and in May of the following year supplied some 400 men to the 2/4th Queen's for service with the 53rd (Welsh) Division. A

Drums and Bugles of the 22nd (County of London) Battalion, The London Regiment, 1909. The drums still bear the battalion's pre-1908 designation: '3rd Volunteer Battalion, The Queen's (Royal West Surrey Regiment)'.

5th (Reserve) Battalion (3/5th) was also formed and was absorbed into the 4th (Reserve) Battalion, Queen's in 1916.

At the beginning of the Second World War the battalion was divided as 1/5th and 2/5th. Both units served through North Africa and Europe, the 1/5th having the distinction of being the first British infantry battalion to enter Berlin. The two battalions were merged as 5th Queen's in 1947. Another amalgamation, this time with the 4th and 6th Battalions of the regiment to form the 3rd Queen's Royal Surreys, occurred in 1961.

6th (Bermondsey) Battalion

In 1868 two Surrey rifle volunteer corps – the 10th, formed in 1860 at Bermondsey and the 23rd, formed 1861 in Rotherhithe – were placed together as the 4th Admin Battalion of Surrey Rifle Volunteers. The 10th and 23rd were amalgamated as the 6th Corps in 1880 and in 1883 redesignated as the 3rd Volunteer Battalion of the Queen's Royal West Surrey Regiment. The battalion contributed a number of its members to the service companies that went to South Africa in 1900. Two men were killed and several wounded while serving with the regular 2nd Battalion.

With the transfer to the Territorial Force in 1908, the 3rd Volunteer Battalion formed the 22nd Battalion of the newly created London Regiment. As such it served throughout the First World War on the Western Front, taking part in the fighting at Loos, High Wood, Messines and Cambrai, Pte. Jack Harvey winning the VC at Peronne in 1918.

The second line battalion formed by the 22nd became part of the 60th Division and saw service in France, Belgium, Macedonia, Egypt and Palestine, Lt. Col. A. D. Borton gaining the Victoria Cross in 1917. A reserve battalion, 3/22nd, was formed in 1915 and was disbanded in August 1919.

The London Regiment was broken up in 1937 and most of its components were converted either to artillery or engineers. The 22nd, however, remained as infantry and rejoined the West Surreys as its 6th (Bermondsey) Battalion.

With the outbreak of war in 1939, the 6th was doubled in strength and divided between the 1/6th and 2/6th Battalions, the 2/6th having its headquarters at New Cross. The senior battalion was at Dunkirk in 1940 and was later to see service in Egypt, Libya, Italy and NW Europe. The 2/6th also fought in both Europe and Africa and was amalgamated after the war with its parent unit.

In 1961 the battalion was amalgamated with the 4th and 5th Queen's West Surreys to form the 3rd Battalion Queen's Royal Surrey Regiment.

7th (Southwark) Battalion

The battalion was raised in 1860 at Lambeth, as the 19th Surrey Rifle Volunteer Corps. It was renumbered 8th in 1880 and then as 4th Volunteer Battalion Queen's West Surrey Regiment in 1883. Several members of the battalion volunteered in 1900 for service in South Africa and were to see action both with the regulars of the West Surreys and the City Imperial Volunteers. One sergeant gained the Distinguished Conduct Medal.

With the transfer in 1908 of the Volunteers to the Territorial Force, the 4th Volunteer Battalion became the 24th Battalion of the London Regiment and part of the 2nd London Division. The 2nd London Division, or as it was renamed the 47th (2nd London), went to France in early 1915. The battalion saw action throughout the Western Front, one of its members, L Cpl. L. J. Keyworth, gaining the Victoria Cross at Givenchy in May 1915.

Formed in 1914 the 2/24th Battalion saw service in France, Salonika, Egypt and

Left
Cornetist of the 24th (County of London) Battalion, The London Regiment. The scarlet tunic has blue collar and cuffs and bears shoulder wings trimmed with white lace. The badges worn are of the pattern introduced in 1920.

Right
Sergeant, 4th Volunteer Battalion, The Queen's (Royal West Surrey Regiment), 1907. The uniform is green with scarlet collar and cuffs. The ancient badge of the Queen's, the Pascal Lamb, can be seen here worn on the cap, collar and pouch-belt.

Officer, Whitgift School Cadet Corps. The School's cadets were associated with the 2nd Surrey RVC, later 1st Volunteer Battalion, The Queen's (Royal West Surrey Regiment), from 1874.

took part in the capture in 1917 of Jerusalem. The 3/24th, later 24th (Reserve) Battalion, remained at home supplying drafts to the 1st and 2nd line units.

When the London Regiment was broken up in 1937, the 24th became known as the 7th (Southwark) Battalion, The Queen's Royal Regiment (West Surrey). In 1939 the battalion was doubled and divided as, 1/7th and 2/7th.

As part of the BEF both battalions saw action in Europe during 1940. The 1/7th, after taking part in the Battle of El Alamein, joined the 7th Armoured Division and served throughout the North African Campaign. It then took part in the invasion of Italy and later that of France in 1944. The 2/7th also served in North Africa and Italy.

In 1947 the 1/7th and 2/7th Battalions were amalgamated as 7th and at the same time converted and transferred to the Royal Artillery as 622 Heavy Anti-Aircraft Regiment.

11th (Home Defence) Battalion

See 30th Battalion

12th (Home Defence) Battalion

The battalion was formed in September 1936 as 23a Group National Defence Companies. It was redesignated as 12th (Home Defence) Battalion Queen's Regiment in 1939 and absorbed into the 10th (HD) Battalion, Middlesex Regt in 1941.

19th Battalion

The battalion was formed in June 1915 at Tunbridge Wells as the 69th Provisional Battalion (TF). The battalion consisted of men from the regiment's territorial battalions that were unfit or unwilling to volunteer for service overseas. It was redesignated as 19th Battalion, West Surreys in 1917 and disbanded in 1919.

30th Battalion

The battalion was formed in 1936 as 4 Group National Defence Companies. It was redesignated as 11th (Home Defence) Battalion Queen's West Surrey Regiment in 1939, Nos. 1 and 2 Independent Companies, Queen's in 1940 and then as 30th Queen's in 1943.

Inter-Company Challenge Shield badge, 4th Volunteer Battalion, The Queen's (Royal West Surrey Regiment). This annual efficiency competition was introduced in 1887.

The Buffs (Royal East Kent Regiment)

4th Battalion

Formation of the 4th Buffs began in 1860 when in August of that year the 4th Admin Battalion of Kent Rifle Volunteers was created. The headquarters of the battalion was at Canterbury and the several corps contained within it were from the Sittingbourne, Ash, Ashford and Wingham areas.

In April 1874 several companies of Cinque Ports rifle volunteers were merged with those of the 4th Admin Battalion to form the 5th Kent (East Kent) Corps. The 5th was renumbered as 2nd in 1880, redesignated 1st Volunteer Battalion, Buffs in 1883 and became the 4th Battalion (TF) in 1908.

As part of the 44th (Home Counties) Division the battalion moved to India in October 1914. It went to Aden in August 1915 and returned to India in January 1916, where it remained until the end of the war.

A 2/4th Battalion was formed in September 1914 which served with the 67th Division in the United Kingdom until disbandment in November 1917. However, in April 1915 one company joined other Kent units to form the Kent Composite Battalion, which served with the 53rd (Welsh) Division overseas. The 3/4th Buffs was formed in 1915, became the 4th (Reserve) Battalion in 1916 and was disbanded in 1919.

After the war the 4th was amalgamated with the 5th Buffs. The new formation was at first known as 4th Battalion, but from 1937 as 4th/5th. In 1939 the battalion was doubled in size, divided, and the 4th and 5th once again listed as separate units. The 4th performed its first duty of the war on lines of communication in France.

It left the UK for Malta in November 1940 and at first served as a Fortress Mobile Reserve unit. Later it joined the 234th Infantry Brigade and lost most of its personnel as prisoners to the Germans on 16 November 1943.

In 1947 the 4th and 5th Battalions were linked once again as 4th/5th. However in 1956, 410 Coast Regiment, Royal Artillery was converted to infantry and amalgamated with part of the 4th/5th Buffs to form a new 5th Battalion. The 4th Battalion now form part of the 5th (Volunteer) Battalion, The Queen's Regiment.

5th (The Weald of Kent) Battalion

The 5th Admin Battalion of Kent Rifle Volunteers was formed in 1861 and contained the several rifle corps that had been raised within the area of Kent

Left
The 2/4th Buffs at the funeral of one of its members, Tonbridge, January 1916. Note guard at 'reversed arms' position.
Right
Stretcher-Bearers, 2nd East Kent Rifle Volunteer Corps. Two members of the group wear on the right upper arm the 'Stretcher-Bearers' badge, consisting of the letters 'S.B.' within a circle.
Below
Member of the Shooting Team, 2nd East Kent Rifle Volunteers. The uniform worn is green and has scarlet collar and cuffs. The letters 'E.K.' are embroidered into the shoulder straps.

known as 'The Weald'. The headquarters of the battalion was at Cranbrook and in 1880 a new battalion was formed by the consolidation of the 5th Admin, known as the 5th Kent (The Weald of Kent) Rifle Volunteer Corps. The 5th became the 2nd (The Weald of Kent) Volunteer Battalion, Buffs in 1883 and in 1900 provided a number of men for service at the front in South Africa.

The Battalion left Southampton for India on the 30 October 1914. In December 1915 it landed at Basra, joined the 35th Indian Brigade and later, saw service in Mesopotamia with the 14th Indian Division.

Second and third line units were formed for service in the First World War. The 2/5th was raised at Ashford in September 1914 and served in the UK with the 67th Division until disbandment in 1917. The 3/5th became the 5th (Reserve) Battalion and was absorbed into the 4th (Reserve) Bn. Buffs in 1916.

After the war the 5th was amalgamated with the 4th Buffs, the new formation

later being known as the 4th/5th Battalion. In 1939 the 4th/5th was doubled in size and subsequently divided, the 5th Battalion serving throughout the Second World War in France, North Africa, Sicily, Italy and Egypt.

The 5th was reunited in 1947 with the 4th, as 4th/5th. In 1956 410 Coast Regiment, Royal Artillery was converted to infantry and together with part of the 4th/5th provided a new 5th Battalion Buffs. The 5th is now represented as elements of the 5th and 6th/7th (Volunteer) Battalions, The Queen's Regiment.

6th (Home Defence) Battalion

See 30th Battalion

10th (Royal East Kent and West Kent Yeomanry) Battalion

Formed in the early part of 1917 by the merger of the two Kent Yeomanry regiments then serving in 3rd Dismounted Brigade, the battalion fought in the Palestine campaign as part of the 74th Division and, for the last months of the war, on the Western Front.

30th Battalion

Formed as 1 Group National Defence Companies in September 1936. Redesignated as 6th (Home Defence) Battalion, The Buffs (Royal East Kent Regiment) in 1939 and as 30th Battalion in 1941. Disbandment was at Dover in 1943.

The King's Own Royal Regiment (Lancaster)

4th Battalion

The 4th originated as a battalion in 1861 upon the formation in Ulverston of the 5th Admin Battalion of Lancashire Rifle Volunteers. The battalion was made up of companies from the Ulverston, Dalton, Cartmel and Broughton-in-Furness areas, and also included one provided by Rossall School. In 1874 the 5th Admin was consolidated to form the 10th Lancashire Rifle Volunteer Corps, consisting of nine companies with headquarters at Ulverston. This in turn became the 1st Volunteer Battalion of the King's Own in 1883.

Members of the 5th Battalion, The King's Own Royal Regiment (Lancaster), at camp. Each man is wearing the brown leather '1903 pattern' bandolier, each of the five pouches holding 10 rounds of ammunition.

As a result of the war in South Africa, and an increase in the number of men wishing to serve with the Volunteers, the 1st Volunteer Battalion was extended to form a 2nd VB. Headquarters of the 1st remained at Ulverston while those of the 2nd were set up at Lancaster. The 1st VB sent over 150 of its members to South Africa, where in addition to being involved in several actions, acted as prison guards at Ladysmith.

During the First World War the 1/4th Battalion saw service on the Western Front where it gained three Victoria Crosses. The 2/4th absorbed the 3/4th in 1916 and together formed the regiment's 4th (Reserve) Battalion.

The battalion was converted to an anti-tank regiment (56th), in November 1938, and as such served in France, Belgium, Burma and India during the Second World War. The battalion became an infantry unit again in 1961, when having dropped its title as R Battery, 380 Light Regiment Royal Artillery, it was amalgamated with the 5th King's Own to form the 4th/5th Battalion, The King's Own Royal Regiment. The 4th/5th are now represented by the 4th (Volunteer) Battalion, King's Own Royal Border Regiment, having previously formed part of the Lancastrian volunteers.

5th Battalion

Formed in 1900 as the 2nd Volunteer Battalion, King's Own from part of the 1st Volunteer Battalion (see 4th Bn), it became 5th in 1908 and during the First World War served as 1/5th on the Western Front. The 2/5th Battalion served in France from 1917 while the 3/5th became the 5th (Reserve) Bn in 1916 and was later absorbed into the 4th (Reserve) Bn The King's Own.

During the Second World War the battalion was converted to an armoured role, becoming 107 Regiment, Royal Armoured Corps and seeing action in NW Europe. Reconstituted as 5th Battalion, King's Own in 1947 and in 1961 amalgamated with R Battery of 380 Light Regiment, Royal Artillery (formerly 4th King's Own), together they formed the 4th/5th Battalion.

12th Battalion

It was formed in 1915 as 41 Provisional Battalion (TF) and became the 12th Battalion King's Own in January 1917, being disbanded in March of the following year.

Above
Corporal of the 5th Battalion, King's Own. The crossed rifles with star above which, according to TF Regulations, are seen here worn on the wrong arm indicate that the wearer is the best shot in his company.
Below
Silver officer's helmet plate of the 1st Volunteer Battalion, Royal Lancaster Regiment. The 'Lion of England' badge was granted to the Regiment by William III.

The Royal Northumberland Fusiliers

4th Battalion

The 1st Admin Battalion of Northumberland Rifle Volunteers was formed in 1860 from several Northumberland companies and the 1st Berwick-on-Tweed Rifle Volunteer Corps. In 1880 the battalion was consolidated to form the 1st Northumberland Rifle Volunteer Corps, consisting of ten companies with headquarters at Alnwick. The corps was redesignated as 1st Volunteer Battalion, Northumberland Fusiliers in 1883, and during the Boer War sent a number of its members to South Africa.

In 1908 the 1st VB, less its Alnwick members, transferred to the Territorial Force as 4th Battalion Northumberland Fusiliers. The Alnwick detachment provided a nucleus for the formation of the regiment's 7th Battalion.

The battalion served with the Northumbrian Division on the Tyne defences until April 1915, when it went to France. It was later reduced to a cadre and joined the 39th Division at Le Havre in August 1918. Also formed was the 2/4th Battalion which served in the 63rd Division until July 1916. The battalion spent the remainder of the war with the 72nd Division in the UK. The 3/4th was formed at

Members of the 5th Battalion, Northumberland Fusiliers at camp in 1909. The party are in 'walking out' dress consisting of scarlet tunics and blue trousers. Each man carries a 'swagger' cane.

B Company, 1st Volunteer Battalion, Northumberland Fusiliers. This company of the battalion was recruited in Morpeth and can be seen here with the Havelock-Allan Trophy, a shooting prize, in August 1894. The uniforms worn by the 1st Volunteer Battalion were grey with scarlet collar and cuffs.

Hexham in 1916 and later became the 4th (Reserve) Battalion. It absorbed the 5th, 6th and 7th Reserve Battalions of the regiment and was disbanded in April 1919.

The Second World War saw the 4th converted to a motor-cycle battalion, serving in France and Belgium in 1940. It became 50th Bn, Reconnaissance Corps in 1941 and served as such in Egypt and Libya. In 1943 the battalion once again became an infantry unit, but in 1944 it was placed into suspended animation and its personnel transferred to three independent machine gun companies.

Reconstituted in 1947 as 4th Royal Northumberland Fusiliers, the battalion amalgamated in 1950 with 588 LAA Regt R.A. (formerly 5th Royal Northumberland Fusiliers) to form 4th/5th Battalion Royal Northumberland Fusiliers. The battalion is now represented by part of 6th (Volunteer) Battalion, Royal Regiment of Fusiliers.

5th Battalion

The several Northumberland rifle corps that were not included in the formation of the 4th Battalion, Royal Northumberland Fusiliers were the 1st (Tynemouth), 8th (Walker) and 9th (Crumlington) Corps which were incorporated in 1861 as the 2nd Admin Battalion of Northumberland Rifle Volunteers. By 1865 only the 8th Corps remained. This became the 2nd in 1880 and subsequently, in 1883, the 2nd Volunteer Battalion Northumberland Fusiliers. Almost a quarter of the battalion volunteered for service in South Africa during the Boer War.

The 1/5th, as part of the Northumbrian Division, served throughout the First World War in France and Belgium. The 2/5th remained in the UK while the 3/5th was absorbed into the 4th (Reserve) Battalion.

In November 1938 the battalion was converted to serve in an anti-aircraft role, adding '53rd Searchlight Regiment' to its title. It transferred to the Royal Artillery in August 1940 and in 1945 became 638 Regiment, Royal Artillery.

When the Territorial Army was reorganised in 1947, 638 Regiment was redesignated as, 588 Light Anti-Aircraft Regiment. In 1950 it once again became an infantry unit when it was reconstituted as 5th Bn Royal Northumberland Fusiliers and at the same time amalgamated with the 4th Battalion as 4th/5th.

6th (City) Battalion

The 6th was a battalion that had its origins in one of the many rifle clubs that formed volunteer corps in 1859. It was the Newcastle Rifle Club that in 1859 formed the 1st Newcastle-on-Tyne Rifle Volunteer Corps. The corps was made up from companies, which in addition to numbers were known by names, e.g. 'Guards', with its men of six foot or more, 'Quaysiders', all dock workers, 'Oddfellows', and even a 'Scottish' Company that were dressed in kilts.

The corps became the 3rd Volunteer Battalion of the Northumberland Fusiliers in 1883 and contributed a large number of volunteers to the service companies that went to South Africa during the Boer War. K Company of the battalion was made up from university students in 1908. Upon transfer to the Territorial Force the company provided the Durham University Contingent of the Officers Training Corps. The remainder of the battalion became the 6th (City) Battalion, Northumberland Fusiliers.

The 1914–18 war record of the 6th, and its second and third line units, was the same as that of the 4th Battalion. In 1938 the battalion was converted as 43rd Battalion (later Regiment), Royal Tank Corps, serving as such in the UK throughout the Second World War.

In November 1956 the 43rd RTR returned to the Royal Northumberland Fusiliers as its 6th (City) Battalion and is now serving as part of the 6th (Volunteer) Battalion, Royal Regiment of Fusiliers.

Left
Pipes and Drums of the 6th Battalion, Northumberland Fusiliers. This battalion was recruited in Newcastle-upon-Tyne and included a complete company of Scotsmen then resident in the city. The scarlet doublets have collars and cuffs in gosling green and are worn with black glengarry caps bearing cocks' feathers.
Right
An officer of the Northumberland Fusiliers TF, painted by R. Caton Woodville c1909. The scarlet tunic has gosling green collar and cuffs and bears silver lace and shoulder cords. A red over white plume is worn in the head-dress. The building in the background is the castle at Alnwick, the headquarters of the 7th Battalion.

7th Battalion

Formed in 1908 as a new unit, but with a strong nucleus provided by the Alnwick members of the 1st Volunteer Battalion, Northumberland Fusiliers (see 4th Battalion). The battalion served with the Northumbrian Division on Tyne defences until April 1915, when it moved to France. In February 1918 the 7th became a pioneer battalion attached to the 42nd Division.

The 2/7th Battalion was formed at Alnwick in September 1914 and joined the 63rd Division in January 1915. It served as a garrison battalion in Egypt from early

Silver plaid-brooch worn by members of the 'Scottish' Company of the 3rd Volunteer Battalion, Northumberland Fusiliers. The figure of St George and the Dragon is the 'ancient badge' of the regiment and has been in use since before 1797.

Two members of the 1st Volunteer Battalion, Northumberland Fusiliers, 1907. The uniforms are grey and have scarlet collars, cuffs and piping.

1917 until disbandment in September 1919. The 3/7th, later 7th (Reserve) Battalion, was absorbed into the 4th (Reserve) in 1916.

Converted to a machine gun battalion, the 7th served in France and Belgium in 1940. It later served in NW Europe and was placed in suspended animation during 1944.

The battalion was re-formed after the war and in 1947 amalgamated with its war time duplicate, the 9th Battalion. The 7th are now represented as part of the 6th (Volunteer) Battalion, Royal Regiment of Fusiliers.

8th Battalion

An 8th (Cyclist) Battalion was intended for the Northumberland Fusiliers in 1908, but this unit shortly after formation became the Northern Cyclist Battalion. The next 8th Bn, a motor-cycle battalion, was formed in 1939 as a duplicate unit of the 4th Battalion. In April 1941, it became 3rd Battalion Reconnaissance Corps, and later 3rd Reconnaissance Regiment, Royal Armoured Corps. The battalion returned to the Northumberland's in 1946 and was disbanded in the following year.

9th (Northumberland Hussars) Battalion

This was formed as the 9th (Service) Battalion, Northumberland Fusiliers at Newcastle in September 1914, as part of the 'New' or 'Kitchener's' Army system. While in France the battalion absorbed the 2/1st Northumberland Hussars Yeomanry and in September 1917 assumed the title 9th (Northumberland Hussars) Battalion (TF). The 9th served with the 61st Division and was disbanded in 1919.

9th (Machine Gun) Battalion

Formed as a duplicate of the 7th Battalion in 1939 it served in France during 1940 and in 1942 was captured by the Japanese in Malaya. It was absorbed into the 7th Battalion in 1947.

10th (Home Defence) Battalion

See 30th Battalion

11th (Home Defence) Battalion

See 30th Battalion

30th Battalion

Formed in September 1936 as 40 Group National Defence Companies it became the 10th (Home Defence) Battalion, Royal Northumberland Fusiliers in 1939 and the following year it was divided to form, 1/10th and 2/10th Battalions. The 2/10th was later designated as the 11th (HD) Battalion but in June 1941 was amalgamated with the 1/10th as 10th Bn. Redesignation as 30th Battalion took place in December 1941. The 30th later served in North Africa and Malta, where it was disbanded in 1945.

35th Battalion

Formed in 1915 as the 21st Provisional Battalion (TF) it became 35th Northumberland Fusiliers in January 1917 and was disbanded in 1919.

36th Battalion

Formed in 1915 as 22nd Provisional Battalion (TF) it became the 36th Bn Northumberland Fusiliers in January 1917 and in 1918, served as a garrison guard battalion in France as part of the 59th Division. Disbandment was in 1919.

The Royal Warwickshire Regiment

5th Battalion

The 1st Warwickshire Rifle Volunteer Corps was formed at Birmingham in 1859. It became the 1st Volunteer Battalion, Royal Warwickshire Regiment in 1883. In 1908, consisting of eighteen companies, it transferred to the Territorial Force as 5th and 6th Battalions. Part of the 1st Volunteer Battalion (A Company) was formed from university students, which in 1908 provided the Birmingham University Contingent of the Officers Training Corps.

About 125 men of the 1st Volunter Battalion volunteered, and saw active service during the Boer War, including that at Elandsfontein, Pretoria, Diamond Hill and Belfast.

The 1/5th Battalion landed at Havre as part of the 48th (South Midland) Division on 22 March 1915, and subsequently saw action in France and Belgium. In November 1917 the battalion was moved to the Italian front, where it took part in the Battle of The Piave and Vittorio Veneto. The First World War second and third line units were the 2/5th Battalion, formed at Birmingham in October 1914 and the 3/5th, formed in May 1915. The former joined the 61st Division at Northampton and proceeded to France in May 1916 where it disbanded in February 1918. The 3/5th remained in the UK, serving as the 5th (Reserve) Battalion from 1916.

The 5th Royal Warwickshire Regiment was converted and transferred as 45th Anti-Aircraft Battalion, Royal Engineers in 1936.

6th Battalion

As previously mentioned, the 6th Battalion was formed in 1908 from part of the 1st Volunteer Battalion Royal Warwickshire Regiment (see 5th Battalion). The 1/6th served during 1914–18 with the 48th Division and its war record follows that of the 1/5th Battalion. The 2/6th was formed in 1914 and saw service in France from 1916 until the end of the war. The 3/6th Battalion was also formed, becoming the 6th (Reserve) in 1916, and was later absorbed into the 5th (Reserve) Battalion.

In December 1936 the 6th Battalion was converted and transferred as 68th Anti-Aircraft Brigade, Royal Artillery.

Rugby School Cadet Corps. The school cadet corps was affiliated to the 2nd Volunteer Battalion, Royal Warwickshire Regiment until its transfer to the OTC in 1908. The uniform worn is scarlet and has a blue collar and cuffs with white piping. In the centre of the helmet plate can be seen the Antelope badge of the Royal Warwickshires, while the collar shows the 'Bear and Ragged Staff' device of the Earl of Warwick. The school Arms are worn on the left arm and indicate that the wearer was a member of the Corps' shooting team on the occasion of its winning the Ashburton Shield in 1894.

7th Battalion

With its headquarters in Coventry, the 7th originated in 1860 as the 2nd Admin Battalion of Warwickshire Rifle Volunteers. The battalion was made up of companies that were recruited from areas that included Warwick, Rugby (where a strong contingent was provided by Rugby School), Stratford-on-Avon and the Saltley Training College.

In 1880 the 2nd Admin became the 2nd Warwickshire Rifle Volunteer Corps, retaining its Coventry headquarters and with twelve companies. The next title change was to that of 2nd Volunteer Battalion, Royal Warwickshire Regiment in 1883, which during the Boer War sent more than 100 of its members to serve in South Africa. When the battalion transferred to the Territorial Force, the bulk of its personnel joined the 7th Battalion, although some went to form two companies of the 8th.

The 1/7th Battalion served as part of the 48th (South Midland) Division throughout the First World War, seeing action on both the Western and Italian fronts, Pte. Arthur Hut gaining the Victoria Cross in Belgium in October 1917. The 2/7th was with the 61st Division in France, while the 3/7th remained in the UK as a reserve battalion.

In 1939 the battalion once again became the 1/7th, having formed the 2/7th as a duplicate unit. It served with the 143rd Infantry Brigade in Europe during 1940, taking part in the action at Comines Canal in May. The 1/7th also took part in the invasion during 1944, and was involved in the fighting around Caen and Mont Pincon. The 2/7th acted as a reserve battalion and remained with the 61st Infantry Division in the UK.

After the war the 1/7th once again became known as the 7th Battalion. The 2/7th continued as such until 1950 when upon transfer, it became 623 LAA Regiment, Royal Artillery. It later became part of 443 LAA Regt and as such amalgamated into the 7th Royal Warwicks in 1961.

The 7th Battalion, Royal Warwickshire Regiment is now represented by part of the 5th (Volunteer) Battalion, Royal Regiment of Fusiliers.

8th Battalion

The 8th Battalion, Royal Warwickshire Regiment was raised at Aston Manor, Birmingham in 1908 being one of the new units of the Territorial Force. However, two companies – B at the Saltley Training School and D at the Dunlop Works, had seen service as volunteers with the 2nd Volunteer Battalion.

Service in the First World War was with the 48th Division on both the Western and Italian fronts. The 1/8th left the 48th Division in September 1918 and moved to St. Riquier where it joined the 25th Division, a member of the battalion L Cpl. Amery gained the VC at Landrecies in November. The 2/8th went to France with the 61st Division in May 1916, remaining there until disbandment in 1918. The 3/8th, later 8th (Reserve) Battalion, was also formed for war service.

During 1940 the 8th Royal Warwicks served in France and Belgium with the 143rd Infantry Brigade.

The 1947 reorganisations of the TA saw the 8th Battalion reconstituted as part of the Army Air Corps and as 18th Battalion, Parachute Regiment. It returned to the Royal Warwickshire Regiment in 1956 and was subsequently amalgamated into the 7th Battalion.

9th Battalion

The 9th was formed in 1939 as a duplicate of the 8th Battalion. It served as part of the 61st Infantry Division in the UK throughout the Second World War and in 1947 was converted as 10 Anti-Aircraft Workshops Battalion, Royal Electrical and Mechanical Engineers.

11th (Home Defence) Battalion

See 30th Battalion

18th Battalion

Formed in 1915 as 81 Provisional Battalion (TF), it became 18th Battalion Royal Warwickshire Regiment in 1917 and was disbanded in January of the following year.

30th Battalion

Formed in September 1936 as 84b Group National Defence Companies, it was redesignated as 11th (Home Defence) Battalion, Royal Warwickshire Regiment in 1939 and then as 30th Battalion in 1941. Disbandment took place at Denbigh in February 1944.

Corporal, 2nd Volunteer Battalion, Royal Fusiliers. The scarlet tunic has the title of the battalion embroidered in white on to the shoulder straps. White metal grenade badges are worn on the blue collar and on the black fur cap.

The Royal Fusiliers (City of London Regiment)

8th (1st City of London) Battalion

The founder of the 8th Royal Fusiliers was Thomas Hughes – author of *Tom Brown's Schooldays*. In 1859 he formed from the Working Men's College in Bloomsbury the 19th Middlesex Rifle Volunteer Corps, which by 1862 consisted of nine companies. The 19th was renumbered 10th in 1880 and redesignated as 1st Volunteer Battalion, Royal Fusiliers in 1883. A large number from the battalion served in South Africa during the Boer War.

The battalion transferred to the Territorial Force as the 1st (City of London) Battalion, The London Regiment (Royal Fusiliers) and as such undertook its first duty of the First World War in 1914 which was to guard the railway line between London and Newhaven. The battalion sailed for Malta in September 1914. It was later relieved by the 2/1st Battalion and, after returning to England, moved subsequently to France.

From Malta the 2/1st Battalion went to Gallipoli. It then moved to Egypt and finally in April 1916 to the Western Front where it was absorbed into the 1/1st Battalion. At this time the 3/1st Battalion was renumbered 2/1st. It served in France and Belgium until disbandment in 1918. A 4/1st Battalion was also formed which became the 1st (Reserve) Battalion, London Regiment in 1916.

In 1937 the 1st London Regiment became the 8th Battalion Royal Fusiliers and as such served with the 8th Army under General Montgomery in North Africa. The battalion later took part in the invasion of Italy and was one of the first units to enter Salerno.

The battalion formed the City of London Battalion, Royal Fusiliers upon amalgamation with 624 LAA Regt, Royal Artillery in 1961 (see 9th Battalion). It now forms part of the 5th (Volunteer) Battalion, Royal Regiment of Fusiliers.

9th (2nd City of London) Battalion

The 9th Royal Fusiliers was formally the 2nd (City of London) Battalion, The London Regiment and was raised as the 46th Middlesex Rifle Volunteer Corps in 1861. The 46th was renumbered 23rd in 1880 and in 1883 redesignated as the 2nd Volunteer Battalion, Royal Fusiliers. The 2nd VB contributed a large number from its ranks to the several Volunteer Service Companies formed by the Royal Fusiliers for the Boer War. Many members also saw action with the Imperial Yeomanry and the City Imperial Volunteers.

In 1908 the 2nd Volunteer Battalion became the 2nd Battalion, London Regiment, and was included in the 1st London Division. It was increased to four battalions during the First World War. The 1/2nd went to Malta in 1914, but after a few months was relieved by the 2/2nd so that it could join the 6th Division on the Western Front. The 2/2nd left Malta in August 1915 and in October joined the 63rd (Royal Naval) Division at Gallipoli. The battalion remained on the peninsula until the evacuation of Helles in January 1916. It spent the next four months in Egypt and then moved to France where it was disbanded. Upon the disbandment of the 2/2nd, the 3/2nd assumed its title. It served in France and Belgium throughout the war. The 4/2nd became the 2nd (Reserve) Battalion, London Regiment in 1916.

The London Regiment was broken up in 1937, the 2nd Battalion becoming the 9th (2nd City of London) Battalion, Royal Fusiliers. During the Second World War the 9th saw action in North Africa and Italy.

The battalion was converted and transferred in 1947 as, 624 Light Anti-aircraft Regiment, Royal Artillery. It served as such until 1961 when upon amalgamation with the 8th Royal Fusiliers formed the City of London Battalion, The Royal Fusiliers. This battalion is now represented by part of the 5th (Volunteer) Battalion, Royal Regiment of Fusiliers.

10th (3rd City of London) Battalion

The 10th Battalion of the Royal Fusiliers was originally formed in 1859 from workers on the London and North Western Railway Company. Its headquarters were at Euston and until 1880 was known as the 20th Middlesex Rifle Volunteer

Corps. It then became the 11th and in 1890, the 3rd Volunteer Battalion, Royal Fusiliers.

With the introduction of the Territorial Force in 1908, the battalion became the 3rd London Regiment, and as such served in Malta, France and Belgium during the First World War. The 2/3rd Battalion took over from the 1/3rd at Malta in December 1914. It later served at Gallipoli and on the Western Front where it was disbanded in 1916. The 3/3rd Battalion assumed the 2/3rd title while serving in France, and the 4/3rd became 3rd (Reserve) Battalion, the London Regiment in 1916.

In 1937 the 3rd London Regiment became the 10th (3rd City of London) Battalion, Royal Fusiliers. It added '69 Searchlight Regiment' to its title in 1938 and in 1940 was transferred to the Royal Artillery in that role.

11th Battalion

Formed in 1939 as a duplicate of the 8th (1st City of London) Battalion it served in the UK throughout the Second World War, and in 1947 was amalgamated with its parent unit.

12th Battalion

The 12th Battalion, Royal Fusiliers was formed in 1939 as a duplicate of the 9th (2nd City of London) Battalion. Amalgamation with the 9th took place in 1947 having served throughout the war in the UK.

13th (Home Defence) Battalion

See 30th Battalion

30th Battalion

Formed in 1936 as 20 Group National Defence Companies, it became 13th (Home Defence) Battalion, Royal Fusiliers in 1939 and 30th Bn in 1941. Disbandment took place in 1943.

4th City of London Regiment

Formed in 1860 as the 2nd Tower Hamlets Rifle Volunteer Corps, it amalgamated in 1868 with the 4th Tower Hamlets to form a battalion of seven companies located at, Hackney, Dalston, Bow, Poplar, Limehouse and Clapton. Designated as 1st Tower Hamlets and later as, The Tower Hamlets Rifle Volunteer Brigade, the battalion served as a volunteer battalion of the Rifle Brigade between 1881 and 1904. It then transferred to the Royal Fusiliers as its 4th Volunteer Battalion and in 1908 became the 4th (City of London) Battalion, The London Regiment.

The 4th was increased to four battalions for service during the Great War. The 1/4th served in Malta, France and Belgium while the 2/4th went from Malta to Gallipoli and then to the Western Front via Egypt. Shortly after reaching France the 2/4th was disbanded, the 3/4th Battalion assuming its title. The 4/4th acted as a reserve unit and in 1916 was absorbed into the 3rd (Reserve) Battalion of the London Regiment.

In 1916 the 4th Battalion, London Regiment became part of the Royal Fusiliers. It was converted to an anti-aircraft role in 1935 and subsequently transferred as 60th AA Brigade, Royal Artillery.

33rd (City of London) Battalion, The London Regiment

See Rifle Brigade

The King's Regiment (Liverpool)

5th Battalion

The 5th Battalion King's was formed in Liverpool as the 1st Lancashire Rifle Volunteer Corps in 1859. Although not the senior volunteer corps, this unit's Commanding Officer, Captain N. P. G. Bousfield, is on record as being the first officer of the Volunteer Force to be commissioned.

The corps becamd the 1st Volunteer Battalion, King's Regiment in 1888 and in 1900 contributed a large number of its members for service in South Africa. The contingent served alongside the regulars and saw action at Laing's Nek, Amersfont and Geluk's Farm.

As the 1/5th King's the battalion served on the Western Front throughout the First World War, Pte. Arthur Procter gaining the Victoria Cross Near Ficheux in June 1916. The 2/5th also fought in France, where it was disbanded in February 1918, while the 3/5th became the 5th (Reserve) Battalion in 1916.

During the Second World War the battalion remained in the UK with the 55th Infantry Division until 1944, when it took part in the D Day Assault landings in Normandy. In 1967 the battalion transferred to the TAVR as D Company, Lancastrian Volunteers and is now represented as part of the 5th/8th (Volunteer) Battalion, the King's Regiment.

6th (Rifle) Battalion

The 5th Lancashire Rifle Volunteer Corps was also known as the 'Liverpool Rifle Volunteer Brigade' and was formed in 1859 from professional and business men of the City. The 5th became the 2nd Volunteer Battalion, King's Regiment in 1888 and during the Boer War contributed to the three volunteer companies that were formed for service in South Africa.

The 2nd Volunteer Battalion became the 6th (Rifle) Battalion, King's Regiment in 1908 and in 1914 provided two battalions for service in France and Belgium and a third, which became part of the regiment's 5th (Reserve) Battalion.

The battalion was converted and transferred in 1936 as 38th Anti-aircraft Battalion, Royal Engineers.

7th Battalion

Formed in Liverpool as the 15th Lancashire Rifle Volunteer Corps in 1860, it

Officers and sergeants, 5th Battalion, The King's (Liverpool Regiment), 1909. The officers are seen in khaki service dress while the NCOs are wearing the green full dress uniform of the volunteer period.

Blackened brass shoulder title worn by the 8th (Irish) Battalion, The King's (Liverpool Regiment).

became the 4th Volunteer Battalion, King's Regiment in 1888 and the 7th Battalion (TF) in 1908. Members of the battalion saw action in South Africa during the Boer War. In the First World War two battalions were formed for war service in France and a third remained at home as the 7th (Reserve). In November 1938 the 7th King's took on an armoured role, transferring as the 40th Royal Tank Corps.

8th (Irish) Battalion

The Liverpool Irish was raised as the 64th Lancashire Rifle Volunteer Corps in 1860, and contained Irishmen then resident in the City of Liverpool. The corps was renumbered as 18th in 1880 and then redesignated, 5th (Irish) Volunteer Battalion, King's Regiment in 1888. In 1900 members from the battalion served with the regular battalions of both the King's and Royal Irish Regiments.

The 8th King's sent two battalions to France during the First World War, 2nd Lt. Edward Baxter of the 1/8th gaining the Victoria Cross near Blairville in April 1916. A third provided a reserve unit which in 1916 was absorbed into the 7th (Reserve) Battalion. The battalion was not re-formed after the war and was disbanded with effect from 31 March 1922.

When the Second World War broke out in 1939 the 'Irish' were re-formed as a duplicate of the 5th King's. Under their old title 8th (Irish) Battalion, they served in the UK until going to Normandy as part of a Beach Group, on 4 June 1944.

In 1947 the battalion transferred to the Royal Artillery as 626 Heavy Anti-Aircraft Regiment.

9th Battalion

The 9th King's, when they were formed in 1861 as the 80th Lancashire Rifle Volunteer Corps, were known as the 'Liverpool Press Guard', its members being recruited from workers in the newspaper and printing trade. The 80th was renumbered 19th in 1880 and in 1888 became the 6th Volunteer Battalion, King's Regiment.

As the 9th King's, the battalion began its war service as part of the Forth Defences. The 2/9th was formed in 1914 and both battalions later fought in France and Belgium. The 3/9th was absorbed into the 7th (Reserve) Battalion in 1916. The 9th King's was re-formed after the war as, 53rd Divisional Royal Engineers.

In 1939 the Territorial Army received the order to increase its strength and form duplicate units. The 5th King's in fact formed two additional battalions, the 8th (Irish) and 9th. The new 9th King's remained in the UK throughout the Second World War and was eventually absorbed into the parent unit in 1947.

10th (Scottish) Battalion

See under The Cameron Highlanders, the Liverpool Scottish.

10th (Home Defence) Battalion

See 15th and 30th Battalions

15th (Home Defence) Battalion

Formed in September 1940 as 2/10th (Home Service) Battalion, King's Regiment it became the 15th in November and, in 1941, transferred to the King's Shropshire Light Infantry as its 8th (HD) Battalion.

25th Battalion

Formed in 1915 at Sherringham as 43 Provisional Battalion (TF) it became 25th Battalion King's Regiment in 1917 and in 1918 served in France as a garrison guard battalion with the 59th Division. The 25th was later disbanded in Egypt.

26th Battalion

Formed in 1915 as 44 Provisional Battalion (TF) it became the 26th King's in 1917 and was disbanded the following year.

30th Battalion

Formed in 1936 as 103a Group National Defence Companies it became the 10th (Home Defence) Battalion, King's Regiment in 1939, 1/10th in 1940 and 30th in 1941. Disbandment took place in 1943.

Left
Senior NCO of the 1st Volunteer Battalion, The King's (Liverpool Regiment). The tunic is green and has a black collar and cuffs. Worn on the collar is the White Horse of Hanover, a badge granted to the regiment by King George I in 1716. **D. J. Barnes**
Right
Officers of the 10th (Scottish) Battalion, The King's (Liverpool Regiment), at camp in Rhyl, 1908. The kilts are in Forbes tartan.
D. J. Barnes

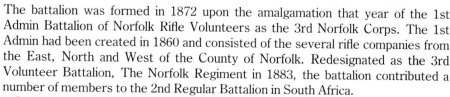

The Royal Norfolk Regiment

4th Battalion

The 4th Battalion, Royal Norfolk Regiment was formed in the City of Norwich as the 1st Norfolk Rifle Volunteer Corps in 1859. In 1872, a 4th Corps was formed by the amalgamation of several other Norfolk companies that were recruited from areas that included, Harleston, Diss, Loddon and Blofield. The two rifle corps became in 1883, the 1st and 4th Volunteer Battalions of the Norfolk Regiment and in 1908 were amalgamated to form the 4th Battalion (TF). Both contributed volunteers for service with the regular battalions in South Africa during the Boer War.

As part of the 54th (East Anglian) Division, the battalion left Liverpool for Gallipoli in July 1915. From there the 1/4th went to Egypt and subsequently took part in the Invasion of Palestine and the battles for Gaza and Jaffa. Both 2/4th and 3/4th Battalions were formed during the First World War. The 2/4th served in the 69th Division and did not move out of the UK, while the 3/4th became the 4th (Reserve) Battalion in 1916.

The battalion went out to Malaya with the 54th Infantry Brigade in 1942 and while taking part in the Battle for Singapore Island (8–15 February) was captured by the Japanese.

The 4th Bn, Royal Norfolk Regiment is now represented as part of the 6th (Volunteer) Battalion, Royal Anglian Regiment.

5th Battalion

The battalion was formed in 1872 upon the amalgamation that year of the 1st Admin Battalion of Norfolk Rifle Volunteers as the 3rd Norfolk Corps. The 1st Admin had been created in 1860 and consisted of the several rifle companies from the East, North and West of the County of Norfolk. Redesignated as the 3rd Volunteer Battalion, The Norfolk Regiment in 1883, the battalion contributed a number of members to the 2nd Regular Battalion in South Africa.

In 1914 the battalion was in the East Anglian Division and later saw service at Gallipoli, Egypt and Palestine. The 2/5th remained in the UK until disbandment in May 1918 while the 3/5th became a reserve unit and was absorbed into the 4th (Reserve) Battalion in 1916.

During the Second World War the 5th Norfolk served in the UK until 1942 when it moved to Malaya where it was subsequently captured by the Japanese. The battalion was not re-formed after the war and was officially disbanded in 1947.

6th (Cyclist) Battalion

Formed at Norwich as a new battalion in 1908 from the cyclist companies of the 1st and 4th Volunteer Battalions, Norfolk Regiment, the 6th formed three battalions during the First World War and remained in the UK on coastal defence duties.

The 6th Norfolks were re-formed in 1920, as East Anglian Divisional Royal Engineers.

6th Battalion

Formed in 1939 as a duplicate of the 4th Battalion at Norwich, it was captured in Malaya by the Japanese in 1942 and amalgamated in 1947 with the parent unit.

Officers of the City of Norwich Rifle Volunteers on the range at Mousehold Heath in 1862. From a coloured lithograph by J. H. Lynch after Claude L. Nurset, published January 1863. **National Army Museum**

7th Battalion

Formed in 1939 as the 7th (Pioneer) Battalion, a duplicate of the 5th at King's Lynn, the battalion was converted to an infantry role in 1940 and during that year saw service in France and Belgium. As part of the 176th Infantry Brigade the 7th was involved in the fighting around Caen and Mont Pincon during 1944. It was placed into suspended animation in 1946 and finally disbanded in 1947.

8th (Home Defence) Battalion

See 30th Battalion

11th Battalion

Formed in 1915 as 61 Provisional Battalion (TF), it became the 11th Norfolk Regiment in 1917 and was disbanded in December of the same year.

12th (Norfolk Yeomanry) Battalion

The battalion was formed in 1917 from personnel of the 1/1st Norfolk Yeomanry, then serving in a dismounted role in Egypt. As part of the 74th Division the battalion later moved to the Western Front.

30th Battalion

Formed in 1936 as No 9 Group National Defence Companies it became the 8th (Home Defence) Battalion, Norfolk Regiment in 1939 and 30th Battalion in 1941. The battalion took part in the Italy and Balkans Campaigns during 1943–5 and was finally disbanded in 1946.

4th Battalion, Lincolnshire Regiment, 1937. In 1937 the Territorial Machine Gun Cup was won by the 4th Lincolns seen here having just received their cup and medals. The 'Sphinx' badge of the regiment, commemorating its service in Egypt in 1801, is displayed on a star by the officers and above a scroll by the other ranks.

The Royal Lincolnshire Regiment

4th Battalion

Both the 4th and 5th Battalions of the Royal Lincolnshire Regiment originated from the rifle volunteers of the county. In 1860, two admin battalions were formed, which in 1880 became the 1st and 2nd Lincolnshire Rifle Volunteer Corps. These in turn became the 1st and 2nd Volunteer Battalions, Lincolnshire Regiment in 1883 and in 1900, the 3rd was formed from part of the 1st Bn. During

the war in South Africa, all three battalions provided men for active service. They served with the regular battalions and were involved in the capture of Johannesburg and Pretoria.

In 1908 the three volunteer battalions were reorganised to form the Lincolns' two new Territorial Force battalions, the 4th and 5th. In 1915 the 1/4th Battalion went to France where it saw a great deal of action on the Western Front. The 2/4th had been formed at the beginning of the war and until 1917 served in Ireland. It arrived in France in February 1917 and later took part in the operations around Ypres and Cambrai. The 3/4th served as the 4th (Reserve) Battalion.

The 4th was re-formed after the war and during the Second World War saw service in Norway, Iceland and NW Europe. In 1950 it was amalgamated with the 6th Lincolns to form the 4th/6th Battalion and now forms part of the 7th (Volunteer) Battalion, Royal Anglian Regiment.

5th Battalion

The origins of the 5th Battalion, Royal Lincolnshire Regiment have already been covered above (see 4th Battalion). During the First World War both the 1/5th and 2/5th saw active service in France and Belgium, the two being amalgamated in 1918. The 3/5th was a reserve unit. After the war the battalion was converted to an anti-aircraft role and transferred to the Royal Engineers in 1936 as 46th AA Battalion.

6th Battalion

Formed in 1939 as a duplicate of the 4th Battalion. The 6th saw service in France during 1940, North Africa, Italy, Egypt, Palestine, Syria and Greece and was finally placed into suspended animation in 1945. Reconstituted as a motor battalion in 1947, in 1950 it was amalgamated with the 4th Battalion to form the 4th/6th Battalion.

13th Battalion

Formed in 1915 as 28 Provisional Battalion (TF) it became 13th Lincolnshire Regiment in 1917 and was disbanded in October of the same year.

The Devonshire Regiment

4th Battalion

Formed in 1852, the 1st Devonshire Rifle Volunteer Corps was the senior volunteer unit in the United Kingdom. It was raised in Exeter and in 1885 became the 1st (Exeter and South Devon) Volunteer Battalion of the Devonshire Regiment. In 1860 several other Devonshire rifle corps from the Exeter area were placed together as the 1st Admin Battalion of Devonshire Rifle Volunteers. This formation became 3rd Corps in 1880 and the 3rd Volunteer Battalion, Devonshire Regiment in 1885.

Both battalions contributed a large number of volunteers for service with the regular battalions in South Africa. In 1908 the 1st and 3rd were merged to form the 4th Battalion, Devonshire Regiment (TF).

In 1914 the 1/4th Battalion left Southampton for India where they served until early 1916. On 2 March the battalion landed at Basra and later formed part of the Tigris River defences. The 2/4th also served in India. It moved to Egypt and was disbanded there in 1918. The 3/4th remained in the UK and served as the 4th (Reserve) Battalion.

During the Second World War the 4th Devons served in the 2nd Gibraltar Brigade, arriving on the rock in May 1940 and leaving in December 1943. After the war an amalgamation took place with the 8th Devonshire Regiment and in 1950 a further merger, this time with the 5th Battalion and the 628 Heavy Regiment, Royal Artillery (see 6th Bn).

Upon the amalgamation in 1958 of the regular battalion of the Devonshire Regiment with that of the Dorsets, forming the Devonshire and Dorset Regiment, the county title was continued by the 4th Battalion. It became known as the Devonshire Regiment (1st Rifle Volunteers) and since 1967 has provided elements of the Devonshire Territorials, the Wessex Yeomanry and the 1st Battalion Wessex Regiment (Rifle Volunteers).

5th (Prince of Wales's) Battalion

The title 'Prince of Wales's' was conferred upon the 2nd Devonshire Rifle Volunteer Corps in 1880. The 2nd had been formed that year by the consolidation of the 2nd Admin Battalion of Devonshire Rifle Volunteers, which had been formed with headquarters at Plymouth in 1860. Also in 1860 the county's 4th Admin Battalion was formed at Newton Abbott. This became the 5th Corps in

1880 and in 1885, the 5th Volunteer Battalion, Devonshire Regiment. At the same time the 2nd Devon RVC became the regiment's 2nd Volunteer Battalion and in 1900 both contributed to the service company that joined Buller's force at Ladysmith.

The year 1908 saw the two battalions amalgamated as the 5th (Prince of Wales's) Battalion (TF). Later numbered as 1/5th, the battalion went out to India in 1914. It left Bombay for Egypt in March 1917, landing at the Suez on 4 April. From there it went to France where it saw a great deal of action on the Western Front as part of the 62nd Division. The 2/5th Battalion left Devonport for Egypt in September 1915 and was disbanded there in July of the following year. A 3/5th was also formed which was absorbed into the 4th (Reserve) Battalion in 1916.

In November 1941 the 5th Battalion was converted to, 86th Anti-Tank Regiment, Royal Artillery and was to serve as such throughout NW Europe. After the war the battalion reverted to infantry and in 1950 was amalgamated with the 4th Devons.

6th Battalion

Formed in 1860 as the 3rd Admin Battalion of Devonshire Rifle Volunteers at Barnstaple, it became 4th Corps, with seven companies, in 1880, and subsequently the 4th Volunteer Battalion, Devonshire Regiment in 1885.

Both the 1/6th and 2/6th Battalions were sent to India at the beginning of the First World War. They later moved to Mesopotamia and served as part of the Tigris River defences and on lines of communications. The 3/6th was also formed and remained in the UK in reserve.

The 6th Battalion served in the UK throughout the Second World War. In 1947 an amalgamation took place with the 9th Devons to form 628th Heavy Regiment, Royal Artillery. However, in 1950 most of the regiment reverted to the Devons as part of an amalgamation with the 4th and 5th Battalions to form the 4th Bn.

Left
Volunteer of the 1st Devonshire Rifles. Th[e]
green uniform has a black collar and cuff[s]
is worn here with a belt displaying the Arm[s]
Exeter, the headquarters of the corps.
Right
Mounted officer of the 4th Battalion,
Devonshire Regiment, 1909. Painted by
R. Caton Woodville.

7th (Cyclist) Battalion

The battalion was formed at Exeter in 1908 from the cyclist sections of the 1st and 5th Volunteer Battalions, Devonshire Regiment. During the First World War, both the 1/7th and 2/7th served on coastal defences in the UK. In 1920 the 7th Devons were to be converted to artillery. This was not accepted by the battalion and it chose to disband.

7th (Haytor) Battalion

This battalion was formed in 1939 as a duplicate of the 5th Battalion. In 1941 the 7th was converted as 87th Anti-Tank Regiment, Royal Artillery and served as such throughout North Africa.

8th Battalion

Formed in 1939 as a duplicate of the 4th Battalion at Yelverton, it served in the UK throughout the war and was amalgamated with the 4th in 1947.

9th Battalion

Formed in 1939 as a duplicate of the 6th Battalion, it served in the UK during the Second World War and amalgamated with the 6th in 1947.

10th (Home Defence) Battalion

See 30th Battalion

15th Battalion

Formed in 1915 as 86th Provisional Battalion (TF), it became the 15th Devons in 1917 and was disbanded in 1919.

16th (Royal 1st Devon and Royal North Devon Yeomanry) Battalion

This battalion was formed by the amalgamation of the two Devonshire yeomanry regiments in 1916. At this time the yeomen were serving in a dismounted role, patrolling the Suez Canal. As part of the 74th (Yeomanry) Division, the battalion fought in Egypt, Palestine and later on the Western Front.

30th Battalion

Formed in 1936 as 80a Group National Defence Companies, it became 10th (Home Defence) Battalion, Devonshire Regiment in 1939, the 30th in 1941, and was finally disbanded in 1945.

The Suffolk Regiment

4th Battalion

The 1st Suffolk Rifle Volunteer Corps was formed at Ipswich in 1859. In 1860 the 1st, together with other corps from the area, were grouped as the 2nd Admin Battalion of Suffolk Rifle Volunteers. The volunteer reorganisations of 1880 saw the battalion consolidated as the 1st Corps of eight companies. The 1st became the 1st Volunteer Battalion Suffolk Regiment in 1887 and during the Boer War contributed to the volunteer service companies that went out to South Africa.

The battalion landed in France on 9 November 1914. It later served in

Musicians of the 2nd Volunteer Battalion, The Suffolk Regiment, 1907.

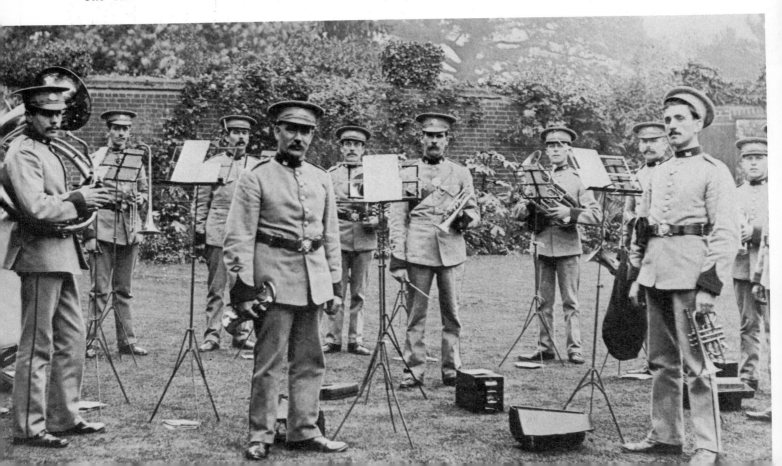

Left
Volunteer of the 1st Suffolk Corps. The uniform of this battalion was green and with black facings.
Right
2nd Volunteer Battalion, The Suffolk Regiment. The subject of this photograph is a retired sergeant and as such he was permitted to wear his uniform with the letter R embroidered into the shoulder strap.
D. J. Barnes

several formations including the Jullundur Brigade, Lahore Division. The battalion joined the 58th Division in February 1918 and was converted to a pioneer role until the end of the war.

The 2/4th Suffolks was formed at Ipswich in 1915 and was disbanded in January of the following year. The reserve battalion, 3/4th, was merged with the 5th Reserve Suffolks and the 1st Reserve Cambridgeshire Regiment to form the Cambridgeshire and Suffolk Reserve Battalion.

After the war the 4th and 5th Battalions, Suffolk Regiment were amalgamated as the 4th, but in 1939 were again separated for war service. As part of the 54th Infantry Brigade, both battalions were captured by the Japanese in February 1942, while taking part in the battle for Singapore Island.

The battalions were once again amalgamated in 1947. In 1960, just after the regular battalion of the Suffolk Regiment had merged with that of the Norfolks, the 4th became known as the Suffolk Regiment. The following year another amalgamation took place, this time with the Cambridgeshire Regiment, to form the Suffolk and Cambridgeshire Regiment. The Suffolk part of the regiment is now represented by the 6th (Volunteer) Battalion, Royal Anglian Regiment.

5th Battalion

The 5th Bn was created in 1860 as the 1st Admin Battalion of the Suffolk Rifle Volunteers. In 1880 the battalion was consolidated and was given the opportunity of taking on the position of the 2nd Corps within the county. However it chose to assume the number held by the senior corps within the battalion, the 6th.

The 6th Suffolk Rifle Volunteer Corps became the 2nd Volunteer Battalion, Suffolk Regiment in 1887 and in 1908 the 5th Battalion (TF). As part of the 54th (East Anglian) Division the battalion served in the First World War at Gallipoli. It later took part in the Invasion of Palestine where it saw action at the several battles for Gaza. Both 2nd and 3rd line battalions were formed which remained in the UK throughout the war.

The 5th Suffolks were amalgamated with the 4th Battalion in 1920.

6th (Cyclist) Battalion

In 1908 the several volunteer cyclist units of the Suffolk and Essex Regiments were organised into the Essex and Suffolk Cyclist Battalion. By 1910 the battalion had been divided, the four Suffolk companies being removed to form the 6th (Cyclist) Battalion, Suffolk Regiment.

The 1/6th served for most of the First World War on defence duty in Saxmundham. It was attached to the 1st Mounted, and later 68th Divisions. A 2/6th was formed which patrolled the coast between Skegness and Sutton-on-Sea. The 3/6th only existed between May 1915 and March 1916. The 6th Battalion was re-formed after the war as 58th Medium Brigade, Royal Garrison Artillery.

6th (Home Defence) Battalion

See 30th and 31st Battalions

Silver helmet plate of the 1st Suffolk Rifle Volunteer Corps.

9th Battalion

See 31st Battalion

14th Battalion

Formed in April 1915 as 64th Provisional Battalion (TF), it became the 14th Suffolks in January 1917 and was disbanded at Holt in March 1919.

15th (Suffolk Yeomanry) Battalion

The battalion was formed in March 1917 from the 1/1st Suffolk Yeomanry, then serving as infantry in Egypt. As the 15th Suffolks, the battalion served with the 74th (Yeomanry) Division in Palestine and on the Western Front.

30th Battalion

Formed in 1936 as 7 Group National Defence Companies, it became the 6th (Home Defence) Battalion, Suffolk Regiment in 1939, the 30th Battalion in 1941 and was disbanded at Yeovil in 1913.

31st Battalion

Formed in 1940 as the 2/6th (Home Defence) Battalion, Suffolk Regiment, it became 9th Battalion in 1940, 31st in 1941 and was disbanded at Saffron Walden in 1946.

Lance Corporal of the 2nd Volunteer Battalion, The Suffolk Regiment, 1907. The grey uniform has scarlet collar, cuffs and piping. The part played by the Suffolk Regiment during the siege of Gibraltar, 1779–83, is represented by the 'Castle' badge worn on the cap and collar.

Private, 3rd Somersetshire Rifle Volunteer Corps, c1878. The 3rd Corps, as a member of the 2nd Admin Battalion of Somersetshire Rifle Volunteers, displays on the shoulder straps of its grey uniforms the abbreviated title as laid down in 'Volunteer Regulations' – '2AB' over '3' over 'Sm'. The battalion numeral is also shown in the centre of the 'Maltese Cross' helmet plate.

The Somerset Light Infantry (Prince Albert's)

4th Battalion

In 1860 the County of Somersetshire organised its existing rifle volunteer corps into three admin battalions. The headquarters of each were – 1st at Bath, 2nd at Taunton and 3rd at Wells. The three battalions became the 1st, 2nd and 3rd Somersetshire Rifle Volunteer Corps in 1880, and in 1882 were the first to be shown in General Orders as having changed to a 'Volunteer Battalion' designation – 1st, 2nd and 3rd Somersetshire Light Infantry.

In 1908 the Somerset Light Infantry were allotted two Territorial Force battalions, the 4th and 5th. These were formed from the members of the three existing volunteer battalions which were amalgamated for this purpose. Headquarters of the 4th Battalion were placed at Bath, its recruitment area being the northern part of the county. As part of the Wessex Division, the battalion sailed for India in October 1914, landing at Bombay on the 9 November. In February 1916, the battalion went to Basra to join the 37th Indian Brigade. It was transferred the same year to the 41st Indian Brigade and served on lines of communication work in Mesopotamia.

Upon formation, the 2/4th Battalion joined the 45th Division, and on 12 December 1914, sailed for India. On 25 September 1917, the battalion landed at Suez and joined the 75th Division near Deir el Balah. From here the 2/4th went to France where it served as a pioneer battalion with the 34th division for the remainder of the war. The 3/4th provided the 4th (Reserve) Bn.

The 4th Somersets fought in NW Europe as part of the 43rd Infantry Division during 1944–5, and was amalgamated with the 5th and 6th battalions of the regiment in May 1950. The title, 4th/5th Battalion was later assumed.

In 1959, the regular battalion of the Somerset Light Infantry was amalgamated with that of the Duke of Cornwall's Light Infantry to form the Somerset and Cornwall Light Infantry. The following year the 4th Battalion was permitted to carry on the old regimental title, and from then on was known as the Somerset Light Infantry (Prince Albert's). The battalion now form part of the 6th (Volunteer) Battalion, Light Infantry.

5th Battalion

This battalion had originally been raised in 1859 as rifle volunteer companies. Headquarters of the 5th Battalion, Somerset Light Infantry was at Taunton, its

recruiting area being south of a line Burnham to Wincanton. The battalion went with the Wessex Division to India in October 1914, and later served in Egypt and Palestine. The 2/5th also served in India while the 3/5th remained at home as a reserve unit.

During the Second World War, the 5th Somersets served in the UK. In 1947 it was converted to 630 Medium Regiment, Royal Artillery and in 1950 reverted to an infantry role and was absorbed into the 4th Battalion.

6th Battalion

Formed in 1939 at Wells as a duplicate of the 4th Battalion, it served in the UK throughout the war, being amalgamated with the 4th and 5th Somersets in 1950 to form the 4th Battalion.

7th Battalion

Formed in 1939 as a duplicate of the 5th Battalion at Taunton, the battalion remained in the UK until 1944, when it took part in the NW Europe operations. It was amalgamated in 1947 with the 5th Battalion and converted to 630 Medium Regiment Royal Artillery.

8th (Home Defence) Battalion

See 30th Battalion

11th Battalion

Formed in 1915 as 85th Provisional Battalion (TF), it became 11th Somersets in 1917 and in 1918 served as a garrison guard battalion. The 11th went to France with the 59th Division in May 1918.

12th (West Somerset Yeomanry) Battalion

This battalion was formed on 4 January 1917 in Egypt, where it had been serving in a dismounted role. The battalion became part of the 74th (Yeomanry) Division, fought in Palestine, and from May 1918, in France and Belgium.

30th Battalion

Formed in 1936 as D and E Companies of 80b Group National Defence Companies, it became 8th (Home Defence) Battalion, Somerset Light Infantry in 1939 and 30th Bn in 1941. The battalion served in North Africa, Sicily and Italy and was disbanded in 1946.

Left
Members of the 1st Volunteer Battalion, Somerset Light Infantry at camp in 1907. The uniforms worn are scarlet with blue facings and white piping. **J. G. Woodroff**
Right
Lieutenant Colonel W. H. Roberts, 4th Battalion, Somerset Light Infantry, presenting Bugle Major Wiltshire to HRH Princess Margaret, Bath, 1 May 1948. **Somerset Light Infantry Museum**

The West Yorkshire Regiment (The Prince of Wales's Own)

5th Battalion

The 1st Yorkshire West Riding Rifle Volunteer Corps was formed at York in 1859. The following year the 1st, together with several other West Riding companies, were grouped as the 1st Admin Battalion of West Riding Rifle Volunteers. The 1st became the 1st Volunteer Battalion, West Yorkshire Regiment in 1887 and during the Boer War 9 officers and 210 men volunteered for service in South Africa. Members of the 1st Service Company were in Hamilton's Brigade, and took part in the actions at Botha's Pass and Alliman's Nek.

In the First World War the 1/5th Battalion served with the 49th (West Riding) Division and while on the Western Front on 19 December 1915, experienced the first attack of phosgene gas. The 2/5th fought in the 62nd Division, and served in France and Belgium throughout the war. The 3/5th was also formed which became the 5th (Reserve) Bn in 1916.

The Second World War saw the battalion divided as 1/5th and 2/5th, the latter eventually becoming the 14th Battalion, West Yorkshire Regiment. The 1/5th served in Iceland as part of the Alabaster Force between 1940 and 1942. The battalion was placed in suspended animation in 1946, reformed in 1947 as 5th, and concurrently amalgamated with the 14th Battalion.

On 25 April 1958 the regular battalion of the West Yorkshire Regiment was amalgamated with that of the East Yorkshires to form – the Prince of Wales's Own Regiment of Yorkshire. Shortly after this the 5th West Yorks and the 4th East Yorks became the new regiment's 3rd Territorial Battalion. The 3rd Prince of Wales's own is now represented as part of 2nd Battalion Yorkshire Volunteers.

6th Battalion

Formed at Bradford in 1859 as the 5th and 6th Yorkshire West Riding Rifle Volunteer Corps, they were amalgamated in 1860 as the 3rd Corps. This became the 2nd Volunteer Battalion, West Yorkshire Regiment in 1887 and the 6th Battalion (TF) in 1908.

The 1/6th Battalion served in the 49th (West Riding) Division on the Western Front throughout the First World War. Cpl. Samuel Meekosha of the battalion gained the Victoria Cross while in action near Yser in France on 19 November 1915. The 2/6th Battalion went to France in January 1917 with the 62nd Division, while the 3/6th remained at home in reserve.

In October 1937 the battalion was converted to an anti-aircraft role and transferred to the Royal Engineers as 49th Battalion.

7th (Leeds Rifles) Battalion

The Leeds Rifles were formed in 1859 as the 11th Yorkshire West Riding Volunteer Corps. Renumbered as 7th in 1860 the corps later consisted of ten companies, mostly recruited from large firms in the Leeds area including Joshua Tetley's Brewery.

As the 3rd Volunteer Battalion, West Yorkshire Regiment, the Rifles sent several of its members out to South Africa during the Boer War.

In the First World War, two battalions served on the Western Front, a third at home in reserve, the 1/7th with the 49th Division and the 2/7th with the 62nd. Cpl. Sanders of the 1/7th won the VC near Thiepval, France in July 1916. Just before the outbreak of the Second World War, the 7th West Yorks were converted to an armoured role and transferred to the Royal Tank Regiment as 45th RTR fighting as such at El Alamein.

The Territorial Army reorganisations of 1947 saw the 45th amalgamated with its wartime duplicate unit 51st RTR as 45/51 RTR. In October 1956, the regiment was converted back to infantry and was once more known as 7th Battalion (Leeds Rifles), The West Yorkshire Regiment. A further amalgamation took place in February 1961, this time with the 8th Battalion to form The Leeds Rifles, Prince of Wales's Own Regiment of Yorkshire. The Leeds Rifles are now represented by elements of 1st and 2nd Battalions Yorkshire Volunteers.

8th (Leeds Rifles) Battalion

The 8th West Yorks was formed in 1908 as part of a double battalion with the 7th (see above). In the First World War the 8th fought as part of the 49th and 62nd Divisions on the Somme, Marne and in the Battle of the Hindenburg Line. The 2/8th also served on the Western Front and was amalgamated with the 1/8th in January 1918. The 3/8th became part of the 7th (Reserve) Bn.

During the Second World War the battalion served in India as 66 HAA Brigade, Royal Artillery. It was renumbered as 466 in 1947, and in 1961 converted back to an infantry role and merged with the 7th Battalion (see above).

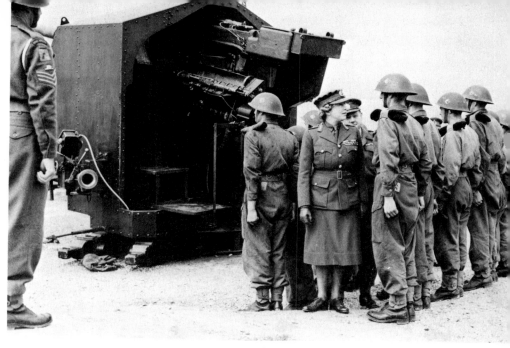

8th (Home Defence) Battalion

Formed in September 1936 as 44 Group National Defence Companies, it became 8th (HD) Battalion, West Yorks in November 1939 and in 1940 was divided as 1/10th and 2/10th Battalions. The same year the 1/10th once again became known as 8th, the 2/10th at the same time being redesignated the 30th. December 1941 saw the 8th absorbed into the 6th (HD) Battalion, East Yorkshire Regiment.

1/10th, 2/10th and 13th (Home Defence) Battalions

See 30th Battalion

14th Battalion

The 14th Bn was originally formed in 1939 as the 2/5th Battalion as a duplicate of the 5th. Under that title they fought as part of the 137th Infantry Brigade at St Omer La Bassee in 1940. The battalion took on an armoured role in 1942 and as 113 Regiment RAC served in the UK for the remainder of the war. Redesignated as 14th West Yorks in 1944, the battalion was placed in suspended animation until 1947 when it was merged with its parent unit.

30th Battalion

Formed at Doncaster in 1940 from part of the 8th (HD) Battalion and originally designated as 2/10th, the battalion became 13th and later 30th Bn. Disbandment was at Falmouth in 1942.

The East Yorkshire Regiment (The Duke of York's Own)

4th Battalion

During 1859–60 five independent companies of rifle volunteers were raised at Hull and designated as – 1st to 4th and 9th Yorkshire East Riding Rifle Volunteer Corps. By 1861 the five corps had been merged under the title of 1st. This became the 1st Volunteer Battalion, East Yorkshire Regiment in 1883, and in 1900, 61 all ranks went out to South Africa to serve with the regular 2nd Battalion of the regiment.

The 1/4th Battalion went to France with the 50th (Northumbrian) Division in April 1915 and subsequently took part in actions on the Somme, Ypres and Arras. On 15 July 1918 the battalion was reduced to cadre strength and moved to the Dieppe area for duty on lines of communications. The 2/4th Battalion was formed in Hull in September 1914 and served with the 63rd Division in the UK until

November 1916 when it left England for duty in Bermuda. The 3/4th became the 4th (Reserve) Battalion in 1916.

During 1940 the 4th East Yorks fought in France and Belgium. The following year it saw service in Egypt, Cyprus and Palestine and in 1942 was captured by the Germans while in Libya.

In 1947 the 4th and 5th Battalions were amalgamated as 4th, and in February 1960 joined the 5th West Yorks to form the 3rd Battalion, Prince of Wales's Own Regiment of Yorkshire. The battalion is now represented by part of 2nd Yorkshire Volunteers.

5th (Cyclist) Battalion

The 5th (Cyclist) Battalion was formed in 1908 from the cyclist personnel of the 1st Volunteer Battalion. Headquarters and four companies were at Hull while the remainder were recruited from around the East Riding. In 1914–18 the battalion served in the UK as part of the Humber defences. After the war it was re-formed as a regiment of the Royal Corps of Signals.

5th Battalion

A new 5th Battalion was formed in 1939 as a duplicate unit of the 4th. The battalion joined the 50th Infantry Division and saw its first action in France during 1940. It fought at El Alamein and throughout North Africa, Pte. Eric Anderson gaining a posthumous Victoria Cross at Akarit on the Wadi, Tripolitania on 6 April 1943. The 5th later took part in the invasion of Sicily and the assault landings in Normandy in June 1944. The battalion was merged with its parent unit in 1947.

6th (Home Defence) Battalion

See 30th Battalion

30th Battalion

Formed in 1936 as 43 Group National Defence Companies, it became 6th (Home Defence) Battalion, East Yorkshire Regiment in 1939 and was renumbered as 30th in 1941. Disbandment was at Spalding, Lincs in 1943.

The Bedfordshire and Hertfordshire Regiment

5th Battalion

Between 1860 and 1864, nine corps of rifle volunteers were formed in the County of Bedfordshire. They all joined the 1st Admin Battalion and in 1880 were amalgamated to form the 1st Bedfordshire Rifle Volunteer Corps of nine companies. This in turn became the 3rd Volunteer Battalion, Bedfordshire Regiment.

In 1900 a new volunteer battalion was raised for the Bedfordshire Regiment in Huntingdonshire. This was numbered 4th, and included personnel from the Huntingdon, St. Ives, Fletton and St. Neots areas. Upon the formation on the Territorial Force in 1908, the 3rd and 4th Volunteer Battalions were amalgamated to form the 5th Bedfords, four companies being found by each county.

As part of the 54th (East Anglian) Division, the 5th Bedfords went out to Gallipoli on 26 July 1915, taking part in the landings at Suvla Bay in August. The battalion moved to Egypt in December 1915 and in 1917 fought in Palestine where Pte. Samuel Needham won the Victoria Cross at Kefr Kasim on 10/11 September. The 2/5th and 3/5th Battalions served in the UK throughout the war.

The battalion was part of the 55th Infantry Brigade when it left India for Singapore in January 1942. It was subsequently captured by the Japanese during the battle for the island between 8 and 15 February.

In 1958 the regular battalion, which had become the Bedfordshire and Hertfordshire Regiment in 1919, was amalgamated with the Essex Regiment to form the 3rd East Anglian Regiment. At this time the 5th Battalion changed its name to the Bedfordshire Regiment. It joined with the Hertfordshire Regiment Territorials in 1961 and from then on was known as the 1st Battalion Bedfordshire and Hertfordshire Regiment. The Bedfordshire elements of the regiment are now represented as part of the 6th (Volunteer) Battalion, Royal Anglian Regiment.

Colour Sergeant, 5th Battalion, Bedfordshire Regiment. The badge worn on the right breast is the Imperial Service Brooch, indicating that the wearer had volunteered to serve overseas if required.

6th Battalion

The 6th Battalion Beds & Herts was formed as a duplicate of the 5th in 1939. It served in the UK throughout the war and was placed in suspended animation from 1946 until 1947, when it was amalgamated with its parent unit.

7th (Home Defence) Battalion

Formed in 1936 as 6 Group National Defence Companies, it became 7th (HD) Battalion, Beds & Herts in 1939 and in 1940 was divided to form the 1/7th and 2/7th Battalions.

10th (Home Defence Battalion

See 30th Battalion

11th Battalion

Formed in 1915 as 68 Provisional Battalion (TF) at Southwold, it became 11th Bedfords in 1917. It was disbanded in 1919 having served with 225 Brigade in the UK.

30th Battalion

Formed as the 2/7th (Home Defence) Battalion in 1940, it became the 10th in the same year, 30th in 1941 and was disbanded in Italy in 1946. The 30th had become part of the 42nd Infantry Brigade in July 1943. The brigade had been formed for internal security duties on lines of communications under Allied Force Headquarters. The 42nd went to North Africa in August 1943 and in November, for deception purposes, was called 57th Division. Its battalions were designated as 'brigades', the 30th becoming the 172nd.

The Royal Leicestershire Regiment

4th Battalion

There were ten volunteer rifle corps formed within the County of Leicestershire from 1859. These were grouped into the 1st Admin Battalion and in 1880, amalgamated as the 1st Leicestershire Rifle Volunteer Corps with headquarters at Leicester and eleven companies.

By 1900 the corps had grown to sixteen companies and was now divided into two battalions. That year a large number volunteered for service in South Africa. Those that went served with the 1st Regular battalion of the regiment, taking part in the actions at Laing's Nek, Belfast and the operations around Lydenberg.

The 1st Leicestershire Rifle Volunteer Corps became the 1st Volunteer Battalion, Leicestershire Regiment in 1883, and in 1908 provided the regiment's 4th and 5th Territorial Battalions. In March 1915 the 1/4th landed in France with the 46th (East Midland) Division. On 30 July the battalion was involved in the 'Liquid Fire' attack at Hooge and a year later took part in the fighting at Gommecourt on the Somme.

The 2/4th Battalion was part of the 59th Division in Ireland. It moved to France in February 1917 but was later reduced to a training cadre and sent back to England where it was absorbed into the 14th Leicesters. The 3/4th became the 4th (Reserve) Battalion in 1916.

The 4th Battalion was converted to, 44th Anti-Aircraft Battalion, Royal Engineers in 1936. It later joined the Royal Artillery as a searchlight regiment and in 1961, as part of 438 Light Anti-aircraft Regiment, reverted to an infantry role. As the 4th Royal Leicesters the battalion amalgamated with the 5th Battalion of the regiment and became the 4th/5th Battalion. It is now represented by the 7th (Volunteer) Battalion, Royal Anglian Regiment.

5th Battalion

Headquarters of the 5th Battalion were at Loughborough, where it was formed in 1908 from part of the 1st Volunteer Battalion, Leicestershire Regiment. The battalion served alongside the 4th Leicesters during the First World War. The 2/4th, however, were stationed in Ireland before moving to the Western Front in 1917. The 3/4th Battalion were absorbed into the 4th (Reserve) in 1916.

The battalion was doubled in strength in 1939, forming two battalions designated as 1/5th and 2/5th. The 1/5th spent a few weeks during 1940 in Norway, and upon returning to England became a training unit with 148 Infantry Brigade in 1942. The 2/5th served in France, 1940, and from 1943 saw action in North Africa and Italy.

The 1/5th and 2/5th were merged as 5th Battalion in 1947. In 1961 the 5th was amalgamated with the regiment's 4th Battalion and from then on was known as the 4th/5th Royal Leicestershires.

6th (Home Defence) Battalion

Formed in 1936 as 45a Group National Defence Companies, it became 6th (Home Defence) Battalion, Leicestershire Regiment in 1939 and was disbanded at Loughborough in 1941.

The Green Howards (Alexandra, Princess of Wales's Own Yorkshire Regiment)

4th Battalion

The 4th Green Howards originated in 1860 as the 1st Admin Battalion of Yorkshire North Riding Rifle Volunteers. Headquarters of the battalion were at Richmond and its components recruited from areas in the North Riding that included Swaledale, Leyburn, Startforth, Bedale and Catterick. The battalion was consolidated as the 1st North Riding Corps in 1880. It became the 1st Volunteer Battalion Green Howards in 1883 and in 1908 provided the regiment's 4th Territorial Battalion.

As part of the 50th (Northumbrian) Division, the 1/4th landed in France on 8 April 1915. It moved on to the Ypres sector and later fought on the Somme and at Arras. One officer of the battalion gained the Victoria Cross near Wancourt in

5th Battalion, Green Howards, in France, March 1917. **Green Howards Museum**

5th Battalion, Green Howards, 1939.
Green Howards Museum

1917. The 2/4th Battalion was formed at Northallerton in September 1914. It served in the UK with the 63rd Division until 1916, when it transferred to the 73rd. A 3/4th was also formed which in 1916 became the regiment's 4th (Reserve) Battalion.

The battalion served in France and Belgium during 1940. It spent a time in Egypt, Cyprus and Palestine the following year and in 1942 was captured by the Germans while taking part in the battle of Gazala in Libya on 1 June.

In 1961 the 4th was amalgamated with the regiment's former 5th Battalion, then serving as 631 Light Regiment, Royal Artillery, to form the 4th/5th Battalion, Green Howards. This battalion is now represented by elements of the 1st and 2nd Battalions, Yorkshire Volunteers.

5th Battalion

The 5th Battalion, Green Howards was created in 1908 from two Yorkshire volunteer battalions, the 2nd Green Howards and the 2nd East Yorkshires. Both these units had originated in 1860 as admin battalions of rifle volunteers and had provided men for war service in South Africa.

The 1/5th Battalion landed with the 50th (Northumbrian) Division at Boulogne on 17 May 1915. It immediately moved on to the Ypres sector and within days took part in the actions at St. Julien and Frezenberg Ridge. The 2/5th was formed at Scarborough in September 1914 and served in the UK until disbandment in March 1918. The 3/5th was absorbed into the 4th (Reserved) Battalion in 1916.

The battalion was with the 150th Infantry Brigade in Libya at the beginning of 1942, and like the 4th Green Howards was captured at Gazala on 1 June.

In 1947 the 5th was reconstituted as 631 Anti Tank-Regiment, Royal Artillery. It later became a light regiment and in 1961 reverted to an infantry role to form upon amalgamation, the 4th/5th Battalion.

6th Battalion

The 6th Battalion was formed in 1939 as a duplicate of the 4th. With the 50th Infantry Division it fought at El Alamein and later took part in the assault landings in Normandy on 6 June 1944. The 6th became 871 (Independent) Movement Light Battery, Royal Artillery in 1947.

7th Battalion

Formed as a duplicate battalion of the 5th Green Howards in 1939, the battalion served in the 50th Infantry Division and while at Tunisia on 20/21 March 1943, one of its officers gained the Victoria Cross. It later took part in the D Day landings of 6 June 1944. The battalion was absorbed into its parent unit in 1947.

8th (Home Defence) Battalion

See 13th and 30th Battalions

10th (East Riding Yeomanry) Battalion

Formed in June 1940 from the 2nd East Riding Yeomanry, the battalion later became the 12th Battalion, Parachute Regiment. As part of the 6th Airborne Division it took part in the parachute drop on D Day.

13th (Home Defence) Battalion

Formed in September 1940 as the 2/8th (HD) Battalion, it was redesignated as 13th in the same year. In June 1941 it was absorbed into the regiment's 8th Battalion.

18th Battalion

Formed as the 24th Provisional Battalion (Territorial Force) at Newcastle in June 1914, it became the 18th Green Howards in January 1917 and served in the UK as such until disbanded in 1919.

30th Battalion

Formed in September 1936 as 42 Group National Defence Companies, it became the 8th Green Howards in 1939 and 30th in 1941. Disbandment was in October 1946 the battalion having served in North Africa and the Italian Campaign of 1944.

Amalgamation parade, 4th Green Howards and 631 Light Regiment, Royal Artillery, to form 4th/5th Battalion. **Green Howards Museum**

The Lancashire Fusiliers

5th (Bury) Battalion

This battalion was formed at Bury as the 8th Lancashire Rifle Volunteer Corps in 1859. In 1883 the corps became the 1st Volunteer Battalion Lancashire Fusiliers, consisting of six companies in Bury and two at Heywood. A large number of volunteers served during the Boer War.

As part of the 42nd (East Lancashire) Division the battalion fought at Gallipoli before moving on to Egypt and France. While on the Western Front, L/Sgt. Edward Smith won the Victoria Cross for his part in the action East of Serre on the 21/23 August 1918. Smith, who also gained the DCM, was killed in France while serving with the 2nd Lancashire Fusiliers in 1940. In all three members of the 2/5th Battalion were also awarded the Victoria Cross. Pte. James Hutchinson by Ficheux on 28 June 1916, Lt. Col. Best-Dunkley at Wieltje on 31 July 1917 and 2nd Lt. John Schofield who was killed at Givenchy on 9 April 1918. A 3/5th Battalion also served in France while the 4/5th became the 5th (Reserve) Battalion Lancashire Fusiliers in 1916.

The Battalion served in France and Belgium during 1940 and after returning to the UK was converted as 108 Regiment Royal Armoured Corps. This regiment was part of the 10th Tank Brigade and acted as a holding and training unit.

The war-time duplicate unit of the 5th Lancashire Fusiliers was designated 2/5th Battalion and served in NW Europe during 1944. Both battalions were reconstituted after the war and amalgamated in 1947 as the 5th (Bury) Battalion, now represented as part of the 5th (Volunteer) Battalion, Royal Regiment of Fusiliers.

6th Battalion

Formed in 1860 at Rochdale as the 24th Lancashire Rifle Volunteer Corps, it became the 12th Bn in 1880 and the 2nd Volunteer Battalion Lancashire Fusiliers in 1883. A number of its members went to South Africa during the Boer War.

In the First World War the 1/6th Battalion formed part of the 42nd (East Lancashire) Division. This division was the first to leave England for foreign service, departing from Southampton on the 10 September 1914. The 42nd Division took part in the action at Helles, Gallipoli before moving to Egypt and the Suez defences. After reaching France in 1917 the 1/6th Lancashire Fusiliers were transferred to the 66th Division at Marcelcave. The 2/6th Battalion was formed at

Mossborough in 1914. It went to France in 1917 and was later absorbed into the 1/6th. The 3/6th was also formed, acting as the 6th (Reserve) Battalion.

In 1939 the 6th was once again divided into two battalions, having doubled its strength for the war. As the 1/6th Battalion a transfer was made in November 1941 to the Royal Armoured Corps. The battalion served as 109 Regiment until February 1944 when it was re-converted to an infantry role. The battalion was reconstituted in 1947, this time to 633 Light Anti-Aircraft Regiment, Royal Artillery.

The 2/6th Lancashire Fusiliers remained in the UK throughout the war and was disbanded in 1946.

7th Battalion

The 7th Battalion was formed as the 56th Lancashire Rifle Volunteer Corps in 1860. It became the 17th Corps in 1880 and the 3rd Volunteer Battalion, Lancashire Fusiliers in 1886. During the Boer War the 3rd VB contributed 119 all ranks to the service companies that were sent out to South Africa. By 1908 the battalion consisted of sixteen companies and, upon transfer to the Territorial Force, provided both the 7th and 8th Battalions of the Lancashire Fusiliers.

The 1/7th and 2/7th Battalions served in France during the First World War, the former seeing action before moving to the Western Front at Gallipoli and Egypt. The 2/7th was absorbed into the 24th (Service) Battalion in 1918, and after the war the 7th transferred in 1936 as 39th Anti-Aircraft Battalion, Royal Engineers. The 3/7th, formed in 1915, became part of the 6th (Reserve) Battalion in 1916.

8th Battalion

This battalion was formed from the 3rd Volunteer Battalion in 1908 (see 7th Battalion). During the First World War the 1/8th served alongside the other Territorial Battalions of the Lancashire Fusiliers in the 42nd Division. The 2/8th fought in France while the 3/8th was amalgamated in 1916 with the third line battalions of the 6th and 7th to form the 6th (Reserve) Battalion, Lancashire Fusiliers.

The 8th was doubled in 1939 and formed the 1/8th and 2/8th Battalions. The 2/8th served in the UK throughout the war, but the senior battalion saw service in 1940 at St Omer-la Bassee and later in India and Burma. The two battalions were amalgamated to form 634 HAA Regiment, Royal Artillery in 1947.

Left
1/5th Battalion, Lancashire Fusiliers, returning to Bury in March 1919.
Right
Drummer of the 1/7th Battalion, Lancashire Fusiliers, giving instruction on the Hotchkiss anti-aircraft gun to American troops, 18 May 1918, near Pas. **Imperial War Museum**

Crude brass shoulder title made by the 6th Battalion, Lancashire Fusiliers, while on overseas service during the First World War.

The Royal Scots Fusiliers

4th Battalion

The 1st Admin Battalion of Ayrshire Rifle Volunteers was formed in 1860 and soon contained the fourteen individual corps of riflemen that had been raised throughout the county. With this number of units the battalion became too large to administer efficiently. Subsequently, in 1873, it was divided into two. The 2nd Admin Battalion had its headquarters in Kilmarnock and included the companies then located in North Ayrshire.

The battalion was consolidated in 1880 as the 1st Ayrshire Rifle Volunteer Corps. This became the 1st Volunteer Battalion, Royal Scots Fusiliers in 1887 and contributed a number of its members to the war in South Africa.

As the 1/4th Royal Scots Fusiliers the battalion served with the 52nd (Lowland) Division throughout the First World War. It landed at Gallipoli in June 1915 and later took part in the action at Gully Revine. From Gallipoli the battalion moved to Egypt as part of the Suez Canal defences. It was involved in the Invasion of Palestine in 1917 and the following year, transferred to the Western Front for the last months of the war. During the Great War three members of the battalion won the Victoria Cross, Pte. Lauder at Cape Helles, Gallipoli and 2nd Lts. Boughey and Craig in Palestine.

The 2/4th Battalion was formed in October 1914 and, as part of the 65th Division, served in Ireland from January 1917 until disbandment in May 1918. The 3/4th Battalion was also raised and served as the 4th (Reserve) Bn.

The 4th was amalgamated with the 5th Royal Scots Fusiliers in 1921 to form the 4th/5th Battalion. During the Second World War the battalion saw action in France in 1940 and later throughout NW Europe. Fusilier Dennis Donnini gained a posthumous Victoria Cross near Hongen in Holland on 18 January 1945.

The 4th/5th Royal Scots Fusiliers is now represented in elements of the 1st and 2nd Battalions, 52nd Lowland (Volunteers).

5th Battalion

When the 1st Admin Battalion of Ayrshire Rifle Volunteers was divided in 1873 (see 4th Battalion), it retained the several corps located in the southern part of the county. The battalion became the 2nd Ayrshire Rifle Volunteer Corps in 1880 and the 2nd Volunteer Battalion Royal Scots Fusiliers in 1887.

The 2nd Volunteer Battalion became the 5th Battalion (TF) in 1908. It joined the Lowland Division and served throughout the First World War alongside the 4th Battalion (see above). A 2/5th was also formed which was absorbed in the 2/4th in January 1916, together with a 3/5th, which became part of the 4th (Reserve) Bn in 1916. After the war the 5th was merged with the 4th to form the 4th/5th Battalion, Royal Scots Fusiliers.

6th Battalion

Formed in 1939 as a duplicate of the 4th/5th Battalion at Kilmarnock, the battalion took part in the campaign in France and Belgium during May 1940. In 1944 it served with the 15th (Scottish) Infantry Division throughout NW Europe. The battalion was disbanded in 1947.

10th (Home Defence) Battalion

See 30th Battalion

11th Battalion

Formed in 1915 as the 11th (Scottish) Provisional Battalion (TF), it transferred to the Royal Scots Fusiliers in 1917, and served with the 59th Division in France as the 11th Garrison Guard Battalion.

12th (Ayr and Lanark Yeomanry) Battalion

This battalion was formed in 1917 from the 1/1st Ayrshire and 1/1st Lanarkshire Yeomanry, then serving in a dismounted role in Egypt. The battalion fought in Palestine and on the Western Front.

30th Battalion

Formed in 1936 as 68a Group National Defence Companies, the unit became 10th (Home Defence) Battalion, Royal Scots Fusiliers in 1939, and the 30th Battalion in 1941. Disbandment was at Perth in 1943.

The Ardeer Company

This independent company was formed in 1913 by the Nobel Explosives Factory at the Ardeer Works, three miles north west of Irvine in Ayrshire. Attached to the 4th Royal Scots Fusiliers, the company was formed with the intention of guarding the factory in the event of war. The company is not shown in the *Army List* after 1922.

Colour Sergeant Galloway, 2nd Volunteer Battalion, Royal Scots Fusiliers, an ex-champion shot of Scotland seen here with numerous cups, medals and badges awarded to him for good shooting.

The Cheshire Regiment

4th Battalion

The 4th Cheshire Regiment originated in 1860 as the 1st Admin Battalion of Cheshire Rifle Volunteers. In 1880 the battalion became the 1st Cheshire Rifle Volunteer Corps of eight companies and in 1887 was redesignated as the 1st Volunteer Battalion, Cheshire Regiment. In 1900 the battalion sent a number of its members to South Africa.

During the First World War the 1/4th went with the 53rd (Welsh) Division to Gallipoli where it took part in the landing at Suvla in August 1915. The division later served in Egypt and Palestine. The 1/4th Cheshires left the 53rd Division in May 1918 and moved to France and the 34th Division.

Both 2nd and 3rd line units were formed. The 2/4th served in the 68th Division until amalgamated with the 2/7th in November 1915, while the 3/4th became the 4th (Reserve) Battalion.

After the war the 4th and 5th Battalions of the Cheshire Regiment were amalgamated as the 4th/5th (Earl of Chester's) Battalion. In 1939, however, the two were divided for war service. The 4th was converted to a machine gun battalion and went with the BEF to France in 1940. Two companies engaged the enemy near Metz and were, according to the Regimental history, 'the first TA troops to fire upon the Germans'. The battalion returned to England via Dunkirk and spent the remainder of the war in the UK. The 4th is now part of the 1st and 2nd Mercian Volunteers.

5th (Earl of Chester's) Battalion

Formed in 1860 as the 2nd Admin Battalion of Cheshire Rifle Volunteers. Headquarters was at Chester and the recruiting area included Runcorn, Weaverham and Frodsham. The title 'Earl of Chester's' was taken into use by the senior company of the battalion in 1870. It was retained in 1880 when the 2nd Admin became the 2nd Cheshire Rifle Volunteer Corps and again in 1887 when the corps became the 2nd (Earl of Chester's) Volunteer Battalion of the Cheshire Regiment. Also formed in 1860 was the county's 3rd Admin Battalion. This became the 3rd Corps and subsequently the 3rd Volunteer Battalion. Headquarters were at Knutsford. Both the 2nd and 3rd Volunteer Battalions sent members to South Africa during the Boer War.

In 1908 the 2nd and 3rd Volunteer Battalions were amalgamated to form the 5th

(Earl of Chester's) Battalion, The Cheshire Regiment. As the 1/5th Cheshires the battalion went to the Western Front in 1915 as the divisional pioneer battalion of the 5th Regular Division. Retaining its pioneer role, the 1/5th transferred to the 56th (1st London) Division in February 1916. Both the 2/5th and 3/5th Battalions were formed during the First World War.

The 5th formed the 4th/5th Battalion Cheshire Regiment upon amalgamation in 1921. The two battalions were divided for war service in 1939, the 5th being stationed in the UK until disbanded in 1947.

6th Battalion

The 6th was formerly the 4th Admin Battalion of Cheshire Rifle Volunteers (1860–80), the 4th Cheshire Rifle Volunteer Corps (1880–7) and the 4th Volunteer Battalion Cheshire Regiment (1887–1908). Headquarters were at Stockport and in addition to Cheshire companies, the battalion also included at one time two from the neighbouring county of Derbyshire.

The 1/6th served with a number of formations throughout France and Belgium during the First World War. The 2/6th was formed at Stockport in 1914 while the 3/6th became part of the 4th (Reserve) Battalion in 1916.

In 1920 the battalion was converted as the 6th Medium Brigade, Royal Garrison Artillery. It was not until 1939 that the regiment once again included a 6th Battalion. A new 6th being formed that year as a duplicate of the 7th at Stockport. It became a machine gun battalion and fought in the Western Desert, taking part in the Battle of El Alamein, and in the Italian Campaign. The 6th was disbanded in 1947.

7th Battalion

The 7th Battalion was formed in 1908 from the 5th Volunteer Battalion, Cheshire Regiment. This was formerly the 5th Cheshire Rifle Volunteer Corps and before that the 5th Admin Battalion of Cheshire Rifle Volunteers.

During the First World War the 1/7th served with the 53rd (Welsh) Division at Gallipoli, Egypt and Palestine. It later moved to the Western Front and fought throughout France and Belgium. The 2/7th was formed at Macclesfield in 1914 and remained in the UK as part of the 68th Division, while the 3/7th became part of the 4th (Reserve) Battalion in 1916.

As a machine gun battalion, the 7th served in France and Belgium during the 1940 campaign. It later saw action in Sicily and Italy. The battalion is now represented in both the 1st and 2nd Mercian Volunteers.

8th (Home Defence) Battalion

See 30th Battalion

23rd Battalion

Formed in 1915 as 46 Provisional Battalion (TF), it became 23rd Bn Cheshire Regiment in 1917 and served as a garrison battalion with the 59th Division in France.

30th Battalion

Formed in 1936 as 103a Group National Defence Companies, the unit became 8th (Home Defence) Battalion, Cheshire Regiment in 1939 and the 30th in 1941. War service was in North Africa and as the British garrison battalion in Rome during 1944/5.

Above
A volunteer battalion of the Cheshire
Regiment, c1907. **D. Barnes**
Below
Bugler of the 1st Cadet Battalion, The
Cheshire Regiment. The battalion was formed
in 1901 at Northenden and wore scarlet tunics
with white collar and cuffs. The 'Acorn' badge
worn on the collar is an old badge of the
Cheshire Regiment and is said to
commemorate their services at the battle of
Dettingen.

The Royal Welch Fusiliers

4th (Denbighshire) Battalion

The 4th Royal Welch Fusiliers was formed in 1860 as the 1st Admin Battalion of Denbighshire Rifle Volunteers. Headquarters were at Ruabon and included were the nine corps that had been raised within the county. The battalion became the 1st Denbighshire Rifle Volunteer Corps in 1880, and four years later, the 1st Volunteer Battalion of the Royal Welsh Fusiliers.

In 1900 the regiment sent three volunteer service companies out to South Africa. They served as part of Barton's Union Brigade and saw action at Rooidam, Kraal Pan and Frederickstadt.

The battalion went to France in 1914 and the following year became the divisional pioneer battalion of the 47th Division. The 2/4th was formed in September 1914 and disbanded at Yarmouth in 1918, while the 3/4th became the 4th (Reserve) Battalion in 1916.

During the Second World War, the 4th served in NW Europe from 25 June 1944. In 1947 it was amalgamated with the 8th Battalion and is now represented by part of the 3rd (Volunteer) Battalion, Royal Welch Fusiliers.

(*Note. The spelling of the regimental name was officially altered in 1920 from 'Welsh' to 'Welch'.*)

5th (Flintshire) Battalion

The battalion originally contained the volunteers from both Flintshire and Carnarvonshire. It was designated as the 1st Flint and Carnarvon Rifle Volunteer Corps in 1880 and then as the 2nd Volunteer Battalion, Royal Welsh Fusiliers in 1884. 127 members of the battalion served with the regular battalions in South Africa during the Boer War.

As part of the 53rd (Welsh) Division, the 1/5th Battalion landed at Suvla Bay, Gallipoli in August 1915. From there it moved to Egypt and Palestine where it was amalgamated with the 1/6th Royal Welsh Fusiliers to form the 5th/6th Battalion.

The battalion was reconstituted as 5th in 1920 and in 1938 converted as 60th Anti-Tank Regiment, Royal Artillery.

6th (Carnarvonshire and Anglesey) Battalion

As previously mentioned above, the 5th Royal Welch Fusiliers was originally recruited in the counties of Flintshire and Carnarvonshire. In 1887 the Carnarvonshire part of the battalion was detached and formed into the 3rd Volunteer Battalion, Royal Welsh Fusiliers with headquarters at Carnarvon. When the 6th Battalion was created in 1908, seven of the eight companies were located in Carnarvonshire. The eighth was found in Anglesey and had its headquarters at Holyhead.

The 1/6th Battalion served alongside the 1/5th during the First World War, and while in Palestine Capt. John Fox Russell RAMC, who was then attached to the 1/6th, gained the Victoria Cross.

The battalion was re-formed after the war and in 1944/5 served throughout NW Europe. In 1947 the battalion was amalgamated with the 9th Royal Welch Fusiliers and converted to 635 Light Anti-Aircraft Regiment, Royal Artillery. In 1955 further re-organisations of the TA amalgamated the regiment with the former 7th Battalion Royal Welch Fusiliers, then serving as 636 LAA Regt, to form 466 (Royal Welch) LAA Regt. The following year the regiment assumed an infantry role and was designated 6th/7th Battalion, Royal Welch Fusiliers. It now forms part of the 3rd (Volunteer) Battalion Royal Welch Fusiliers.

7th (Merionethshire and Montgomeryshire) Battalion

As the name suggests, the battalion was recruited from two counties. However it was not until 1937 that this title was assumed, the battalion being previously known as the 7th (Montgomery) Bn.

Montgomeryshire had raised five corps of rifle corps of rifle volunteers during 1860/1, but all these were disbanded by the end of 1876. It was in 1897 that the county once again provided rifle volunteers when in that year it raised the 5th Volunteer Battalion of the South Wales Borderers. The battalion was recruited throughout the county and also included a whole company formed by members of Aberystwyth University.

In 1908 the university contingent of the battalion became part of the Senior Division of the Officers Training Corps. The remainder provided the 7th Royal Welch Fusiliers. During the First World War the 1/7th Battalion served at Gallipoli, Egypt and Palestine while the 2/7th and 3/7th remained in the UK.

The 7th fought in NW Europe during 1944/5. In 1947 it was amalgamated with the 10th Battalion as 636 LAA Regiment, Royal Artillery and in 1955 merged with the former 6th Royal Welch Fusiliers, then serving as 635 LAA Regt to form a new LAA Regiment numbered as 446. This in turn became the 6th/7th Battalion Royal Welch Fusiliers and is now part of the 3rd (Volunteer) Battalion of the same regiment.

8th (Denbighshire) Battalion

Formed in 1939 as a duplicate of the 4th Battalion, the 8th served throughout the Second World War in the UK with 115 Infantry Brigade, and in 1947 was amalgamated with the 4th.

9th (Carnarvonshire and Anglesey) Battalion

Formed in 1939 as a duplicate of the 6th Battalion, it served in the UK throughout the war and was amalgamated with the 6th in 1947.

10th (Merionethshire and Montgomeryshire) Battalion

This battalion was formed as a duplicate of the 7th Battalion in 1939. In 1942 the

Territorials of the Royal Welsh Fusiliers, c1910. Painted by R. Caton Woodville. Note the black 'Flashes' worn on the back of the tunic collars. This distinction was granted to the 23rd Royal Welsh Fusiliers in 1834.

battalion was converted to 6th Battalion (Royal Welch) The Parachute Regiment and as part of the 2nd Para Brigade, fought at Cassino in May 1944. The battalion reverted to its former role and title in 1946, and the following year was absorbed into the 7th Battalion.

1/11th and 2/11th (Home Defence) Battalions

See 30th and 31st Battalions

14th Battalion

See 31st Battalion

23rd Battalion

Formed in 1915 as 47th Provisional Battalion (TF), it became 23rd Bn Royal Welsh Fusiliers in 1917 and was disbanded in 1919.

24th (Denbighshire Yeomanry) Battalion

This battalion was formed in 1917 from the 1/1st Denbighshire Hussars, then serving in Egypt in a dismounted role. From Egypt the battalion moved to Palestine as part of the 74th (Yeomanry) Division. It later went to France for the remaining months of the war.

25th (Montgomery and Welsh Horse Yeomanry) Battalion

Formed in 1917 from dismounted yeomen of the two regiments, the battalion took part in the Palestine campaign and for the last months of the war fought on the Western Front.

30th Battalion

Formed in 1936 as 105a Group National Defence Companies, the unit became the 11th (Home Defence) Battalion, Royal Welch Fusiliers in 1939 and the following year was divided to form 1/11th and 2/11th Battalions. In 1941 the two battalions were re-numbered as 30th and 31st and subsequently disbanded at the end of the war.

31st Battalion

Formed in 1940 as the 2/11th (Home Defence) Battalion, Royal Welch Fusiliers, it became the 14th Bn by the end of the year, and the 31st Bn in 1941.

Sergeant of the 1st Volunteer Battalion, The South Wales Borderers, 1907. The scarlet tunic has white collar, cuffs and piping. The sergeant wears his red sash over the right shoulder and the khaki cap from his service dress.

The South Wales Borderers

The Brecknockshire Battalion

In 1908 the South Wales Borderers were allotted just one territorial battalion, which bore no number, just the designation The Brecknockshire Battalion. The Brecknocks were formed in 1860 when the county grouped its rifle volunteers into an admin battalion. Seven independent corps were formed which in 1880 were amalgamated as the 1st Brecknockshire Rifle Volunteer Corps. This in turn became the 1st Volunteer Battalion, South Wales Borderers in 1885.

The battalion provided volunteers for the several service companies that were sent out to South Africa in 1900. In 1914 the battalion sailed from Southampton with the Home Counties Division and after reaching Bombay on the 3 December, transhipped for Aden. The battalion returned to India in August 1915. Both 2/1st and 3/1st Battalions were formed for war service.

In 1922 the battalion was amalgamated with the 3rd Battalion Monmouthshire Regiment and ceased to exist as an independent unit.

5th (Home Defence) Battalion

See 30th Battalion

30th Battalion

Formed in 1936 as 106a Group National Defence Companies, the unit became the 5th (HD) Battalion, South Wales Borderers in November 1939, and the 30th Bn in 1941. Disbandment was in 1943.

See also the Monmouthshire Regiment.

The King's Own Scottish Borderers

4th (The Border) Battalion

In 1861 the several rifle corps that had been formed since 1859 in the counties of Roxburghshire and Selkirkshire were grouped together as an admin battalion. The additional title 'The Border' was added in 1868, and was continued in 1880 when the battalion was consolidated as the 1st Roxburgh and Selkirk (The Border) Rifle Volunteer Corps. The new corps consisted of nine companies which in 1881 were allotted to the Royal Scots Fusiliers as one of its volunteer battalions. Seven years later, however, the battalion was transferred to the KOSB.

The 4th KOSB also owes its origins to the regiment's former 2nd Volunteer Battalion. This battalion was formally the 1st Berwickshire Rifle Volunteer Corps which had been formed in 1880 by the amalgamation of the seven corps then in existence within the county. Both battalions contributed a number of its members to the several volunteer service companies that went out to South Africa.

The two battalions were merged in 1908 to form the 4th KOSB. Headquarters and six companies were provided by the Roxburgh Bn while the remaining two were supplied by the 2nd Volunteer Battalion.

As part of the 52nd (Lowland) Division, the battalion left Liverpool for Gallipoli in 1915. It then went to Egypt where it took part in the operation at Dueidar and in 1917 was involved in the invasion of Palestine. The last months of the war were spent on the Western Front. The 2/4th Battalion was formed in 1914 and served in the 65th Division until January 1916 when it was absorbed into the 2/5th, while the 3/4th became the 4th (Reserve) Battalion in 1916.

During the Second World War, the battalion saw action in NW Europe. In 1961 it was amalgamated with the 5th KOSB to form the 4th/5th Battalion, and is now represented in both the 1st and 2nd Battalions, 52nd Lowland Volunteers.

5th (Dumfries and Galloway) Battalion

The 5th Battalion, King's Own Scottish Borderers was recruited from three counties in Scotland Dumfriesshire, which formed ten companies of rifle volunteers from 1860, Kirkcudbrightshire and Wigtownshire. In 1860 the several rifle corps formed by the last two counties were grouped together under the title the Galloway Admin Battalion of Rifle Volunteers. The ten Dumfriesshire companies were merged in 1880 as the 1st Dumfriesshire Rifle Volunteer Corps. That same

year the Galloway units were amalgamated. Both battalions were later to join the KOSB as volunteer battalions.

During the Boer War 95 members of the 3rd VB joined the regular battalions in South Africa. Three men from the Galloway Rifles were mentioned for gallantry at the capture of Commandant Wolmarans and 30 Boers near Damhoek in August 1901.

The two battalions were merged in 1908 to form the 5th (Dumfries and Galloway) Battalion, KOSB. The 1/5th served in Gallipoli, Egypt and Palestine before moving to the Western Front for the last months of the war. While in Belgium Sgt. Louis McGuffie won the Victoria Cross at Wytschaete on 28 September 1918. The 2/5th Battalion was formed in September 1914, moved to Ireland in 1917 and was disbanded in May 1918. The 3/5th became part of the 4th (Reserve) Battalion in 1916.

Left
Two members of the 6th Battalion, King's Own Scottish Borderers, trying on their life-belts before the Rhine crossing in 1945. **KOSB Museum**
Right
6th Battalion, King's Own Scottish Borderers, moving up into the Reichswald Forest in February 1945. **KOSB Museum**

In 1939 the battalion was doubled in strength, the Dumfriesshire companies remaining as the 5th (Dumfriesshire) Battalion and the Galloway contingent forming the new 7th (Galloway). The 5th served throughout NW Europe during 1944/5 and was once more joined with the Galloway personnel in 1947.

The 5th was merged with the 4th Battalion in 1961 to form the 4th/5th Battalion, King's Own Scottish Borderers.

6th (The Border) Battalion

Formed in 1939 as a duplicate of the 4th Battalion, it served in NW Europe during 1944/5 and was amalgamated with the 4th in 1947.

7th (Galloway) Battalion

This battalion was formed in 1939 as a duplicate of the 5th Battalion. In 1943 the 7th was converted to an Air Landing Battalion and, while serving in the 1st Airborne Division, took part in the operation at Arnhem. The battalion was placed into suspended animation due to the heavy casualties incurred at the battle. Later, in 1947, it was amalgamated with the 5th.

8th (Home Defence) Battalion

See 30th Battalion

30th Battalion

Formed in 1936 as 68b Group National Defence Companies, the unit became 8th (Home Defence) Battalion, KOSB in 1939 and the 30th Bn in 1941. Disbandment was in 1943.

The Cameronians (Scottish Rifles)

5th Battalion

The 5th Cameronians originated as the 1st Lanarkshire Rifle Volunteer Corps, which was formed in Glasgow during 1859/60. The 1st Lanarks soon consisted of two battalions recruited from the western part of the city. Whole companies were formed from the staff of leading Glasgow firms. One was also raised by the University of Glasgow.

The 1st Lanarks became a volunteer battalion of the Cameronians in 1881, and in 1900 contributed a large number to the volunteer service companies of the regiment that went out to South Africa. In 1908 transfer to the Territorial Force was as the 5th Battalion Cameronians. The University Company, however, became part of the Senior Division of the Officers Training Corps.

The battalion was at its Princess Street headquarters when war was declared in 1914. It went to France in November and subsequently served on the Western Front throughout the war. While in France, Sgt. John Erskine, who was later killed at Arras, won the Victoria Cross for his part in the action at Givenchy on 22 June 1916.

Both second and third line battalions were formed by the 5th. The 2/5th became part of the 65th Division and served in the UK while the 3/5th absorbed the regiment's other third line units in 1916.

After the war the 5th and 8th Cameronians were amalgamated to form the 5th/8th Battalion. In 1938 an anti-aircraft role was assumed, and eventually in 1940, a transfer was made to the Royal Artillery as 56th Searchlight Regiment.

6th (Lanarkshire) Battalion

In 1873 the several rifle volunteer companies that had been formed in the Hamilton, Uddington, Strathaven, Bothwell, Wishaw, Motherwell and Ballatyre areas of Lanarkshire were amalgamated as the 16th Lanarkshire Rifle Volunteer Corps. The 16th was re-numbered 2nd in 1880, and seven years later became the 2nd Volunteer Battalion, Cameronians. During the Boer War the battalion contributed 132 of its members to the service companies that went to South Africa. Six men from this number served with the Scottish Volunteer Cyclist Company.

The 1/6th Battalion went to France in March 1915 where it joined the 8th Division at Estaires. It later transferred to the 51st Division and then to the 33rd

Division as a pioneer unit. The 2/6th Battalion was formed in September 1914 and later served as No 18 Battalion of the 65th Division, after amalgamation with the 2/7th Cameronians. It moved to Ireland in January 1917 and was disbanded in May of the following year. The 3/6th merged with the 3/5th and became part of the 5th (Reserve) Battalion.

The 6th served with the 52nd Infantry Division in France at the beginning of the Second World War, and later during 1944/5, throughout NW Europe. In 1947 it merged with its war-time duplicate battalion, the 10th, and in 1950 became the 6th/7th Cameronians after amalgamation. The battalion is now represented by elements of the 1st and 2nd Battalions, 52nd Lowland Volunteers.

7th Battalion

The 3rd Lanarkshire Rifle Volunteer Corps was created during 1859/60, and consisted of companies made up from volunteers from the Glasgow area. Included in the corps were large contingents from two of the city's leading firms – Messrs Cogan's Spinning Factory and the Etna Foundry. Two further companies were made up entirely of 'total abstainers' and members of temperance organisations.

The 3rd Lanarks joined the Cameronians as one of its volunteer battalions in 1881, and during the Boer War 98 of its members saw active service with the regiment in South Africa. During the First World War the 1/7th Battalion served in Gallipoli, Egypt, Palestine and on the Western Front. 2nd and 3rd line battalions were also formed by the battalion for war service.

At the beginning of the Second World War the 7th Battalion fought in France. It later served throughout NW Europe. The battalion was amalgamated with the 6th Cameronians in 1950 to form the 6th/7th Battalion.

8th Battalion

The 8th Cameronians was formed in 1859 as the 4th Lanarkshire Rifle Volunteer Corps and was recruited from the northern part of the City of Glasgow. It contained one company made up from employees of one of the city's breweries. In 1887 the 4th became the 4th Volunteer Battalion, Cameronians and contributed a large number from its ranks for service in South Africa, during the Boer War.

The 1/8th Battalion served alongside the 1/7th throughout the First World War. The 2/8th was absorbed into the 2/5th during the war and the 3/8th was merged into the 5th (Reserve) Battalion in 1916. The battalion was amalgamated with the 5th Cameronians in 1920 to form the 5th/8th Battalion.

The 5th/8th assumed the additional title 56th Searchlight Regiment in 1938.

Party from the 1st Lanarkshire Rifle Volunteer Corps showing various orders of dress. The uniforms were grey with blue collar, cuffs and piping and the piper's tartan is Douglas.

The following year, as a result of the order to expand existing TA units, the former 8th Battalion was re-formed as 57th Searchlight Regiment. Both regiments were transferred to the Royal Artillery in 1940.

9th Battalion

Formed in 1939 as a duplicate of the 7th Battalion, the 9th saw action with the 15th (Scottish) Infantry Division during 1944/5 and was amalgamated with the 7th in 1947.

10th (Lanarkshire) Battalion

Formed in 1939 as a duplicate of the 6th Battalion, the 10th served in the UK throughout the war and was eventually amalgamated with the 6th in 1947.

1/11th and 2/11th Battalions

See 13th and 30th Battalions

13th (Home Defence) Battalion

Formed in September 1940 from part of the 11th (Home Defence) Battalion and designated as 2/11th, the battalion became the 13th in November 1940 and the following year joined the 11th to form the 30th Cameronians.

15th Battalion

Formed in 1915 as the 10th (Scottish) Provisional Battalion (TF), it became the 15th Cameronians in January 1917 and was disbanded in 1919.

30th Battalion

Formed in 1936 as 69 Group National Defence Companies, the unit became the 11th (Home Defence) Battalion, Cameronians in 1939, and in 1940 was divided to form the 1/11th and 2/11th Battalions. In 1941 these two units were merged to form the 30th Battalion.

The 46th Middlesex Rifle Volunteer Corps: skirmishing in 1875. Painted by R. Simkin.
5th (V) Bn, Royal Regiment of Fusiliers Museum

The 46th Middlesex Rifle Volunteer Corps in 1876, having just changed their uniforms from grey to scarlet. Painted by R. Simkin.
5th (V) Bn, Royal Regiment of Fusiliers

This page:
Above
Representatives from five City Battalions of the London Regiment c1910. Painted by R. Caton Woodville.
Left
The Robin Hood Rifles – Officer c1868. Painted by W. Younghusband.

Facing page:
Above left
Cyclist, 13th Middlesex Rifle Volunteer Corps 'Queen's Westminsters'.
Above right
13th Middlesex Rifle Volunteer Corps 'Queen's Westminsters'. Member of the Mounted Infantry Section.
Below
Party of volunteer cyclists. From a series of postcards published by Raphael Tuck & Sons.

"13th Middx ~
"Queen's Westminster" R·V· Cyclist.

Queen's Westminster Volrs
~ Mounted Infantry ~

VOLUNTEER CYCLIST CORPS.

Facing page: Above
Postcard published by the 9th Volunteer
Battalion, Royal Scots. The card shows a
corporal of the battalion in full dress uniform,
Lieutenant Colonel James Clark, who became
Commanding Officer in 1904, and the
battalion's headquarters at 7 Wemyss Place,
Edinburgh.
Below
Plate taken from 'Records of the Scottish
Volunteer Force 1859–1908' by Lieutenant
General Sir James Moncrieff Grierson
(published 1909) showing a selection of
uniforms worn by volunteers of the Argyll and
Sutherland Highlanders. Left to right: 3rd
Admin Battalion, Renfrewshire; 3rd
Volunteer Battalion; 3rd Stirlinghsire RVC;
1st Admin Battalion, Stirlingshire; 4th
Volunteer Battalion.

This page: Above left
Sergeant, a volunteer battalion of the Royal
Fusiliers c1890. Painted by C. A. Collins.
P. Bronson
Above right
10th (Scottish) Battalion, The King's Liverpool
Regiment c1910. Painted by R. Caton Woodville.
Below
The London Scottish. Painted by F. O. Beinne.

67th (2nd Home Counties) Division

56th (1st London) Division

47th (2nd London) Division

42nd (East Lancashire) Division

60th (London) Division

74th (Yeomanry) Division

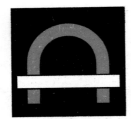

57th (West Lancashire) Division

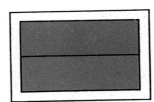

46th (North Midland) Division

59th (North Midland) Division

58th (London) Division

55th (West Lancashire) Division

51st (Highland) Division

The Royal Inniskilling Fusiliers

5th Battalion

The 5th Battalion Royal Inniskilling Fusiliers (TA) was formed in 1947 and was soon to consist of companies located at Londonderry, Magherafelt, Omagh, Enniskillen and Dungannon. The battalion now forms part of the 4th (Volunteer) Battalion, Royal Irish Rangers, North Irish Militia.

The Gloucestershire Regiment

4th (City of Bristol) Battalion

The battalion was formed as the 1st Gloucestershire (City of Bristol) Rifle Volunteer Corps in 1859. It became the 1st Volunteer Battalion of the Gloucestershire Regiment in 1883, and provided a number of personnel for service in South Africa during the Boer War.

The 1/4th Battalion saw action with the 48th (South Midland) Division throughout France and Flanders during the First World War. The battalion also served in Italy. The 2/4th also fought on the Western Front, while the 3/4th absorbed the regiment's other third line units to form the 4th (Reserve) Battalion.

During the Second World War the battalion served as part of the air defences of Britain, having converted to 66th Searchlight Regiment in November 1938, and eventually transferring to the Royal Artillery in 1940.

5th Battalion

In 1860 the Gloucestershire rifle volunteers that had been formed outside Bristol were grouped as the 1st Admin Battalion. With headquarters at Gloucester, the battalion was consolidated as the 2nd Gloucestershire Rifle Volunteer Corps in 1880. It contained ten companies and in 1883 provided the 2nd Volunteer Battalion of the regiment.

For the service of its members in the Boer War, the battalion was awarded the battle honour 'South Africa 1900–02'. In the First World War no less than sixteen honours were earned by the 5th. One member, Francis George Miles, won the Victoria Cross while in France. The battalion, re-numbered 1/5th, served throughout France, Flanders and later in Italy. The 2/5th also saw a great deal of action on the Western Front while the 3/5th merged with the 3/4th in 1916.

While on active service in France during 1940, the first Military Medal awarded to a territorial in the Second World War was won by a member of the 5th Bn. Converted to 48th Battalion, Reconnaissance Regiment, the battalion was sent to NW Europe in 1944.

The battalion reverted to its former title after the war and in 1967 provided elements of the Royal Gloucestershire Hussars (T) and the Wessex Volunteers.

6th Battalion

The 6th was formerly the regiment's 3rd Volunteer Battalion. It was formed in 1900 and had its headquarters in Bristol. As the 1/6th, the battalion served in France, Belgium and Italy during the First World War. The 2/6th also served on the Western Front.

In November 1938 the 6th Bn was converted to an armoured role and as the 44th Battalion, Royal Tank Regiment saw service during the Second World War in North Africa, Sicily and Italy.

7th Battalion

Formed in 1939 from B and D Companies of the 5th Battalion, the battalion spent three years in Northern Ireland, and later became a training unit. In 1947 the 7th was re-amalgamated with the 5th Battalion.

8th (Home Defence) Battalion

See 30th Battalion

17th Battalion

Formed in 1914 as the 82nd Provisional Battalion (TF), it became the 17th Battalion, Gloucestershire Regiment in 1917 and was disbanded in May 1919.

30th Battalion

Formed in 1936 as 84c Group National Defence Companies, the unit became 8th (Home Defence) Battalion, Gloucestershire Regiment in 1939, and the 30th Bn in 1941. The battalion was occupied on various guard duties throughout the war. It had the honour to guard Badminton House while HM Queen Mary was living there as a guest of the Duke of Beaufort. The 30th later became No 29 Primary Training Centre and was disbanded in 1943.

The Worcestershire Regiment

7th Battalion

The senior company of the battalion was formed at Wolverly in November 1859. This was designated as the 1st Worcestershire Rifle Volunteer Corps and in 1860 was linked with other rifle companies in the area to form the county's 1st Admin Battalion of Rifle Volunteers. In 1880 the battalion was consolidated as the 1st Worcestershire, its headquarters being at Hagley and the establishment set at eleven companies. The corps became the 1st Volunteer Battalion, Worcestershire Regiment in 1883 and during the Boer War contributed two detachments for service in South Africa.

On the 31 March 1915, the 1/7th Battalion landed at Boulogne and as part of the 48th (South Midland) Division took part in the Somme battles of 1916. The following year the division was in the Ypres sector, moving to Italy in November. The 2/7th also served on the Western Front while the 3/7th absorbed the 3/8th and provided the Worcester's 7th (Reserve) Battalion.

Having served in France during 1940 the battalion later moved to India and Burma. It now forms part of the 1st and 2nd Mercian Volunteers.

8th Battalion

The 8th Worcesters originated from the county's 2nd Admin Battalion of Rifle Volunteers. Formed in 1860, the battalion was consolidated in 1880 as the 2nd Worcestershire Corps, its headquarters being at Worcester. The 2nd later became the 2nd Volunteer Battalion Worcestershire Regiment and contributed 130 of its members to the volunteer service companies that served with the regular battalions in South Africa.

The battalion served with the 48th Division in France, Belgium and Italy. It returned to France in September 1918 where it joined the 25th Division. The 2/8th was formed in September 1914 and served in France and Belgium with the 61st Division. The reserve battalion, 3/8th, was absorbed into the 3/7th in 1916.

After returning from France in 1940, the battalion remained in the UK for the remainder of the war. It was amalgamated with the 10th Battalion in 1947 and subsequently converted to 639 Heavy Regiment, Royal Artillery.

1st Volunteer Battalion, The Worcestershire Regiment, c1907. Clearly seen on the collar is the 'Star' pattern badge of the regiment.

9th Battalion

Formed in 1939 as a duplicate of the 7th Battalion. The battalion was stationed in the UK throughout the war and in 1947, amalgamated with the 7th Battalion.

10th Battalion

Formed as a duplicate of the 8th Battalion in 1939, it served in the UK throughout the war and was amalgamated with the 8th to form 639 Regiment, Royal Artillery in 1947.

The East Lancashire Regiment

4th Battalion

The 2nd Lancashire Rifle Volunteer Corps was formed at Blackburn in 1859 and in 1880 merged with the 62nd Lancashire Corps at Clitheroe. Redesignation as the 1st Volunteer Battalion, East Lancashire Regiment took place in 1889, and as the 4th Battalion (TF) in 1908.

The battle honour, 'South Africa 1900–02' was granted to the battalion in recognition of the service of its members in the Boer War. Further honours were gained by the battalion during the First World War which took it to Egypt, Gallipoli and France. The 2/4th was formed in 1914 and was amalgamated with the 1/4th while in France. The 3/4th merged with the 3/5th and provided the 4th (Reserve) Battalion.

The battalion formed the 4th/5th East Lancashire Regiment upon amalgamation in 1920. However, the 4th Battalion title was once again in use from 1939 on the formation of the 5th Duplicate Battalion. The 4th served with the BEF in France during 1940. It remained in the UK for the remainder of the war and is now represented as part of the 4th (Volunteer) Battalion, Queen's Lancashire Regiment, having formed part of the Lancastrian Volunteers in 1967.

5th Battalion

The 5th East Lancashire Regiment originated in 1860 as the 3rd Admin Battalion of Lancashire Rifle Volunteers. This unit was made up from a number of individual companies that were located from areas including – Rossendale, Accrington, Burnley and Fleetwood.

In 1880 the 3rd Admin Battalion was amalgamated as the 3rd Lancashire Rifle Volunteer Corps, consisting of twelve companies. It later became the 2nd Volunteer Battalion, East Lancashire Regiment and in 1908, the 5th Battalion (TF).

Members of the battalion served in South Africa during the Boer War. The 1/5th saw action in Egypt, Gallipoli and France during the First World War, one of its members 2nd Lt. Alfred Smith gaining the Victoria Cross at Gallipoli in 1915. The 2/5th also served in France while the 3/5th became part of the 4th (Reserve) Battalion in 1916.

The 5th was amalgamated with the 4th East Lancs to form the 4th/5th Battalion in 1920. In 1939 it was separated for war service and as the 5th Battalion, fought in NW Europe during 1944 and was disbanded in 1947.

6th (Home Defence) Battalion

See 30th Battalion

30th Battalion

Formed in 1936 as 101 Group National Defence Companies, the unit became the 6th (Home Defence) Battalion, East Lancashire Regiment in 1939, 30th Bn in 1941 and was disbanded in 1943.

Far left
Corporal of the 23rd (County of London) Battalion, The London Regiment. The cap badge of the battalion is based on that of the East Surrey Regiment and displays in the centre a shield bearing the Arms of Guildford.
J. G. Woodroff
Left
Colour Sergeant V. Douch of the 23rd (County of London) Battalion, The London Regiment. He wears the Queen's South Africa Medal with six bars and the Volunteer Long Service award.
Below
Members of the 1st Surrey Rifle Volunteer Corps at Wimbledon during the 1870s.
National Army Museum

The East Surrey Regiment

5th Battalion

The battalion originated in 1860 upon the formation that year of the 1st Admin Battalion of Surrey Rifle Volunteers. The 1st Admin was made up from several rifle corps located in areas that included – Croydon, Brixton, Wimbledon and Battersea. In 1880 the battalion was consolidated to form the 3rd Surrey Rifle Volunteer Corps, consisting of seven companies. As the 2nd Volunteer Battalion, East Surrey Regiment, redesignated as such in 1887, the corps was well represented in South Africa during the Boer War.

The battalion embarked at Southampton, for India, in October 1914. In December 1917 it joined the 18th Indian Division and served as part of Force D of the Mesopotamia Expeditionary Force. The 2/5th served with the 67th Division in the UK while the 3/5th absorbed the 3/6th and formed the East Surrey's 5th Reserve Battalion.

The 5th East Surrey Regiment was converted in 1938 into 57th Anti-Tank Regiment, Royal Artillery.

6th Battalion

The 2nd Admin Battalion of Surrey Rifle Volunteers was formed in 1860, and in 1880 was consolidated as the 5th Surrey Rifle Volunteer Corps consisting of eight companies with headquarters at Kingston. The 5th was redesignated as 3rd Volunteer Battalion, East Surrey Regiment in 1887 and during the Boer War contributed a number of volunteers for the war in South Africa.

As part of the Home Counties Division, the battalion went to India in 1914. A year was later spent as part of the Aden Field Force. The 2/6th remained in the UK throughout the war, while the 3/6th became part of the 5th (Reserve) Battalion in 1916.

The battalion was split in 1939 to form the 1/6th and 2/6th East Surreys. Both formed part of the BEF that went to France in 1940. The 1/6th later served in North Africa and Italy. The 2/6th remained in the UK for the remainder of the war.

In May 1961 the battalion was amalgamated with the 23rd London Regiment to form the 4th Battalion, Queen's Royal Surrey Regiment. The 4th Battalion now forms part of the 5th and 6/7th (Volunteer) Battalions of the Queen's Regiment.

7th (23rd London) Battalion

The 7th East Surrey Regiment was formerly the 23rd London Regiment. The 7th title being assumed in 1937. The battalion originated from two Surrey rifle volunteer corps, the 7th, raised at Southwark in 1859, and the 26th which was formed at Clapham in 1875. With a combined strength of nine companies, the two corps were amalgamated as the 7th Bn in 1880. This title was changed to 4th Volunteer Battalion, East Surrey Regiment in 1887 and to 23rd (County of London) Battalion, The London Regiment in 1908.

The 1/23rd Londons served on the Western Front during the First World War. It saw a great deal of action at Loos and High Wood and later in the Ypres sector. The 2/23rd landed at Havre in June 1916 and after serving in France, moved to Salonika in November of the same year, Egypt in June 1917 and back to France in May 1918. The 3/23rd became part of the 21st (Reserve) Battalion, London Regiment in 1916.

After spending a year under the title of 7th (23rd London) Battalion, The East Surrey Regiment, the battalion was converted to an armoured role in 1938. As 42nd Battalion, Royal Tank Regiment it fought at El Alamein and throughout the Western Desert campaign.

In 1956 the battalion reverted to its former infantry status, serving as part of the East Surreys and under the title of 23rd London Regiment (TA). On 1 May 1961 the 23rd was amalgamated with the 6th Battalion East Surrey Regiment to form the 4th Battalion Queen's Royal Surrey Regiment (see 6th Battalion).

8th (Home Defence) Battalion

Formed in 1939 as 3 Group National Defence Companies, the unit became the 8th (Home Defence) Battalion in 1939 and in 1941 was absorbed into the 8th (Home Defence) Battalion of the Queen's Royal West Surrey Regiment.

The First Surrey Rifles

Formed in 1859 at Camberwell as the 1st Surrey (South London) Rifle Volunteer Corps. The corps soon reached a strength of eight companies and in 1881 became a volunteer battalion of the East Surrey Regiment.

In 1908 the 1st Surreys transferred to the Territorial Force as the 21st (County of London) Battalion, The London Regiment and, as such, served in France, Belgium, Salonika, Egypt and Palestine during the First World War. Both 2/21st and 3/21st Battalions were also formed. The battalion became part of the East Surrey Regiment in 1916 and in 1935 was converted to – 35th Anti-Aircraft Battalion, Royal Engineers.

Right
5th Battalion, East Surrey Regiment, India, during the First World War. The designation '5' over 'E.Surrey' is stitched in white on to a red diamond and worn on the side of the helmet.
Left
6th Battalion, East Surrey Regiment. Over 90% of the battalion volunteered for foreign service and they can be seen here wearing their 'Imperial Service' brooches. The battalion bore the distinction of placing the words 'Imperial Service' below their title in the 'Army List'.
J. G. Woodroff

The Duke of Cornwall's Light Infantry

4th Battalion

In 1860 the several Cornwall rifle corps located within the western part of the county were grouped together as the 1st Admin Battalion of Cornwall Rifle Volunteers. The battalion became the 1st Cornwall Rifle Volunteer Corps in 1880 and in 1885 was renamed the 1st Volunteer Battalion, Duke of Cornwall's Light Infantry. The battalion contributed a number of men to the volunteer service companies that went out to South Africa during the Boer War.

As part of the Wessex Division the 1/4th DCLI left Southampton for India in October 1914. It later served for a year in Aden, and from February 1917 was part of the Suez defence force. In June 1917 the battalion transferred to the 75th Division, with which it took part in the invasion of Palestine. The 2/4th Battalion also served in India while the 3/4th absorbed the 2/5th and served as the 4th (Reserve) Battalion.

The 4th was amalgamated with the 5th Battalion to form the 4/5th DCLI in 1921. In 1939, however, the strength of the battalion was doubled and subsequently divided as 4th and 5th. The 4th Battalion remained in the UK throughout the Second World War.

In 1947 it was amalgamated with the 5th to form once again, the 4th/5th Battalion. The regular battalion of the DCLI was amalgamated with the Somerset Light Infantry in 1959 to form the Somerset and Cornwall Light Infantry. A year later the 4/5th was permitted to adopt the former county title. The Duke of Cornwall's Light Infantry are now represented in the 6th Light Infantry Volunteers.

5th Battalion

The 5th Battalion was formed from the 2nd Admin Battalion of Cornwall Rifle Volunteers. This battalion was created in 1860 from the rifle companies in the eastern part of Cornwall. In 1880 it became the 2nd Cornwall Rifle Volunteer Corps of nine companies and in 1885 the 2nd Volunteer Battalion, DCLI.

Several members from the battalion saw active service in South Africa. During the First World War a number of men, those that were willing to serve overseas, transferred to the 1/4th Battalion. Those that remained were later trained as pioneers and eventually went with the 61st Division to France in 1916. As no third line battalion was formed, the 2/5th acted as a reserve unit.

In 1921 the 5th was amalgamated with the 4th to form the 4/5th Battalion, DCLI. When war was declared in 1939 the strength of the battalion was doubled and the two battalions once again separated. The 5th fought throughout NW Europe in 1944 and was once again merged with the 4th in 1947.

7th (Home Defence) Battalion

See 30th Battalion

30th Battalion

This battalion was formed as the 7th (Home Defence) DCLI Battalion from part of the 10th (HD) Battalion Devonshire Regiment in 1940. Renumbered as 30th in 1941, it was disbanded in 1946. The battalion served in North Africa and in June 1944 joined the 2nd Sudan Defence Force Brigade with which it served in an administative capacity and on internal security duties.

Quarter-Master and staff of the 5th Battalion, Duke of Wellington's Regiment, c1909.
D. J. Barnes

The Duke of Wellington's Regiment (West Riding)

4th Battalion

In 1860 the several rifle corps that had been formed in the Halifax area during 1859/60 were amalgamated as the 4th Yorkshire West Riding Rifle Volunteer Corps. The 4th later included companies from Brighouse and Checkheaton and in 1883 was redesignated as the 1st Volunteer Battalion, Duke of Wellington's Regiment.

The battalion contributed to the volunteer service companies that served during the Boer War. In 1914 the 1/4th spent the first months of the war on coastal defence duties near Hull and Grimsby. It landed in France in April 1915 and served on the Western Front with the 49th Division. The 2/4th went to France with the 62nd Division while the 3/4th was amalgamated with the 3/5th to form the 4th (Reserve) Battalion.

The 4th Duke's were converted to 58th Anti-Tank Regiment, Royal Artillery in 1938, and during the Second World War saw action in North Africa, Italy and Palestine. The battalion continued service with the Royal Artillery in different roles until May 1961, when upon amalgamation, reverted to infantry as The West Riding Battalion. The battalion is now represented by elements of the 1st and 2nd Battalions Yorkshire Volunteers.

5th Battalion

The services of a corps of rifle volunteers formed in Huddersfield were accepted on 3 November 1859. This was numbered as 10th Yorkshire West Riding and in 1880, after amalgamation with companies from Holmfirth, Saddleworth and Mirfield, became 6th. Redesignated as 2nd Volunteer Battalion, Duke of Wellington's Regiment, the corps provided a number of volunteers for service in the Boer War. In 1908 the 2nd formed the 5th Battalion and part of the 7th.

During the First World War the 1/5th served on the Western Front with both the 49th and 62nd Divisions. One officer from the battalion, 2nd Lt. James Huffam, gained the Victoria Cross while attached to the 2nd Battalion of the regiment. Also, Pte. Henry Tandy went on record as the most decorated private of the war. His awards being in addition to the Victoria Cross – the Distinguished Conduct and Military Medals. The 2/5th also served in France and Belgium while the 3/5th was absorbed into the 3/4th to form the 4th Reserve Battalion.

In 1936 the battalion was converted as – 43 Anti-Aircraft Battalion, Royal Engineers. It later transferred to the Royal Artillery and in 1944 moved to France for duty as a garrison regiment. The battalion was re-converted to an infantry role in 1957, when upon amalgamation formed the 5th/7th Duke of Wellington's Regiment.

6th Battalion

The 6th Battalion, Duke of Wellington's was formerly the regiment's 3rd Volunteer Battalion, and before that, the 9th Yorkshire West Riding Rifle Volunteer Corps. This corps had originated in 1860 and included companies from areas in the West Riding that included – Skipton-in-Craven, Settle, Burnley and Bingley.

A number of volunteers from the battalion served with the regular battalions in South Africa during the Boer War. In 1914–18 both the 1/6th and 2/6th served in France and Belgium while the 3/6th absorbed the 3/7th to form the 6th (Reserve) Battalion.

In 1939 the battalion was divided as the 1/6th and 2/6th. The 1/6th took part in the occupation of Iceland during 1940–2 while the 2/6th adopted an armoured role in 1942 as 114th Regiment Royal Armoured Corps, after seeing action in France during May 1940. With the conversion of the 2/6th the 1/6th reverted to its former title and as the 6th Duke's fought in NW Europe after landing in Normandy in 1944. The 114 Regiment RAC, which had served in the UK in a tank delivery role, was redesignated in 1944 as the 11th Battalion, Duke of Wellington's. In 1947 it was amalgamated with the 6th Battalion to form – 673 Heavy Anti-Aircraft Regiment, Royal Artillery. This regiment eventually became part of 382 Medium Regiment and in 1961 became part of the West Riding Battalion. (See 4th Battalion.)

7th Battalion

Formed in 1908 from part of the 2nd Volunteer Battalion, Duke of Wellington's Regiment, the battalion had its headquarters at Milnsbridge and was recruited from the Colne Valley area. Both the 1/7th and 2/7th Battalions served on the Western Front during the First World War, the latter being broken up in 1918 after the Battle of Arras. The 3/7th formed the 6th (Reserve) Battalion after amalgamation with the 3/6th in 1916.

The 7th was once again organised as 1/7th and 2/7th Battalions for war service in 1939. The 1/7th served in Iceland and NW Europe while the duplicate battalion fought in France during 1940 and was later converted to 115 Regiment, Royal Armoured Corps.

In 1944 115 Regiment RAC was reconverted to infantry under the title 12th Battalion, Duke of Wellington's. In 1947 it was amalgamated with the 7th Battalion which in 1957 merged with the 5th to form the 5th/7th Battalion, Duke of Wellington's Regiment.

11th Battalion

See 6th Battalion

12th Battalion

See 7th Battalion

Musician of the 5th Battalion, Duke of Wellington's Regiment, c1912. The scarlet tunic has white piping, chevrons and lace and is worn with the sergeants' red sash. The badge worn on the collar is that conferred on the 76th Regiment of Foot (2nd Battalion, Duke of Wellington's) in 1807 to commemorate its long service in India and consists of an elephant with howdah. The musicians' 'Lyre' badge is worn above the chevrons and three efficiency stars below.

The Border Regiment

4th (Westmorland and Cumberland) Battalion

In 1860 the eleven independent rifle corps that had been formed within the county of Cumberland were grouped together as the 1st Admin Battalion of Cumberland Rifle Volunteers. At the same time, the six corps of the County of Westmorland became that county's 1st Admin Battalion. During 1880 the battalions were consolidated as the 1st Cumberland and 1st Westmorland Rifle Volunteer Corps. These in turn became the 1st and 2nd Volunteer Battalions of the Border Regiment which in 1908 were amalgamated to form the 4th Battalion (TF).

Both battalions contributed volunteers for service at the front during the war in South Africa. In 1914 both the 1/4th and 2/4th went out to India where they served throughout the war. During this period the 1/4th took part in the Third Afghan War of 1919. The 3/4th, which was formed during the First World War, was amalgamated with the 3/5th Battalion in 1916 to form the 4th (Reserve) Battalion.

In 1939 the battalion was divided to form the 4th (Westmorland) and 6th (East Cumberland) Battalions. The 4th went to France with the BEF in 1940 and was to see action around Amiens before the retreat to Dunkirk. The battalion moved to Egypt in 1941 and was to serve in the Western Desert until February 1942 when it went to India. The 4th Border Regiment later served throughout Burma in Wingate's Chindit Force.

The 4th Battalion is now represented as part of the 4th (Volunteer) Battalion, King's Own Royal Regiment, having transferred to the T&AVR in 1967 as part of the Lancastrian Volunteers.

5th (Cumberland) Battalion

The 5th Battalion was formed in 1900 when several companies of the 1st Volunteer Battalion, Border Regiment were withdrawn and designated as 3rd (Cumberland) Volunteer Battalion. Headquarters were at Workington and the establishment of the battalion authorised eight companies.

The 1/5th Battalion landed in France at the beginning of the First World War and served with the 50th Division on lines of communications. In February 1918 the battalion was converted and transferred to the 66th Division as its pioneers. The 2/5th served in the 65th Division, which consisted of regiments from the

Lowlands of Scotland. In January 1916 it was absorbed into the 2/4th Battalion of the Royal Scots Fusiliers. The 3/5th was a reserve unit and became part of the 4th (Reserve) Battalion.

The 5th fought as part of the BEF in France during 1940 and in 1941 was converted to an armoured role under the title of 110 Regiment, Royal Armoured Corps. The unit served in the UK for the rest of the war, and in 1944 reverted to infantry under its former title.

The battalion was amalgamated in 1947 with its war-time duplicate unit, the 7th Border Regiment, and concurrently transferred as 640 Heavy Anti-Aircraft Regiment, Royal Artillery.

6th (East Cumberland) Battalion

Formed in 1939 as a duplicate of the 4th Battalion, the 6th served in the UK until 1944 when it took part in the assault landings in Normandy. In 1947 the battalion was converted to 8th Army Recovery Company, Royal Electrical and Mechanical Engineers.

7th (Cumberland) Battalion

Formed in 1939 as a duplicate of the 5th Battalion, the 7th served in the UK throughout the war, and in 1947 was amalgamated with the 5th to form 640 HAA Regt Royal Artillery.

8th (Home Defence) Battalion

See 30th Battalion

30th Battalion

Formed in 1936 as 100 Group National Defence Companies, the group contained men from Westmorland, Cumberland and Lancashire and in 1939 was redesignated as the 8th (Home Defence) Battalion, Border Regiment. Re-numbered as 30th in 1941, the battalion was disbanded at Ulverston in 1942.

Above
1/4th Battalion, Border Regiment in Burma, 1916. **King's Own Royal Border Regiment Museum**
Left
Private Little of the 4th Battalion, Border Regiment in Burma 1944. **King's Own Royal Border Regiment Museum**
Right
5th Battalion, The Border Regiment, learning to use the Bren for anti-aircraft defence. **King's Own Royal Border Regiment Museum**

The Royal Sussex Regiment

4th Battalion

The County of Sussex formed two admin battalions of rifle volunteers in 1860. In 1874 these were merged as the 1st and subsequently, in 1880, consolidated as the 2nd Sussex Rifle Volunteer Corps, consisting of eleven companies and headquarters at Worthing. Later, and as the 2nd Volunteer Battalion, Royal Sussex Regiment, the corps sent a number of volunteers to the war in South Africa. They served with the 1st Regular Battalion of the regiment, and saw action at Welkom Farm, the Zand River, Doornkop, Johannesburg, Pretoria, Diamond Hill and Retief's Nek.

During the First World War, the 1/4th served with the 53rd (Welsh) Division at Gallipoli, Egypt and Palestine, finally moving to France in May 1918 when they joined the 34th Division at Proven. The 2/4th was raised at Horsham, and later merged with the 3/4th as 4th (Reserve) Battalion.

The 4th went to France again in 1940, and before returning to England, saw action at St Omer La Bassee. They later served as a lorried infantry battalion at El Alamein, and subsequently in Iraq, Persia and Palestine. In 1943 the 4th was amalgmated with the 5th Battalion Royal Sussex to form the 4th/5th (Cinque Ports) Battalion and is now represented as part of 6th/7th (Volunteer) Battalion, Queen's Regiment.

5th (Cinque Ports) Battalion

The battalion was formed in 1880 when four companies of rifle volunteers located at Hastings, Battle, Ticehurst and Lewes were amalgamated as the 1st Cinque Ports Corps. The following year the corps became a volunteer battalion of the Royal Sussex Regiment, but although ranked as 3rd, did not assume this title.

Members of the corps volunteered for service with the regular forces in South Africa, and arrived in time to take part in Lord Robert's march on Pretoria. During the First World War, the 1/5th performed various guard duties, including a stay at the Tower of London where it relieved the Guards regiments of most of their duties until 1915. That year the battalion went to France where it undertook the work of pioneers with the 48th Division. The end of the war saw the 1/5th in Italy and Austria where it gained the battle honours – 'Piave', 'Vittorio Veneto' and

'Italy 1917–18'. The 2/5th Battalion was formed in November 1914, and was later absorbed into the 3/5th as a reserve unit.

In 1940 the 5th suffered some 354 casualties while serving with the BEF in France and Belgium. It returned to England via Dunkirk and in 1943 was amalgamated with the 4th Royal Sussex to form the 4th/5th (Cinque Ports) Battalion.

6th (Cyclist) Battalion

Formed in 1859, the 1st Sussex Rifle Volunteer Corps was located at Brighton. It became the 1st Volunteer Battalion, Royal Sussex Regiment in 1887, and as such contributed a number of its members to the volunteer service companies that fought in South Africa. In 1908 the battalion was instructed to transfer to the Territorial Force as part of the Royal Field Artillery. However, this was not accepted by the battalion and the 1st VB did not continue service with the TF. In 1912 it was decided that the Brighton volunteers could remain as infantry, the transfer then being made as the 6th (Cyclist) Battalion, Royal Sussex Regiment.

The 1/6th was attached to the 1st Mounted Division at the beginning of the First World War. Service was in the UK until disbandment in December 1919. The 2/6th went to India in 1916 while the 3/6th was absorbed into the 4th (Reserve) Battalion, Royal Sussex Regiment in 1916.

Sentry and guard of the 5th (Cinque Ports) Battalion, Royal Sussex Regiment.

6th Battalion

A new 6th Royal Sussex was formed in 1939 when in that year the 4th was increased in strength and formed into two battalions. The 6th returned from France in 1940 and remained in the UK until amalgamation with the 4th/5th in 1947.

7th (Cinque Ports) Battalion

Formed as a duplicate of the 5th Battalion in 1939. The battalion served on lines of communications duties in France during 1940, suffering heavy casualties before returning to England. In 1942 the 7th was converted to an air defence role, continuing service as 109 Light Anti-Aircraft Regiment, Royal Artillery.

1/8th and 2/8th (Home Defence) Battalions

See 30th and 11th Battalions

11th (Home Defence) Battalion

Formed in 1940 at Uckfield as the 2/8th (HD) Battalion, this title was changed by the end of 1940 to the 11th Bn, and in 1941 a merger took place with the 8th (HD) Battalion.

15th Battalion

Formed in 1915 as the 70th Provisional Battalion (TF), it became 15th Bn Royal Sussex Regiment in 1917 and was disbanded at Cambridge in the following year.

16th (Sussex Yeomanry) Battalion

This battalion was formed in 1917 from members of the 1/1st Sussex Yeomanry while serving as infantry in Egypt. The battalion later went to France as part of the 74th (Yeomanry) Division.

30th Battalion

Formed in 1936 as 5 Group National Defence Companies, the unit became 8th (Home Defence) Battalion, Royal Sussex Regiment in 1939, and was later divided as 1/8th and 2/8th Battalions. The 2/8th became the 11th (HD) Bn which in 1941 once again became part of the 8th. Redesignation as the 30th Battalion was also in 1941.

Left
Colonel W. H. Campion, CB, VD, Honorary Colonel of the 2nd Volunteer Battalion, Royal Sussex Regiment and later the 4th Battalion from 1903 until 1923.
Right
Bugler of the 2nd Volunteer Battalion, Royal Sussex Regiment. The khaki service dress bears the arm title 'ROYAL SUSSEX' over '2' over 'V', embroidered in white on a red backing. The cap is the 'Brodrick' pattern.
R. J. Marrion

White metal helmet plate of the 4th volunteer Battalion, Hampshire Regiment. The badge of the battalion, a 'Dog Gauge', is seen in the centre of the plate. This device was used to measure dogs in the New Forest.

The Royal Hampshire Regiment

4th Battalion

The 1st Admin Battalion of Hampshire Rifle Volunteers was formed in 1860 from the several rifle companies that had been formed around the Winchester, Romsey, Andover and Basingstoke areas. Re-named as 1st Hampshire Corps in 1880 and 1st Volunteer Battalion Hampshire Regiment in 1885, the battalion consisted of eighteen companies by 1900 and that year sent a large contingent to South Africa.

The 1/4th Battalion left Southampton for India on 9 October 1914. It moved to Mesopotamia in March 1915, where its headquarters and one company were captured by the enemy after being besieged at Kut Al Amara between December 1915 and April 1916. The 2/4th reached Karachi in January 1915. It went to Egypt and manned the Suez defences in 1917, finishing the war in France with the 62nd Division. The 3/4th was formed in March 1915 and later became the 4th (Reserve) Battalion of the Hampshire Regiment.

During 1939 the battalion was doubled in size and divided into 1/4th and 2/4th. The former saw a great deal of action during the Second World War, serving in North Africa, Italy, Egypt, Palestine, Syria, Greece and Austria. The 2/4th, after serving in North Africa, took part in the Invasion of Sicily and Italy in 1943. In May 1944 Capt. Richard Wakeford gained the Victoria Cross near Cassino, and between 2 May and 27 July 1945, the battalion served on special duty in Crete.

The 4th Battalion formed the 4th/5th Royal Hampshire Regiment upon amalgamation in 1961 and is now represented as elements of the 1st and 2nd Wessex Volunteers.

5th Battalion

The 4th Admin Battalion of Hampshire Rifle Volunteers was formed in 1860 and included the rifle corps then in existence at Southampton, Lymington, Christchurch, Lyndhurst and Bournemouth. The 4th Admin was consolidated as the 2nd Hampshire Corps in 1880, containing nine companies with headquarters at Southampton. In 1885 part of the corps was detached to form the 4th Hampshire Rifle Volunteer Corps, and the title – 2nd Volunteer Battalion Hampshire Regiment assumed.

Members of the battalion served during the Boer War. In 1914 the 1/5th was sent out to India where it remained until the end of the war. The 2/5th also served in India, but was later moved to Egypt. The 3/5th became part of the 4th (Reserve) Battalion, Hampshire Regiment in 1916.

In 1921 the 5th was merged with the 7th Hampshires to form the 5th/7th Battalion. This title was retained until 1939, when the strength of the battalion was doubled and the 5th and 7th were made separate units. During the Second World War the 5th saw action that included the battles fought at Tunis, Salerno, Naples and Monte Cassino.

The battalion spent a time after the war, 1948–56, under the title of 14th Battalion, The Parachute Regiment. With the restored title of the 5th Royal Hampshires, it was amalgamated in 1961 with the 4th Battalion to form 4th/5th Battalion.

6th (Duke of Connaught's Own) Battalion

The battalion was formed as the 2nd Admin Battalion of Hampshire Rifle Volunteers. It subsequently became the 3rd Hampshire Rifle Volunteers Corps and then the 3rd VB, the Hampshire Regiment.

The 2nd Admin Bn had been created in 1860 from the rifle volunteers that had been raised around the Portsmouth area. In 1893, the battalion was granted the privilege of including 'Duke of Connaught's Own' in its title, His Royal Highness having been made Hon Colonel that year.

A number of volunteers from the battalion, including a Maxim gun detachment, went to South Africa in 1900. In 1914 the 1/6th served in India and Mesopotamia, while members of the 2/6th remained in the UK as reserves.

In 1938 the 6th Hampshires were converted to an anti-tank role and subsequently transferred to the Royal Artillery as 59th Anti-Tank Regiment.

Left
Prince Henry of Battenberg in the uniform of the 5th (Isle of Wight 'Princess Beatrice's') Volunteer Battalion, The Hampshire Regiment in 1890. Prince Henry became the Honorary Colonel of the battalion in 1885 and wears the green uniform and silver pouch-belt badge displaying the Tower of Carisbrooke Castle. **J. G. Woodroff**

7th Battalion

The battalion originated in 1885 when part of the 2nd Hampshire Rifle Volunteer Corps was removed to form the 4th Corps. The 4th became the 4th Volunteer Battalion, Hampshire Regiment and by 1900 consisted of eleven companies, including one known as the 'New Forest Scouts'.

Members of the battalion served alongside regular troops in South Africa during the Boer War. In the First World War active service of the 1/7th and 2/7th took

Right
1/9th Battalion, Hampshire Regiment at Russian Island, Siberia 1919. **Imperial War Museum**

Centre
Members of the 9th (Cyclist) Battalion, Hampshire Regiment, c1912. The cap badge worn here consists of a cycle wheel with a rose in the centre.

Right
4th Volunteer Battalion, The Hampshire Regiment. The scarlet jacket has a white collar and cuffs.

them to India, Aden and Mesopotamia. A 3/7th was also formed which served as a reserve unit.

In 1921 the amalgamation took place between the 5th and 7th Battalions. Later the 7th was re-formed for war service in 1939 and subsequently saw action throughout NW Europe. With the re-formation of the Territorial Army in 1947, the 7th was transferred to the Royal Artillery as, 642 LAA/SL Regiment.

8th (Isle of Wight 'Princess Beatrice's') Battalion

In 1880 the several corps of rifle volunteers that had been raised since 1859 on the Isle of Wight were formed into a battalion designated as the 1st Isle of Wight Rifle Volunteer Corps. The new corps consisted of eight companies with headquarters at Newport. The corps was redesignated as 5th (Isle of Wight, Princess Beatrice's) Volunteer Battalion of the Hampshire Regiment in 1885, Her Royal Highness being the wife of Prince Henry of Battenburg, the battalion's Hon Colonel.

The battalion sent a number of its members to fight in the Boer War. In 1915 the battalion left Liverpool for Gallipoli, moving that same year to Egypt. The 2/8th was at first known as 3/8th, and served as part of the 4th (Reserve) Battalion. The 8th Hampshires were converted to an artillery role in 1937.

8th and 13th (Home Defence) Battalions

See 30th Battalion

9th (Cyclist) Battalion

The 1/9th went to India in February 1916, having been formed at Southampton in 1911. From India, the battalion moved to Siberia and other parts of Russia in 1918, returning to England via Canada in November of the following year. The 2/9th served in the UK while the 3/9th became part of the 4th (Reserve) Battalion. The 9th was not re-formed after the war.

17th Battalion

Formed in 1915 as 84th Provisional Battalion (TF), it became 17th Hampshire Regiment in January 1917 and was disbanded in 1919.

30th Battalion

Formed in 1936 as 82 Group National Defence Companies, the unit became 8th (Home Defence) Battalion in 1939 and the following year was divided as 1/8th and 2/8th, and then as 8th and 13th Battalions. In 1941 the two were amalgamated and redesignated the 30th Bn.

The South Staffordshire Regiment

5th Battalion

The 5th Battalion, South Staffordshire Regiment originated from the 3rd Staffordshire Rifle Volunteer Corps, which was formed in 1880 by the amalgamation of several rifle volunteer companies situated in Walsall, Bloxwich, Brownhills, Cannock and Wednesbury. These units had been raised during 1959/60, and had previously constituted the 5th Admin Battalion of Staffordshire Rifle Volunteers. The corps was re-named as 2nd Volunteer Battalion, South Staffordshire Regiment in 1883 and later gained the battle honour 'South Africa 1900–02' for its service during the Boer War.

With the exception of a month's visit to Egypt in 1916, the 1/5th served with the 46th (South Midland) Division throughout France and Belgium during the First World War. The 2/5th went to Ireland with the 59th Division in April 1916. It returned to England in January 1917, and then moved to France on the 25 February. The 3/5th became a reserve unit, and together with the 3/6th Battalion, formed the 5th (Reserve) Battalion.

Service during the Second World War was in NW Europe, the battalion taking part in the battles around Caen in 1944. The 5th South Staffordshire Regiment formed part of the 5th/6th (T) Battalion, Staffordshire Regiment in 1967, and later, the Light Infantry and Mercian Volunteers. They are now represented as elements of the 2nd Battalion Mercian Volunteers.

6th Battalion

The 4th Admin Battalion of Staffordshire Rifle Volunteers was formed in 1860. In 1880 it was consolidated as the 4th Staffordshire Rifle Volunteer Corps consisting of twelve companies and headquarters at Wolverhampton. The 4th became the 3rd Volunteer Battalion, South Staffordshire Regiment in 1883, and in 1908 formed the 6th Battalion (TF).

Members of the battalion served with regular troops during the Boer War. In 1914 the 1/6th fought on the Western Front while the 2/6th went to Ireland before moving to France in 1917. During the Second World War, the battalion was divided as, 1/6th and 2/6th. Both battalions served in the NW Europe campaign of 1944. The 6th was converted to 643 LAA Regiment, Royal Artillery in 1947.

7th Battalion

Formed at Brownhills as a duplicate of the 5th Battalion, the 7th landed in France on the 29 June 1944 and was later placed in suspended animation having sustained heavy casualties incurred at Falaise. The 7th was merged with the 5th in 1947.

9th and 16th (Home Defence) Battalions

See 30th Battalion

30th Battalion

Formed in 1936 as 104B Group National Defence Companies, the unit became 9th (Home Defence) Battalion in 1939. The following year it was separated first as 1/9th and 2/9th, and then as 9th and 16th Battalions. In 1941 the two were amalgamated and redesignated as 30th.

The Dorset Regiment

4th Battalion

The 4th Dorsets originated in 1860 as the 1st Admin Battalion of Dorsetshire Rifle Volunteers. Included in the battalion were the 1st to 12th Corps, all raised within the county during 1959/60. The battalion was consolidated as the 1st Dorsetshire Rifle Volunteer Corps in 1880, consisting of eleven companies with headquarters at Dorchester.

The 1st Corps became the 1st Volunteer Battalion of the Dorset Regiment in 1887 and in 1900 contributed a number of men for service with the regular 2nd Battalion of the regiment in South Africa. The volunteers served under Buller and were present at the battle of Alleman's Nek.

During the First World War, the 1/4th Battalion served in India and Mesopotamia. The 2/4th were also stationed in India, later moving to Egypt and Palestine. The 3/4th became the 4th (Reserve) Battalion and went to Ireland in 1918. In 1939 the 4th was doubled in strength and constituted as the 4th and 5th Battalions. Both served in the 130th Infantry Brigade and saw action in NW Europe during 1944–5.

The regular battalion of the Dorset Regiment became the Devonshire and Dorset Regiment upon amalgamation in 1958. At that time the county title 'Dorset Regiment' continued to be used by the 4th Battalion. The Dorset Regiment now forms part of the 1st Battalion Wessex Regiment (Rifle Volunteers), having provided one company of the Dorset Territorials in 1967.

5th Battalion

Formed in 1939 as a duplicate of the 4th Battalion, the headquarters was at Poole and the battalion saw service throughout NW Europe during 1944–5.

6th (Home Defence) Battalion

See 30th Battalion

30th Battalion

Formed in 1936 as 81 Group National Defence Companies, the unit transferred to the Dorsets as 6th (Home Defence) Battalion in 1939 and was re-numbered as 30th in 1941. The battalion served with 43rd Infantry Brigade which had been formed for internal security duties in N Africa and Sicily, and was for a period known for deception purposes as 120 Infantry Brigade. The 30th left the brigade in 1943 and went to Gibraltar as part of its defence force.

The South Lancashire Regiment (The Prince of Wales's Volunteers)

4th Battalion

In 1880 the 9th and 49th Lancashire Rifle Volunteer Corps were amalgamated to form a corps of seven companies with headquarters at Warrington. The former corps had been formed at Warrington in 1859 while the 49th originated in 1862 at Newton-le-Willows. The 9th Corps became the 1st Volunteer Battalion of the South Lancashire Regiment in 1886 and during the Boer War contributed a large number of volunteers to the service companies that went to fight in South Africa.

During the First World War the 1/4th Battalion served in a pioneer role, joining the 3rd Division in France in February 1915. Later it transferred to the 55th Division with which it saw action in 1916 at the Somme, at Ypres and the battle of Cambrai. The 2/4th Battalion also served in France, while the 3/4th merged with the 3/5th in 1916 to form the 4th (Reserve) Battalion.

In 1939 the battalion was divided to form the 1/4th and 2/4th South Lancashire Regiment. The former served in the UK throughout the war while the 2/4th later became the 13th Battalion Parachute Regiment, and was involved in the Normandy landings of the 6 June 1944.

The battalion now forms part of the 5th/8th (Volunteer) Battalion, The King's Regiment, having provided part of the Lancastrian Volunteers in 1967.

5th Battalion

The 21st Lancashire Rifle Volunteer Corps was formed in 1880 by the amalgamation of the 47th and 48th Corps, both being raised in 1860 as St Helens and Prescot respectively. The 21st became the 2nd Volunteer Battalion South Lancashire Regiment in 1886 and in 1900 sent a number of its members to fight in South Africa. The volunteers joined the 1st regular battalion of the regiment, and were involved in the action at Botha's Pass.

Both the 1/5th and 2/5th Battalions served in France and Belgium during the First World War. The 3/5th joined the 3/4th and together formed the regiment's 4th Reserve Battalion. In the Second World War the battalion assumed an air defence role and was converted as 61st Searchlight Regiment, Royal Artillery.

6th (Home Defence) Battalion

See 30th Battalion

4th Battalion, South Lancashire Regiment, at Caton, 1910. **D. J. Barnes**

14th Battalion

Formed in 1915 as 49th Provisional Battalion (TF). Became 14th South Lancashire Regiment in January 1917 and was disbanded in June 1919.

30th Battalion

Formed in 1936 as 104A Group National Defence Companies, the unit became the 6th (Home Defence) Battalion, South Lancashire Regiment in 1939, the 30th in 1941 and was disbanded in 1943.

The Welch Regiment

4th (Carmarthenshire) Battalion

In 1880 the 1st Pembrokeshire Rifle Volunteer Corps was formed by the amalgamation of several rifle companies raised since 1859 in Pembrokeshire, Haverfordwest, Cardiganshire and Carmarthenshire. The strength of the unit was ten companies and its headquarters located at Haverfordwest. The 1st Pembrokeshire later became the 1st Volunteer Battalion of the Welsh Regiment, and after the Boer War assumed the battle honour 'South Africa 1900–02' in recognition of its service.

During the First World War the 1/4th Battalion saw duty first in Scotland on the Forth and Tay defences. In 1915 it joined the 53rd Welsh Division and sailed for Gallipoli. Before the end of the year the battalion had moved to Egypt, where it took part in the defence of the Suez Canal. The next move was to Palestine and the battalion saw action in the Gaza battles and the capture of Jerusalem. The 2/4th was formed in April 1915, and that same year was absorbed into the 2/4th Battalion of the King's Shropshire Light Infantry. A 3/4th was also formed which, together with the regiment's other third-line units, formed the 4th (Reserve) Battalion.

When the Territorial Force was re-formed after the First World War the recruiting area of the 4th Welch was confined to Carmarthenshire, and subsequently the additional title 'Carmarthenshire' was added. In 1939, when the 15th duplicate battalion was formed, the title changed to 4th (Llanelly) Battalion, the headquarters of the unit being in that town.

During the Second World War, the 4th fought in NW Europe. It was amalgamated in 1947 with the 15th Battalion under its former title 4th (Carmarthenshire). It is now represented by part of the 4th (Volunteer) Battalion, Royal Regiment of Wales.

(*Note. The spelling of the regimental name was altered officially in 1920 from 'Welsh' to 'Welch'.*)

5th (Glamorgan) Battalion

The 5th Welch Regiment was formally the 3rd Volunteer Battalion, previously the 2nd Glamorganshire Rifle Volunteer Corps. This corps had been formed in 1880 by the amalgamation of several of the county's rifle companies that had been raised since 1859.

Members of the battalion served in South Africa with regular troops during the Boer War. In 1914–18, the 1/5th fought in Gallipoli, Egypt and Palestine while the 2/5th was absorbed into the 2/6th Battalion, Cheshire Regiment while stationed at Bedford in 1915. The 3/5th became part of the 4th (Reserve) Battalion in 1916.

For the Second World War, the battalion was again separated as 1/5th and 2/5th. The former served in NW Europe during 1944–5 and on the 16 August 1944, Lt. Tasker Watkins gained the Victoria Cross for his part in an action fought on the Falaise Road. The 2/5th Battalion remained in the UK throughout the war and was amalgamated with the parent battalion in 1947.

The 5th Battalion Welch Regiment now forms part of the 3rd (Volunteer) Battalion, Royal Regiment of Wales.

6th (Glamorgan) Battalion

The 3rd Glamorganshire Rifle Volunteer Corps was formed at Swansea in 1859. It became a volunteer battalion of the Welsh Regiment in 1881 and, during the war in South Africa, its members fought alongside the regulars of the regiment.

The 1/6th Battalion landed at Havre in October 1914 and spent a time on lines of communications work. It was later converted to a pioneer role and served as such for the remainder of the war with the 1st Division. The 2/6th was formed in Swansea, and in November 1915 was absorbed into the 2/5th Battalion, Royal Welsh Fusiliers. The 3/6th became part of the 4th (Reserve) Battalion Welsh Regiment in 1916.

In 1921 the 6th was amalgamated with the regiment's 7th (Cyclist) Battalion. Just prior to the Second World War, the additional title '67th Searchlight Regiment' was added and in 1940 the battalion, in its new air defence role, transferred to the Royal Artillery.

6th Battalion

A new battalion, numbered the 6th, was added to the regiment in October 1956. This was formerly the 16th (Welch) Battalion, Parachute Regiment and had been formed in March 1947. The 6th now form part of the 3rd (Volunteer) Battalion, Royal Regiment of Wales.

7th (Cyclist) Battalion

The 7th Welsh was considered a new unit upon its formation in 1908, although many of its members had transferred from the former 2nd Volunteer Battalion of the regiment. Headquarters were at Cardiff and the several companies were situated around the County of Glamorganshire.

Both the 1/7th and 2/7th Battalions served in the UK throughout the First World War. The 3/7th provided personnel for the 3rd Provisional Cyclist Company and was disbanded in March 1919. The 7th was not re-formed after the war, its members being absorbed into the 6th Battalion.

15th (Carmarthenshire) Battalion

Formed in 1939 as a duplicate of the 4th Battalion, the 15th served in the UK throughout the Second World War and was amalgamated with the 4th Battalion in 1947.

16th (Home Defence) Battalion

See 30th Battalion

17th (Home Defence) Battalion

See 31st Battalion

Sergeant of the 7th Battalion, The Welsh Regiment. The green tunic has a scarlet collar on which is borne the 'Dragon of Wales'. The leather shoulder-belt carries a silver whistle and chain.

24th (Pembrokeshire and Glamorganshire Yeomanry) Battalion

This battalion was formed in 1917 by the amalgamation in Egypt of the two regiments the 1/1st Pembroke Yeomanry and 1/1st Glamorgan Yeomanry. The battalion later moved to Palestine where it took part in the battles of Beersheba and Sheria. In 1918 it was withdrawn for service on the Western Front.

30th Battalion

Formed in 1936 as 106B Group National Defence Companies, it became the 16th (Home Defence) Battalion, Welch Regiment in 1939 and 30th in 1941. Disbandment was in 1944.

31st Battalion

Formed as 106C Group National Defence Companies in 1936 it was transferred to the regiment as 17th (Home Defence) Battalion in 1939. Re-numbered as 31st in 1941 and was disbanded in 1943.

The Black Watch (Royal Highland Regiment)

4th (City of Dundee) Battalion

The battalion was formerly the 1st Volunteer Battalion of the Black Watch, and before that the 1st Forfarshire Rifle Volunteer Corps formed at Dundee in November 1859.

During the Boer War, 97 members of the battalion served in South Africa. In February 1915 the 1/4th went to France where it fought throughout the First World War. The 2/4th was formed in September 1914 and remained in the UK until disbandment in 1917. The 3/4th merged with the regiment's other third line units in 1916 and formed the 4th (Reserve) Battalion. In 1921 the 5th (Dundee and Angus) Battalion, Black Watch was formed by amalgamation, the two battalions having been merged on a temporary basis during the First World War.

When the Territorial Army was doubled in 1939, the battalion was separated into 4th and 5th Battalions. The 4th, after returning to England from France in 1940, went to Gibraltar as part of its defence force. It served on the Rock until 1943 when it returned to the UK. The 4th and 5th were reunited in 1947 and now form companies of the 51st Highland Volunteers.

5th (Angus and Dundee) Battalion

The 5th Black Watch was formed in 1908 by the amalgamation of the 2nd and 3rd Volunteer Battalions of the regiment. In 1861 the several rifle corps raised in Forfarshire, outside of the City of Dundee, were organised into two admin battalions. These were merged as 1st Admin Battalion in 1874 and subsequently formed the 2nd Forfarshire Rifle Volunteer Corps in 1880, and the 2nd Volunteer Battalion in 1887.

The 3rd Volunteer Battalion, Black Watch was recruited at Dundee and was formerly the 3rd Forfarshire (Dundee Highland) Rifle Volunteer Corps, previously the 10th. During the Boer War the two battalions contributed over 200 volunteers for service at the front.

In 1914 the 1/5th Battalion went to France and served as pioneers in the 8th Division. It later transferred to other formations and saw action throughout the Western Front. Both the 2/5th and 3/5th Battalions were short-lived. The former was absorbed into the 2/4th in November 1915 while the third line unit became part of the 4th (Reserve) Battalion.

The 5th was amalgamated with the 4th, as 4th/5th Battalion, in 1921. In 1939, however, it was separated, resuming its former number. The battalion saw action at the battle of El Alamein and later served in Libya, Sicily and NW Europe, where it was involved in the assault landings at Normandy. The 5th was once again amalgamated with the 4th in 1947.

6th (Perthshire) Battalion

The 1st Perthshire Rifle Volunteer Corps was formed in 1880 by the consolidation of the several volunteer companies then in existence throughout the county. The 1st later became the 4th Volunteer Battalion of the Black Watch, and as such contributed men to the Volunteer Service companies that went to South Africa during the Boer War.

Throughout the First World War, the 1/6th Battalion served on the Western Front with the 51st Highland Division. The 2/6th remained in the UK while the 3/6th became part of the 4th (Reserve) Battalion in 1916.

After the First World War the battalion was amalgamated to form the 6th/7th (Perth and Fife) Battalion. In 1939, however, the two battalions were separated for war service. After returning to England from France in 1940, the 6th Battalion later served in N Africa, Italy and Greece. In 1947 it was once again united with the 7th, and from 1967 provides part of the 51st Highland Volunteers.

7th (Fife) Battalion

From 1860 there were nine individual rifle corps formed within the County of Fifeshire. These were merged as the 1st Corps in 1880 and designated as 6th (Fifeshire) Volunteer Battalion, Black Watch in 1887.

The battalion was awarded the battle honour 'South Africa 1900–02' for the service of its members during the Boer War. In 1914–18 the 1/7th served with the 51st Highland Division throughout France and Belgium, while the second and third line battalions remained at home.

The 6th/7th Black Watch was formed upon amalgamation in 1921. In 1939 the battalion was divided for war service and the 7th sent to Egypt, Libya, N Africa, Sicily, Italy and NW Europe. The 6th and 7th were amalgamated as 6th/7th Battalion in 1947.

8th (Cyclist) Battalion

See the Highland Cyclist Battalion

8th (Home Defence) Battalion

See 30th Battalion

9th (Home Defence) Battalion

Formed in September 1936 as 64 Group National Defence Companies, the unit became 9th (HD) Battalion, Black Watch in 1939. In 1941 it was absorbed into the 8th (HD) Battalion.

13th (Scottish Horse) Battalion

This battalion was formed in Egypt by the Scottish Horse Yeomanry serving in a dismounted role. As part of the 27th Division, the battalion moved to Salonika and the Macedonian front in October 1916. It later went to France where it remained for the rest of the war.

14th (Fife and Forfar Yeomanry) Battalion

Formed December 1916 in Egypt from the yeomen of the 1/1st Fife and Forfar Yeomanry then serving as infantry in the 2nd Dismounted Brigade, the battalion took part in the Invasion of Palestine in 1917. In 1918 it went with the 74th (Yeomanry) Division to France and Flanders.

30th Battalion

Formed in 1936 as 62nd Group National Defence Companies, the unit became the 8th (Home Defence) Battalion, Black Watch in 1939, the 30th Bn in 1941, and was finally disbanded in 1943.

The Tyneside Scottish

Formed in 1939 as a duplicate of the 9th Battalion Durham Light Infantry and designated 12th (Tyneside Scottish) Battalion. The title 'Tyneside Scottish' was a revival of that used during the First World War by the several service battalions of the Northumberland Fusiliers that were raised by scotsmen in the Tyneside area.

Before the end of 1939, the battalion was transferred to the Black Watch and re-named the 1st Battalion the Tyneside Scottish. As such it went with the BEF to France in 1940, served in Iceland between October 1940 and December 1941, and fought in NW Europe during 1944. The battalion was transferred to the Royal Artillery as 670 LAA Regiment in 1947.

The Oxfordshire and Buckinghamshire Light Infantry

4th Battalion

In 1875 the several rifle corps that had been formed in Oxfordshire excluding that raised by the University, were merged as the 2nd Oxfordshire Rifle Corps. Headquarters was located at Oxford and the establishment authorised six companies. The 2nd became the 2nd Volunteer Battalion, Oxfordshire Light Infantry in 1887 and in 1900 provided a number of its members for service with regular troops in South Africa.

In March 1915, the 1/4th Battalion landed with the 48th (South Midland)

Members of the 2nd Oxfordshire Rifle Volunteer Corps on the ranges.

Division in France. It fought on the Western Front until November 1917, when it moved to Italy. The 2/4th joined the 61st Division, which went to France in May 1916 and the following year took part in the Battle of Cambrai. On the 28 April, 1917, CSM Edward Brooks won the Victoria Cross for his part in an action at Fayes, near St Quentin. Another member of the battalion, L/Cpl. Alfred Wilcox, also gained the VC the following year.

In 1940 the battalion went to France as part of the BEF and, after suffering heavy casualties at St Omer-La Bassee, returned to England where it remained for the rest of the war.

The battalion was amalgamated in 1947 with its war-time duplicate unit, the 5th Bn and in 1958 assumed the title – Oxfordshire and Buckinghamshire Light Infantry. The regular battalion had, by this time, become the 1st Green Jackets. With the transfer to the T&AVR in 1967, the regiment formed part of the Oxfordshire Territorials and the 4th (Volunteer) Battalion, Royal Green Jackets.

Sergeant of the Buckinghamshire Battalion, c1910. The dark grey tunic has a scarlet collar and is worn with a black leather pouch-belt bearing a whistle and chain. The badge worn on the belt has the letters 'BVRC' in the centre. The head-dress badge consists of a 'Maltese Cross' with, in the centre, the figure of a swan taken from the County Arms.

11

2nd Volunteer Battalion, The Oxfordshire Light Infantry. The scarlet tunic has a white collar bearing bugle horn badges. Embroidered on to the shoulder straps is the designation '2' over 'V' over a bugle horn over 'OXFORD'.

The Buckinghamshire Battalion

The Bucks Battalion of the regiment, when formed in 1908, was not allotted a number. It was, however, due to its position in the order of precedence of the several counties in the Volunteer Force, ranked after the 4th Battalion from Oxfordshire.

The first company of rifle volunteers was formed in Buckinghamshire during 1859. Others followed and in 1875 an amalgamation of these corps took place to form the 1st Bucks Rifle Volunteers. The corps had its headquarters at Great Marlow and included companies located at Wycombe, Aylesbury, Slough and Eton College.

The corps did not change its name when it became a volunteer battalion of the Oxfordshire Light Infantry in 1881. It remained as the 1st Bucks and as such contributed a number of volunteers from its ranks for service in South Africa.

As part of the 48th (South Midland) Division, the 1/1st Bucks Battalion fought on the Somme and at Ypres. In 1917 it moved to the Italian Front where it saw action at the Piave River and Vittorio Veneto. The 2/1st Battalion, which was formed in August 1914, also served on the Western Front, being disbanded at Germaine in February 1918. A third line unit was formed which joined the 3/4th Battalion as the 4th (Reserve) Battalion.

In 1939 the Bucks Battalion was divided as 1st and 2nd. The 1st suffered heavy casualties while serving with the BEF in France but in 1944 was able to play an important part in the Normandy assault landings. The 2nd Bucks remained in the UK.

In 1947 the two battalions were amalgamated and at the same time converted and transferred as 645 LAA Regiment, Royal Artillery.

5th Battalion

Formed in 1939 as a duplicate of the 4th Battalion, the 5th served in the UK throughout the war and was amalgamated with its parent unit in 1947.

The Essex Regiment

4th Battalion

The 4th Battalion Essex Regiment was formerly the 1st Volunteer Battalion, and previously the 1st Essex Rifle Volunteer Corps which had been formed in 1859. During the Boer War a large number volunteered for service at the front. The men joined the City Imperial Volunteers as well as several volunteer service companies formed by the Essex Regiment.

In 1915 the 1/4th Battalion landed with the 54th (East Anglian) Division at Suvla Bay, Gallipoli. The battalion later served in Egypt, as part of the Suez defences, and in the Invasion of Palestine. The 2/4th Battalion remained in the UK throughout the war, while the 3/4th amalgamated with the regiment's other third line units to form the 4th (Reserve) Battalion.

During the Second World War, the battalion was divided as 1/4th and 2/4th. The former served in West Africa, the Middle East, where it took part in the Battle of El Alamein, and Italy. The 2/4th remained in the UK. In 1961 the battalion assumed the title 4th/5th and now forms part of the 5th (Volunteer) Battalion, Royal Anglian Regiment.

5th Battalion

The 1st Admin Battalion of Essex Rifle Volunteers was formed in 1860, and in 1880 was consolidated as the 2nd Essex Corps, consisting of eight companies, with the headquarters at Braintree. The corps was redesignated as 2nd Volunteer Battalion, Essex Regiment in 1883 and contributed men to the several volunteer service companies formed by the regiment for service in South Africa.

During the First World War, the 1/5th Battalion served in Gallipoli, Egypt and Palestine. The 2/5th remained in the UK with the 69th Division, while the 3/5th was absorbed into the 4th (Reserve) Battalion.

In 1939 the 5th Essex was divided to form, the 1/5th (West) and 2/5th (East) Battalions. They served alongside each other in West Africa and the Middle East, where the 2/5th was subsequently placed in suspended animation and the 1/5th renumbered as 5th. The battalions were merged in 1947 as 646 HAA Regiment, Royal Artillery.

6th Battalion

The battalion was formed as the 5th Essex Rifle Volunteer Corps at Plaistow in 1860. It became the 3rd Corps in 1880 and the 3rd Volunteer Battalion Essex Regiment in 1883. In 1900 the battalion consisted of thirteen companies, from which a large number volunteered for service in South Africa.

As part of the 54th (East Anglian) Division, the 1/6th served at Gallipoli, Egypt and Palestine during the First World War. The 2/6th remained in the UK while the 3/6th became part of the 4th (Reserve) Battalion.

The battalion was converted and transferred as 64th and 65th Searchlight Regiments, Royal Artillery in 1940, having been duplicated as the 1/6th and 2/6th the previous year.

7th Battalion

The 7th Battalion was formerly the regiment's 4th Volunteer Battalion and was raised at Silvertown as the 9th Essex Rifle Volunteer Corps in 1859. Several members of the battalion served in South Africa during the Boer War, earning for the 7th Essex, its first battle honour.

During the First World War, the battalion provided three separate battalions. The 1/7th saw action at Suvla Bay during the Gallipoli Campaign, Egypt, and in the invasion of Palestine. The 2/7th remained in the UK, while the 3/7th was absorbed into the 4th (Reserve) Battalion. In 1935 the battalion was converted to an anti-aircraft role and was transferred as 59 AA Brigade, Royal Artillery.

Four members of the 3rd or 4th Volunteer Battalion, The Essex Regiment. Two types of head-dress are being worn: the 'Brodrick' and the later service cap. The tunics are scarlet with white collar and cuffs.

7th (Home Defence) Battalion

See 30th Battalion

8th (Cyclist) Battalion

In 1908 the cyclist personnel of the several Essex Regiment volunteer battalions were included in a battalion designated as the Essex and Suffolk Cyclists. Three years later the Essex members of the battalion were detached and organised as the 8th (Cyclist) Battalion of the Essex Regiment.

During the First World War the 1/8th provided men for the 7th and 8th Provisional Cyclist Companies serving in the UK throughout the war. Both the 2/8th and 3/8th Battalions were raised and subsequently disbanded in 1919 and 1916 respectively.

15th Battalion

Formed in 1915 as 65th Provisional Battalion (TF), the battalion joined the Essex Regiment as its 15th Battalion in 1917 and in 1918 was organised as a garrison guard battalion. The 15th went to France in 1918 and served with the 59th Division until disbandment in 1919.

16th Battalion

Formed in 1915 as 66th Provisional Battalion (TF), it became the 16th Bn, the Essex Regiment in January 1917 and was disbanded in the following December.

17th Battalion

This battalion numbered the 17th Essex in 1917, had been formed as the 67th Provisional Battalion (TF) in 1915. The battalion was disbanded in 1919.

30th Battalion

Formed as 8 Group National Defence Companies in 1936, the unit became the 7th (Home Defence) Battalion, Essex Regiment in 1939 and the 30th in 1941. Disbandment was in 1943.

Young volunteer of the Essex Regiment. This photograph was taken in Romford which was the headquarters of several companies of the regiment's 1st Volunteer Battalion.
J. G. Woodroff

The Sherwood Foresters (Nottinghamshire and Derbyshire Regiment)

5th Battalion

The 1st Admin Battalion of Derbyshire Rifle Volunteers was formed in 1860. It included corps from around the Derby area, and in 1880 was consolidated as the 1st Derbyshire Rifle Volunteer Corps of twelve companies. The 1st Derbys became the 1st Volunteer Battalion, Sherwood Foresters in 1887.

The battalion contributed to the volunteer service companies that served with regular troops during the Boer War. In the First World War one member of the 1/5th Battalion, Sgt. William Johnson, gained the Victoria Cross at Ramicourt in France on 3 October 1918. The 2/5th also fought on the Western Front while the battalion's third line unit remained in the UK as the 5th (Reserve) Battalion, Sherwood Foresters.

In 1939, the battalion was separated to form the 1/5th and 2/5th, and as such served in France with the BEF during 1940. The 1/5th later went out to Malaya and while taking part in the Battle of Singapore Island, was captured by the Japanese. As the 1/5th was thereby in a state of suspended animation, the 2/5th was redesignated as the 5th (Derbyshire) Battalion. Its war service was in N Africa, Italy, Egypt, Palestine, Syria and Greece.

The 5th was re-formed in 1947, amalgamated with the 8th Battalion as 5th/8th in 1961, and after 1967 provided elements of the 1st Battalion Mercian Volunteers and the 3rd (Volunteer) Battalion, Worcestershire and Sherwood Foresters.

6th Battalion

The 6th was formerly the regiment's 2nd Volunteer Battalion, previously the 2nd Derbyshire Rifle Volunteer Corps, which had been raised in 1859. Members of the battalion served with the regular 1st Battalion in South Africa during the Boer War. In the First World War the 1/6th served on the Western Front as did the 2/6th after a period of service in Ireland between 1914 and 1917. The 3/6th was absorbed into the 3/5th and formed part of the 5th (Reserve) Battalion.

In 1936 the 6th Foresters were converted to an anti-aircraft role and transferred as 40th AA Battalion, Royal Engineers.

7th (Robin Hood) Battalion

The battalion was formed as the 1st Nottinghamshire (Robin Hood) Rifle Volun-

Band and mascot of the 6th Battalion, Sherwood Foresters, c1910.

teer Corps at Nottingham in 1859. It became a volunteer battalion of the Sherwood Foresters in 1881 but although serving as 3rd, did not change its rifle volunteer title. By 1900 the battalion consisted of eighteen companies and sent a large contingent to South Africa during the Boer War.

Both the 1/7th and 2/7th Robin Hoods fought on the Western Front throughout the First World War. Capt. Charles Vickers of the 1/7th gained the Victoria Cross at the Hohenzollern Redoubt in France on 14 October 1915, and a famous Royal Flying Corps pilot, Capt. Albert Ball VC, DSO, MC had originally been enlisted in the 2/7th in October 1914.

In 1936 the 7th Foresters transferred to the Royal Engineers as 42nd Anti-Aircraft Battalion.

8th (Nottinghamshire) Battalion

In 1860 the several Nottinghamshire rifle companies that had been formed in the county as opposed to the City of Nottingham, were placed together as the 1st Admin Battalion. It was consolidated as the 2nd Notts Corps of eight companies in 1880, and in 1887 became the 4th (Nottinghamshire) Volunteer Battalion of the Sherwood Foresters.

In 1900 almost a quarter of the battalion volunteered for service in South Africa. A strong contingent was to serve with the regular 1st Battalion which took part in Lord Robert's march to Pretoria and the actions at the Zand River, Doornkop and Diamond Hill.

Both the 1/8th and 2/8th Battalions served in France and Belgium during the First World War, Lt. Col. Bernard Vann gaining the Victoria Cross while attached to the 1/6th Battalion in September 1918. During the Second World War the battalion, with the exception of a short period in April 1940 when it went to Norway, remained in the UK.

In 1947 the 8th was amalgamated with its war time duplicate unit, the 9th Battalion and in 1961 formed the 5/8th Battalion upon amalgamation.

9th Battalion

Formed in 1939 as a duplicate of the 8th (Nottinghamshire) Battalion it was known for a time as the 2/8th. After returning from France in 1940, the battalion was converted to an armoured role and transferred as 112 Regiment Royal Armoured Corps. The regiment served in the UK throughout the war and was re-converted to infantry and placed into suspended animation in 1944. The 9th was amalgamated with the 8th in 1947.

10th and 15th (Home Defence) Battalions

See 30th Battalion

30th Battalion

Formed in 1936 as 45B Group National Defence Companies, it became 10th (Home Defence) Battalion, Sherwood Foresters in 1939 and the following year was at first divided as 1/10th and 2/10th, and then re-numbered as 10th and 15th Battalions. In 1941 the two units were amalgamated as 10th and before the end of the year, redesignated as 30th. Disbandment was in November 1942.

Shako badge of the Robin Hood Rifles. Drawn by W. Younghusband.

The Robin Hood Rifles, c1865. The uniform is green with black collar and cuffs. A crowned bugle horn badge with the reversed letters 'RR' is worn on the shako. Painted by W. Younghusband.

The Loyal Regiment (North Lancashire)

4th Battalion

The 4th Battalion was formed as the 6th Admin Battalion of Lancashire Rifle Volunteers in 1861. It was consolidated as the 11th Lancashire Corps in 1880 and then redesignated as the 1st Volunteer Battalion North Lancashire Regiment in 1883. The battalion was recruited from the Preston, Leyland and Chorley areas and provided in 1900 a large contingent of volunteers for service in South Africa.

During the First World War both the 1/4th and 2/4th Battalions fought on the Western Front. A 3/4th was also formed which together with the 3/5th provided the regiment's 4th (Reserve) Battalion. The battalion assumed an anti-aircraft role in 1938 and in 1940 was transferred to the Royal Artillery as 62nd Searchlight Regiment.

5th Battalion

Formed at Bolton in 1860 as the 27th Lancashire Rifle Volunteer Corps, the 27th was amalgamated in 1876 with the 82nd Corps of Hindley and in 1880 re-numbered as 14th. Redesignated as the 2nd Volunteer Battalion, Loyals in 1883, the battalion was later awarded the battle honour 'South Africa 1900–02' for the services of its members during the Boer War.

Both the 1/5th and 2/5th Battalions served on the Western Front during the First World War, the 2/5th acting as a pioneer battalion for the 57th Division. The 3/5th became part of the 4th (Reserve) Battalion in 1916 and the 4/5th, one of the few fourth line units to be formed, was amalgamated with the 1/5th while in France.

The battalion was converted and equipped with motor cycles in 1939. It went to Malaya in 1942, having been redesignated as 18th Reconnaissance Corps the previous year. While taking part in the battle for Singapore Island, was captured by the Japanese.

The 5th was reconstituted in 1947 and in 1967 transferred to the T&AVR as part of the Lancastrian Volunteers. It is now included in the 4th (Volunteer) Battalion Queen's Lancashire Regiment.

6th Battalion

Formed in 1939 as a duplicate of the 5th Battalion, it became the 2nd Battalion Reconnaissance Corps in 1941 and was absorbed into the 5th Battalion in 1947.

14th Battalion

Formed in 1915 as 42nd Provisional Battalion (TF), it joined the Loyals as its 14th Battalion in 1917, being disbanded by the end of the same year.

Musician of the 1st Volunteer Battalion, The Northamptonshire Regiment. The uniform is grey and has scarlet collar cuffs and piping.

The Northamptonshire Regiment

4th Battalion

The 4th Battalion originated in 1860 as the 1st Admin Battalion of Northampton-shire Rifle Volunteers. The 1st Admin contained the nine independent rifle corps that were formed within the county between 1859–67. The battalion became the 1st Corps in 1880, the 1st Volunteer Battalion, Northamptonshire Regiment in 1887, and the 4th Battalion (TF) in 1908.

A number of volunteers from the battalion served in the Boer War. In the First World War the 1/4th fought at Gallipoli and later in Egypt and Palestine. The second and third line units remained at home, the latter as the 4th (Reserve) Battalion.

In 1937 the 4th Northamptons were converted to an anti-aircraft role and joined the Royal Engineers as its 50th AA Battalion. With the outbreak of the Second World War, a new 4th Battalion was created from the 5th, which had been doubled in strength for war service. The 4th served in NW Europe throughout 1944–5 and in 1947 was amalgamated with its parent unit.

The original 4th Battalion had transferred to the Royal Artillery. It served in several gunner roles until 1961, when as part of 438 LAA Regiment, it was converted back to the infantry and amalgamated with the 5th Battalion to form the 4th/5th Northamptons. The 4th/5th are now represented as elements of the 5th and 7th (Volunteer) Battalions Royal Anglian Regiment.

5th (Huntingdonshire) Battalion

The 5th was originally raised in 1914 as the Huntingdonshire Cyclist Battalion. During the First World War it raised three battalions, which served throughout the war in the UK on defence duties.

In 1920 the battalion joined the Northamptonshire Regiment as its 5th (Huntingdonshire) Battalion, and as such served in France, N Africa, Sicily, Italy and Austria during the Second World War. The 5th was amalgamated in 1961 with the original 4th Northamptons, then serving as part of 438 LAA Regiment, Royal Artillery.

9th Battalion

Formed in 1915 as the 62nd Provisional Battalion (TF), it became the 9th Northamptons in 1917 and was disbanded in 1919.

The Royal Berkshire Regiment (Princess Charlotte of Wales's)

4th Battalion

The 4th Battalion originated as the 1st Admin Battalion of Berkshire Rifle Volunteers, which included the twelve corps that were formed within the county from 1859. The 1st Admin was consolidated as the 1st Corps in 1873, containing thirteen companies and headquarters at Reading. In 1881 the corps provided the 1st Volunteer Battalion of the Royal Berkshire Regiment.

The battalion sent a number of its members to fight in the Boer War. In 1915 the 1/4th went to France with the 48th Division and fought on the Somme in 1916. It served at Ypres and then on to the Italian front. The 2/4th also served in France and Belgium, while the 3/4th formed the 4th (Reserve) Battalion at home.

The battalion again went to France in 1940, and after returning to England the same year, remained in the UK for the remainder of the war. In 1947 the 4th was amalgamated with its war-time duplicate unit to form the 4th/6th Battalion, Royal Berkshires. The battalion formed part of the Royal Berkshire Territorials in 1967 and is now represented by part of the 2nd Battalion, Wessex Regiment (Volunteers).

5th (Hackney) Battalion

The 5th Battalion was originally formed in 1912 to replace the Paddington Rifles, a battalion of the London Regiment. As the 10th (County of London) Battalion, The London Regiment (Hackney), the battalion served during the First World War at Gallipoli, Egypt and Palestine. The 2/10th fought in France and the 3/10th formed the 10th (Reserve) Battalion of the London Regiment.

In 1937 the 10th Londons became the 5th (Hackney) Battalion of the Royal Berkshire Regiment. It took part in the assault landings in Normandy in 1944 and in 1947 was transferred as 648 HAA Regiment, Royal Artillery.

6th Battalion

Formed in 1939 as a duplicate of the 4th Battalion at Reading, the 6th served in the UK throughout the war and was amalgamated with the 4th in 1947 to form the 4th/6th Royal Berkshires.

7th (Stoke Newington) Battalion

Formed in 1939 as a duplicate of the 5th (Hackney) Battalion, the 7th was amalgamated with the 5th in 1947.

8th (Home Defence) Battalion

See 30th Battalion

30th Battalion

Formed as 84A Group National Defence Companies in 1936, the unit became the 8th (Home Defence) Battalion, Royal Berkshire Regiment in 1939, the 30th in 1941 and was disbanded in 1945.

1st Volunteer Battalion, Royal Berkshire Regiment. The subject of this photograph wears a cavalry pattern ammunition bandolier and is a member of the battalion's mounted infantry company which was formed in 1886.

Two musicians of the 1st Volunteer Battalion, Royal Berkshire Regiment. The scarlet tunics have blue collars and cuffs and bear bandsmen's wings trimmed with white lace. The 'Dragon' badge of the Regiment, awarded for service during the China War of 1840–42, is seen here worn on the collars. **J. G. Woodroff**

Grey shako worn by HRH Prince Christian of Schleswig–Holstein while serving as the Honorary Colonel of the 1st Admin Battalion of Berkshire Rifle Volunteers. The numeral '12' is that of the 12th Berkshire Corps which had its headquarters at Windsor Great Park.
National Army Museum

The Queen's Own Royal West Kent Regiment

4th Battalion

The 1st Kent Rifle Volunteer Corps was formed in 1877 by the amalgamation of several Kent rifle companies that had been in existence since 1859. With headquarters at Tonbridge, and forming eight companies, the corps later became the 1st Volunteer Battalion of the Royal West Kent Regiment. It sent a number of volunteers to South Africa during the Boer War and in 1908 provided the regiment's 4th and 5th Territorial Battalions.

During the First World War, the 1/4th Battalion served in India. The 2/4th was merged for a short period with other county second-line units, under the title Kent Composite Battalion. Thee battalions were eventually amalgamated as the 2/4th West Kents and as such served at Gallipoli and Egypt. The 3/4th Battalion was at first known as the 2/4th, being re-numbered in June 1915. The battalion fought on the Western Front throughout the war, acting for a time in 1917, as a pioneer unit. The 4th (Reserve) Battalion of the Royal West Kent Regiment was formed as the 4/4th Battalion.

The 4th Battalion went to France as part of the BEF in 1940 and was subsequently involved in the fighting at St Omer-la Bassee. It later took part in the Battle of El Alamein, before moving on to Iraq, India and Burma. On 8 April 1944 L/Cpl. John Harman won the Victoria Cross for his part in the battle of Kohima, Assam.

The 4th was amalgamated in 1947 with the 5th West Kents, to form the 4th/5th Battalion. This battalion is now represented by the 5th (Volunteer) Battalion, Queen's Regiment.

5th Battalion

The 5th Battalion, Royal West Kent Regiment was formed in 1908 from part of the regiment's 1st Volunteer Battalion (see 4th Battalion above). The 1/5th was stationed in India until 1917 when it moved to Mesopotamia. The 2/5th was formed in June 1915 and remained in the UK throughout the war. The 3/5th was also formed: it became part of the 4th (Reserve) Battalion in 1916.

During the Second World War, the 5th, after returning from France in 1940, saw service in Egypt, Iraq, Syria and Italy. The battalion was amalgamated in 1947 with the 4th West Kents to form the regiment's 4/5th Battalion.

1/5th Battalion, Royal West Kent Regiment, with Turkish prisoners captured at Ramadi, 28/29 September 1917. **Imperial War Museum**

6th Battalion

When the Territorial Force was created in 1908, a 6th (Cyclist) Battalion title was allotted to the Royal West Kent Regiment. However, this unit was eventually made an independent entity and can be seen in the Kent Cyclist Battalion section.

A new 6th Battalion was formed in 1939 as a duplicate of the 4th. It served first in France during 1940, then in N Africa, Sicily and Italy, and was eventually placed into suspended animation while in Greece.

7th Battalion

Formed in 1939 as a duplicate of the 5th Battalion, the 7th remained in the UK throughout the war, having served initially in France in 1940.

8th (Home Defence) Battalion

See 30th Battalion

30th Battalion

Formed in 1936 as 2nd Group National Defence Companies, the unit became the 8th (Home Defence) Battalion, West Kents in 1939, the 30th Bn in 1941, and was disbanded in 1943.

Cyclists of the 2nd Volunteer Battalion, Queen's Own (Royal West Kent Regiment). Green uniforms with black facings are worn, each man having a cycle-wheel badge on the right upper arm.

20th London Regiment

The regiment was first organised as a battalion in 1860, when a number of rifle volunteer corps from the western part of Kent were grouped as the 1st Admin Battalion of Kent Rifle Volunteers. In 1880, the battalion was consolidated as the 3rd Kent (West Kent) Corps. Headquarters were located at Blackheath and the establishment authorised eleven companies.

Two other Kent rifle volunteer units to be formed in 1859–60, the 26th Corps, the sixteen companies of which were recruited from the Royal Arsenal at Woolwich, and the 4th, also at Woolwich. These battalions were amalgamated as the 4th Kent Rifle Volunteer Corps in 1880. In 1883 the 3rd and 4th Kent Corps became the 2nd and 3rd Volunteer Battalions of the Royal West Kent Regiment and in 1908 were amalgamated to form the 20th (County of London) Battalion, The London Regiment (Blackheath and Woolwich).

Members of both battalions served in South Africa during the Boer War. In 1914–18 the 1/20th fought as part of the 47th Division in France and Belgium, while the 2/20th went first to France then to Salonika, returning in 1918 for the last months on the war to the Western Front.

The 3/20th became the 20th (Reserve) Battalion and in 1916 all three battalions were included as part of the Queen's Own Royal West Kent Regiment. The 20th assumed the title 20th London Regiment (Queen's Own) in 1922 and in 1935 was converted and transferred as 34th Anti-Aircraft Battalion, Royal Engineers.

The King's Own Yorkshire Light Infantry

4th Battalion

The 4th KOYLI was first organised as a battalion in 1860, when in that year several rifle volunteer companies from the Wakefield area were grouped as the 3rd Admin Battalion of Yorkshire West Riding Rifle Volunteers. In 1880 the battalion was consolidated to form the 5th West Yorks Corps, which consisted of eleven companies.

The 5th became the 1st Volunteer Battalion KOYLI in 1883, and during the Boer War sent eight officers and 243 other ranks to serve with the regular troops, in South Africa. Upon transfer to the Territorial Force in 1908, the 1st Volunteer Battalion was divided to form the regiment's 4th and 5th Battalions, the former retaining the Wakefield headquarters.

As part of the 49th (West Riding) Division, the 1/4th Battalion saw action during the First World War on the Western Front. The 2/4th, served with the 62nd Division in France and Belgium, while the 3/4th remained in the UK as the 4th (Reserve) Battalion.

The 4th also served with the 49th Division during the Second World War, seeing its first action in the Norwegian Campaign of 1940. They later took part in the invasion of Europe in 1944. In 1939 the 4th had formed a duplicate unit which was designated as the 2/4th Battalion. It joined the 46th Division and served on lines of communication work in France during 1940. The battalion went to North Africa in 1943 and saw service with the First Army throughout the campaign. The 2/4th later served in Italy and Greece.

The two battalions were amalgamated in 1947, and later, elements of the old 5th Battalion were included to form the 4th/5th KOYLI. The battalion is now represented by part of the 5th Bn, The Light Infantry (Volunteers).

5th Battalion

Formed in 1908 from part of the 1st Volunteer Battalion, KOYLI and the 2nd Volunteer Battalion, York and Lancaster Regiment, the battalion served with the 62nd Division on the Western Front during the Great War and also formed second and third line units.

A change occurred in 1938, when the battalion became anti-aircraft and added 53 LAA Regiment to its title. It eventually transferred to the Royal Artillery in 1940.

Facing page:
Left
Band-Master W. Lofthouse, 5th Yorkshire West Riding Rifle Volunteer Corps, c1862.
York Castle Museum
Right
29th Yorkshire West Riding Rifle Volunteer Corps, c1875. The subject of this photograph is a Sergeant Instructor of Musketry.
York Castle Museum
Below
Glengarry badge of the 1st Volunteer Battalion, The King's Own Yorkshire Light Infantry. The King's Own (Yorkshire Light Infantry) was designated as such in 1887, having been known from 1881 as the King's Own Light Infantry (South Yorkshire Regiment).

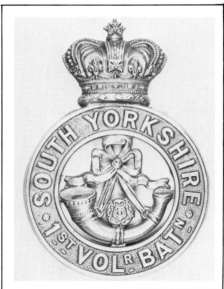

6th (Home Defence) Battalion

This battalion was formed at Doncaster from part of a home defence battalion of the West Yorkshire Regiment. It became the 30th Battalion in 1941 and once again the 6th in 1942. The battalion was disbanded in 1944.

9th (Yorkshire Dragoons) Battalion

In 1942 the Yorkshire Dragoons Yeomanry was converted to a motor battalion while serving as a mounted unit in the Middle East. As 9th KOYLI, it became a lorried infantry battalion in 1944, fought on the Anzio beachhead and later took part in the attack south of Rome.

30th Battalion

See 6th Battalion

The King's Shropshire Light Infantry

4th Battalion

The 4th KSLI was formed in 1908 by the amalgamation of the regiment's 1st and 2nd Volunteer Battalions. Both battalions dated from 1859, and were formerly the 1st and 2nd Shropshire Rifle Volunteer Corps.

During the Boer War, each battalion contributed a number of its members for service at the front. They fought with the 2nd Regular Battalion, KSLI and were involved in actions that included the Zand River, Vredfortweg Rhenoster Spruit and Barberton. During the war, the volunteer service companies sponsored by the 1st and 2nd Volunteer Battalions marched over 1,000 miles.

In October 1914, the 1/4th Battalion left Southampton for India. It later moved to Singapore, from where it sent detachments to the Andaman Isles, and in April 1915, two companies to Hong Kong. The battalion left for home, via Ceylon and Cape Town, in 1917, reaching Plymouth on the 27 July. Two days later it was sent to France. The French Croix de Guerre avec Palme was awarded by the French Government to the battalion for its gallantry at Bligny on 6 June 1918. Both second and third line units were formed by the 4th Battalion. The 2/4th remained in the UK while the 3/4th became the 4th (Reserve) Battalion of the King's Shropshire Light Infantry.

The 4th KSLI went to Europe again in 1944, and was soon involved in heavy fighting at Odon and Mount Pincon. Sgt. G. H. Eardley MM being awarded the Victoria Cross for his part in an attack east of Overloon on the 16 October. The 4th Battalion now form part of the 5th Light Infantry (Volunteers).

5th Battalion

Formed in 1939 as a duplicate of the 4th Battalion, the 5th remained in the UK throughout the war.

8th (Home Defence) Battalion

See 30th Battalion

Members of F (Bridgnorth) Company, 1st Volunteer Battalion, King's Shropshire Light Infantry, 1898. The shooting team are seen here with the 'County Challenge Trophy'.
G. Archer Parfitt

10th (Shropshire and Cheshire Yeomanry) Battalion

Formed in 1917 from the regiments of 1/1st Shropshire and 1/1st Cheshire Yeomanry, then serving in Egypt in a dismounted role. As the 10th KSLI the yeomen fought as part of the 74th (Yeomanry) Division in Palestine, and later in France and Belgium.

30th Battalion

The 30th KSLI was originally formed as the 2/10th (Home Defence) Battalion of the King's Regiment (Liverpool). It was transferred to the KSLI as its 8th (HD) Battalion in 1941, and that same year assumed the title – 30th Battalion. The 30th was redesignated as No 99 Primary Training Centre in 1942, and was disbanded in September of the following year.

Above left
Officer of the 2nd Shropshire Rifle Volunteer Corps. The uniform is grey with black collar, cuffs and cord. The black leather pouch-belt carries a silver whistle and chain with in the centre a 'Maltese Cross' plate.
G. Archer Parfitt

Above right
Colour Sergeant of the 2nd Shropshire Rifle Volunteer Corps. The uniform worn is grey with black collar, cuffs and piping. The three efficiency stars worn on the lower right arm indicate that the wearer has been returned as efficient on fifteen occasions. **D. J. Barnes**

Left
Lieutenant T. G. Hector, MC of the 4th Battalion, King's Shropshire Light Infantry with Regimental Colour. The Croix De Guerre, awarded to the battalion by the French Government, is attached to the pikehead.
G. Archer Parfitt

The Middlesex Regiment
(Duke of Cambridge's Own)

5th Battalion

See 7th Battalion

7th Battalion

The 3rd Middlesex Rifle Volunteer Corps was formed at Hampstead in 1859, and in 1880 was merged with other Middlesex rifle companies at Barnet, Hornsey, Highgate, Tottenham and Enfield. The latter corps was recruited from the Royal Small Arms Factory. The 3rd Corps became the 1st Volunteer Battalion, Middlesex Regiment in 1881. During the Boer War over 300 members went out to South Africa, a number joining the City Imperial Volunteers as well as the volunteer service companies of the Middlesex Regiment.

As the 1/7th, the battalion spent the First World War in France and Belgium, except a few months' service during 1914–15 at Gibraltar. The 2/7th also served in Gibraltar, leaving in August 1915 for Egypt and service in the Western Frontier Force. The 2/7th left for France in May 1916 and owing to an outbreak of typhus, upon arrival was placed into quarantine, and subsequently disbanded. In January 1917 the 3/7th was re-numbered as 2/7th. It served in the UK throughout the war and was disbanded in November 1917. A 4/7th was also formed. This absorbed other reserve battalions of the regiment and in 1916 formed the 7th (Reserve) Battalion.

The 7th was divided in 1939 to form the 1/7th and 2/7th Battalions. Organised as a machine gun battalion, the 1/7th went to France with the BEF in 1940. Subsequent service was in N Africa, Sicily and NW Europe. The 2/7th, also as machine gunners, moved from N Africa to Italy in 1944, and then to Palestine in January 1945.

In 1961 the 5th Battalion of the Middlesex Regiment was formed by the amalgamation of the 7th, 8th and 9th Battalions. The 5th now forms part of the 6th/7th (Volunteer) Battalion Queen's Regiment.

8th Battalion

The battalion was formed in 1859 as the 16th Middlesex Rifle Volunteer Corps. Recruited from Hounslow, the corps was merged with others in the south-west Middlesex area in 1880, to form the 8th Corps. The 8th later became the 2nd

EGH DAY, JUNE 15TH
4

Volunteer Battalion, Middlesex Regiment and as such contributed a number of its members to the volunteer service companies that went to South Africa during the Boer War.

The 1/8th Battalion served in Gibraltar and on the Western Front during the First World War. The 2/8th was also stationed in Gibraltar. It later moved to Egypt and was eventually disbanded in 1916 while serving in France. Upon the disbandment of the 2/8th, the 3/8th assumed its title. The 4/8th became part of the 7th (Reserve) Battalion in 1916.

The battalion was doubled in strength and divided to form the 1/8th and 2/8th Battalions in 1939. The 1/8th went to France with the BEF in 1940, returning to England via Dunkirk the same year. The battalion remained in England until 1944, when on 20 June it landed in Normandy.

The 2/8th was formed from the Ealing and Uxbridge companies of the 8th Battalion, and took part in the NW Europe Campaign during 1944–5.

In 1947 the 1/8th and 2/8th were amalgamated and subsequently transferred as the 11th Battalion, Parachute Regiment. It remained as such until 1956, when it was redesignated as 8th Battalion, Middlesex. The 8th joined the remaining two territorial battalions in 1961 to form the 5th Battalion Middlesex Regiment.

9th Battalion

During 1859, two Middlesex Rifle Volunteer Corps were formed and numbered as 9th and 18th. The former had its first headquarters at Lord's Cricket Ground in St John's Wood, while the 18th was recruited in Harrow and included a large contingent from Harrow School. The two corps were re-numbered as 5th and 9th in 1880 and in 1899 amalgamated under the title of 5th Middlesex (West Middlesex) Volunteer Rifle Corps. The 5th became the 9th Middlesex Regiment in 1908.

During the Boer War over 200 members of the battalion served at the front. In 1914–18 the 1/9th was stationed in India and Mesopotamia, while the 2/9th and 3/9th remained at home.

9th Battalion, Middlesex Regiment, forming a Guard of Honour at Harrow School. A company of the battalion was located at Harrow.

33rd Middlesex Rifle Volunteer Corps, c1864. The 33rd were raised in Tottenham and wore grey uniforms with scarlet cord. **Haringey Archives Committee**

In 1938 the battalion was transferred to Anti-Aircraft Command and converted to a Searchlight unit. It became part of the Royal Artillery in 1940 under the title of 60th SL Regiment. After serving in several gunner roles, the regiment was eventually re-absorbed in 1961 into the Middlesex Regiment, as part of the 5th Battalion.

10th Battalion

The 10th was considered a new unit when formed in 1908, despite the fact that over 300 members of the old 2nd Middlesex Volunteer Corps had transferred into it. On 30 October 1914, the 1/10th left Southampton for India, where it remained throughout the First World War. The 2/10th went to Gallipoli with the 53rd (Welsh) Division and later moved to Egypt where it was disbanded in 1918.

The 3/10th Battalion was formed at Ravenscourt Park in 1915 and saw active service in France with the 1st South African Brigade during 1917. The battalion later became the 11th Entrenching Battalion and was disbanded in February 1918. The 4/10th was absorbed into the 7th (Reserve) Battalion in 1916.

The 10th was reconstituted after the First World War as part of Home Counties Divisional Signals.

10th (Home Defence) Battalion

See 30th Battalion

30th Battalion

Formed in 1936 as 22 Group National Defence Companies, the unit became the 10th (Home Defence) Battalion, Middlesex Regiment in 1939 and was re-numbered as 30th in 1941.

32nd Battalion

Formed in 1915 as 63rd Provisional Battalion (TF), it became the 32nd Battalion, Middlesex Regiment in 1917 and was disbanded in 1919.

7th City of London Regiment

The 7th London Regiment was formed in 1861 as the 3rd London Rifle Volunteer Corps. It became a volunteer battalion of the King's Royal Rifle Corps in 1881, and in 1908 transferred to the Territorial Force as the 7th (City of London) Battalion, The London Regiment.

The regiment served on the Western Front throughout the First World War, and in 1916 became part of the Middlesex Regiment. In 1922 the 7th was amalgamated with the 8th London Regiment (Post Office Rifles) under the title 7th London Regiment (Post Office Rifles). In 1939 the 7th was converted and transferred as 32 AA Battalion, Royal Engineers.

Princess Louise's Kensington Regiment

The regiment was first known as the 4th Middlesex Rifle Volunteer Corps formed in 1859. It became a volunteer battalion of the King's Royal Rifle Corps in 1881. Headquarters of the regiment moved to Kensington in 1885, and in 1908 the transfer to the Territorial Force was as 13th (County of London) Battalion, The London Regiment (Kensington). The title 'Princess Louise's' was later assumed.

In 1914, the 1/13th went to France. The 2/13th spent a short time in Ireland on security duties and later moved on to Salonika and Palestine. The 13th London became part of the Middlesex Regiment in 1916 and in 1937 adopted the title Princess Louise's Kensington Regiment, The Middlesex Regiment.

Badge of the 41st Middlesex Rifle Volunteer Corps. The centre of the device shows three muskets above three bayonets, the 41st having been raised by the Enfield Small Arms Factory.

Men of the 1/7th Battalion, Middlesex Regiment, cleaning their machine-gun near the Mareth Line, Tunisia, in 1943. **Imperial War Museum**

Increased to two battalions in 1939, the Kensingtons were organised as machine gun units. The 1st Battalion served with the BEF in France and Belgium during 1940 and later saw action in Italy. The 2nd acted in a support role with 49th Infantry Division and fought in NW Europe during 1944–5. In 1947 the two battalions were merged and subsequently re-organised as an army phantom signal regiment.

19th London Regiment (St Pancras)

The 19th London Regiment was formed as the 29th Middlesex Rifle Volunteer Corps at St Pancras in 1860. It became the 17th Corps in 1880, and the following year was allotted to the Middlesex Regiment as one of its volunteer battalions.

Having transferred to the Territorial Force in 1908 as the 19th Battalion of the London Regiment, the two battalions served during the First World War throughout France and Belgium (1/19th), Salonika and Palestine (2/19th). In 1916 the 19th became part of the Middlesex Regiment and in 1935 was transferred to the Royal Engineers as 33rd AA Battalion.

The King's Royal Rifle Corps

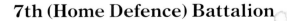

7th and 8th Battalions (Queen Victoria's Rifles)

The predecessor of the 7th and 8th Battalions, KRRC was the 1st Middlesex Rifle Volunteer Corps, which owed its origins to the formation in 1803 of the Duke of Cumberland's Sharpshooters. The 'Sharpshooters' later became the Royal Victoria Rifle Club, and in 1859 provided the County of Middlesex with its first corps of rifle volunteers. Another Middlesex rifle corps was the 11th (St George's), which was formed in 1860, became the 11th in 1880, and in 1892 was amalgamated with the 1st with the title of 1st Middlesex (Victoria and St George's) Rifle Volunteer Corps.

In 1908 the 1st Middlesex was merged with the 19th Middlesex Corps (formed in Bloomsbury in 1860), as the 9th (County of London) Battalion, The London Regiment (Queen Victoria's). During the First World War both the 1/9th and 2/9th Battalions served on the Western Front, while the 3/9th remained at home as the 9th (Reserve) Battalion.

In 1937 the 9th London Regiment became the Queen Vitoria's Rifles, The King's Royal Rifle Corps. At the outbreak of war in 1939 the 'Victoria's' were divided into two battalions. The 1st Battalion was equipped with motor cycles, and in 1940 was lost during the defence of Calais. The battalion was redesignted as 7th Battalion, KRRC in 1941 and two years later, placed into suspended animation. The 2nd Battalion, Queen Victoria's, remained in the UK throughout the war and was redesignated as 8th KRRC in 1941.

The 7th and 8th were amalgamated as Queen Victoria's Rifles, the King's Royal Rifle Corps in 1947. In 1961 an amalgamation took place with the Queen's Westminsters to form The Queen's Royal Rifles. This battalion is now represented by part of the 4th (Volunteer) Battalion, Royal Green Jackets.

7th (Home Defence) Battalion

See 30th Battalion

8th (Home Defence) Battalion

See 14th Battalion

9th and 10th Battalions (The Rangers)

The 9th and 10th Battalions, KRRC were formed from the Central London Rangers, formally the 12th Battalion of the London Regiment. The Rangers were formed at Grays Inn in 1860, under the title of 40th Middlesex Rifle Volunteer Corps. The 40th became the 22nd in 1880 and the 12th London in 1908.

Members of the battalion served with the CIV during the war in South Africa. In the First World War both the 1/12th and 2/12th served on the Western Front, while the 3/12th became part of the 9th (Reserve) Battalion.

In 1937 the 12th London Regiment was redesignated as The Rangers, The King's Royal Rifle Corps, and two years later was divided into two battalions for war service. The 1st and 2nd Rangers were redesignated as 9th and 10th Battalions, KRRC in 1941. The 9th saw service in Greece and Crete during 1941 and later in the following year, fought at El Alamein. The 10th remained in the UK throughout the war.

In 1947 the 'Rangers' were reconstituted and transferred from KRRC to the Rifle Brigade as The Rangers, The Rifle Brigade (Prince Consort's Own) and was later amalgamated with the London Rifle Brigade (see 7th and 8th Battalions, Rifle Brigade).

Left
22nd Middlesex Rifle Volunteer Corps, c1870. This officer wears a grey uniform with red collar, cuffs and piping and, as a member of the St Martin's Division of the 22nd, bears on his pouch-belt a plate showing the figure of St Martin cutting his cloak in half to share it with a beggar. **National Army Museum**
Right
Corporal of the 9th (County of London) Battalion, The London Regiment. A 'Scout' badge is being worn above the chevrons on the right arm. **D. Millbery**

The Wiltshire Regiment (Duke of Edinburgh's)

4th Battalion

The 4th Battalion, the Wiltshire Regiment originated in 1859, and was formerly the regiment's 1st and 2nd Volunteer Battalions, previously the 1st and 2nd Wiltshire Rifle Volunteer Corps. In 1900 the two battalions sent a number of volunteers out to South Africa, the 1st VB contingent being under the command of Viscount Folkestone.

In October 1914, the 1/4th Battalion went to India, where it remained until September 1917. From India the battalion moved to the Suez area, and from there to Palestine. The 2/4th also served in India, while the 3/4th remained at home as the 4th (Reserve) Battalion.

During the Second World War, the battalion served in the 43rd Infantry Division and fought throughout NW Europe during 1944–5. In 1967 the battalion became part of the Royal Wiltshire Territorials and now forms part of the 1st Battalion The Wessex Regiment.

5th Battalion

Formed in 1939 as a duplicate of the 4th Battalion, the 5th served in the 43rd Infantry Division throughout NW Europe and was converted in 1947 as 651 LAA Regiment, Royal Artillery.

6th (Home Defence) Battalion

See 30th Battalion

30th Battalion

Formed as 83 Group National Defence Companies in 1936, the unit joined the Wiltshire Regiment as its 6th (Home Defence) Battalion in 1939 and became 30th in 1941.

Three members of the 1st Wiltshire Volunteer Rifle Corps. The khaki uniforms are of the type introduced c1904 and bear the cloth arm titles 'WILTS' over '1' over 'VRC'.

The Manchester Regiment

5th Battalion

The 4th Admin Battalion of Lancashire Rifle Volunteers was formed in 1860 and included corps from areas of Lancashire that included Wigan, Swinton, Leigh, Worsley and Flixton. In 1880 the battalion was consolidated as the 4th Lancashire Rifle Volunteer Corps, consisting of thirteen companies and headquarters in Manchester. The 4th later became the 1st Volunteer Battalion of the Manchester Regiment and as such contributed a large number of volunteers for service in South Africa.

During the First World War, the 1/5th Battalion served in Gallipoli, Egypt, France and Belgium. Pte. Alfred Wilkinson gained the VC at Marou, France in October 1918. The 2/5th also fought on the Western Front, while the 3/5th became the 4th (Reserve) Battalion.

The battalion again went to France in 1940, and after returning to England via Dunkirk was re-formed as 111 Regiment Royal Armoured Corps. As an armoured unit, the battalion served in the UK and in 1943 was re-converted to infantry and placed in suspended animation. The 5th Battalion became 652 HAA Regiment, Royal Artillery in 1947.

6th Battalion

Formed at Manchester in 1859 as the 6th Lancashire Rifle Volunteer Corps, the battalion joined the Manchester Regiment as its 2nd Volunteer Battalion in 1881. Part of the battalion was formed from members of Manchester University, which in 1908 provided a contingent of the Senior Division, Officers Training Corps.

Members of the battalion served during the Boer War. In the First World War, the battalion was increased to include second and third line units, and active service was seen in Gallipoli, Egypt and on the Western Front.

The 6th/7th Battalion, Manchester Regiment was formed by amalgamation in 1921, and in 1936 a transfer was made to the Royal Artillery as 65 AA Brigade.

In 1939 the 5th Battalion was doubled in size and subsequently split to form the 5th and 6th Battalions. The new 6th remained in the UK throughout the war, and was eventually disbanded in 1947.

Left
5th (Ardwick) Volunteer Battalion, The Manchester Regiment. The cap badge of the regiment at this time was the Arms of the City of Manchester. **D. J. Barnes**
Right
Mounted Infantry Section of the 4th Volunteer Battalion, Manchester Regiment, in stable dress, c1894.

7th Battalion

Another Manchester rifle corps to be raised in 1859 was the 40th, later 16th, Lancashire. This became the 4th Volunteer Battalion, Manchester Regiment in 1888, and in 1908 the regiment's 7th Battalion (TF). Members of the 4th Volunteer Battalion served during the Boer War.

In 1914–18 the 1/7th saw service in Gallipoli and Egypt before moving to France in 1917. The 2/7th also served on the Western Front, while the 3/7th became part of the 5th (Reserve) Battalion in 1916. The 7th Battalion was amalgamated after the war to form the 6th/7th Manchester Regiment.

A new 7th Manchesters was formed in 1939 as a duplicate of the 8th Battalion. The 7th was organised as a machine gun unit and served throughout NW Europe during 1944–5. The 7th was disbanded in 1947.

8th (Ardwick) Battalion

Formed in 1860 and ranked second in Manchester, the 33rd Lancashire Corps became the 20th in 1880 and the 5th (Ardwick) Volunteer Battalion, Manchester Regiment in 1888. Members of the battalion fought alongside regular troops in South Africa during the Boer War. In 1914–18 action was seen in Gallipoli and Egypt before moving to the Western Front in 1917.

The battalion went to France with the BEF in 1940, and after returning to England was re-formed and sent to Malta as part of its defence force. From Malta, the 8th moved to Syria and then on to Egypt, Palestine and Italy. The 8th Manchesters became part of the Lancastrian Volunteers in 1967 and now form part of the 5th/8th (Volunteer) Battalion, King's Regiment.

Signal Section, 6th Battalion, The Manchester Regiment. Each man wears the crossed-flags signallers' badge on the lower left arm.

9th Battalion

The 23rd Lancashire Rifle Volunteer Corps was formed at Ashton-under-Lyne in 1860. It became the 7th Corps in 1880 and the 3rd Volunteer Battalion, Manchester Regiment in 1888.

As the 1/9th Manchesters, the battalion served in Gallipoli where in August 1915 Lt. William Furshaw won the Victoria Cross. From Gallipoli the battalion moved on to Egypt, and then, in 1917, to France. The 2/9th also fought on the Western Front.

The 9th was converted to machine gunners in 1938 and the following year was divided as the 1/9th and 2/9th Battalions. The 2/9th eventually left the regiment to become 88th Anti-Tank Regiment, Royal Artillery. The 1/9th, which was later redesignated as 9th, returned from France in 1940 and was to see subsequent service in Italy and Greece.

The battalion transferred to the T&AVR as part of the Lancastrian Volunteers. It now forms part of the 5/8th (Volunteer) Battalion, King's Regiment.

10th Battalion

The battalion originated in Oldham and was formed as the 31st Lancashire Rifle Volunteer Corps in 1860. The 31st became part of the 7th Corps in 1880, but two years later was removed to form the 22nd Lancashire. As the 6th Volunteer Battalion Manchester Regiment, the Oldham volunteers fought during the Boer War. In the First World War, the battalion served alongside the regiment's other territorials in Gallipoli, Egypt, France and Belgium. In 1938 the 10th was converted and transferred as 41st (Oldham) Royal Tank Regiment.

11th (Home Defence) Battalion

See 30th Battalion

28th Battalion

Formed in 1915 as 45th Provisional Battalion (TF), it became the 28th Manchesters in 1917 and was disbanded the following year.

30th Battalion

Formed in 1936 as 102 Group National Defence Companies, the unit became 11th (Home Defence) Battalion the Manchester Regiment in 1939, the 30th in 1941, and was disbanded in 1943.

4th Volunteer Battalion, The Manchester Regiment. The numerous badges worn on the left arm, together with the medals on the right breast, are awards received from shooting competitions. The subject of the photograph was the best shot in his company – see crossed rifles with star above on lower left arm – and has gained five bars to his Queen's South Africa Medal.

The North Staffordshire Regiment (The Prince of Wales's)

5th Battalion

In 1880 the 2nd Staffordshire Rifle Volunteer Corps, which had been raised in 1859 at Longton, was merged with other rifle corps from the county to form a battalion consisting of eleven companies and headquarters at Stoke-on-Trent. Also known as the 'Staffordshire Rangers', the 2nd Corps became the 1st Volunteer Battalion, North Staffordshire Regiment in 1883, and as such sent a large number of its members to South Africa during the Boer War.

Both the 1/5th and 2/5th Battalions fought on the Western Front during the First World War, L/Cpl. John Thomas of the 2/5th gaining the Victoria Cross at Fontaine, France on 30 November 1917. The 3/5th Battalion remained at home as the 5th (Reserve) Battalion.

In 1936 the battalion was converted and transferred as 41st AA Battalion, Royal Engineers. It later became part of the Royal Artillery, and served in several roles until 1961 when, as part of 441 AA Regiment, it was re-formed as infantry and concurrently amalgamated with the 6th North Staffs to form the 5th/6th Battalion. After 1967 the battalion was represented by the 5th/6th (T) Bn, the Staffordshire Regiment, which later formed part of the Light Infantry and Mercian Volunteers. The battalion now forms elements of the 1st Mercian Volunteers.

6th Battalion

The 6th Battalion North Staffordshire Regiment originated from the 2nd Admin Battalion of Staffordshire Rifle Volunteers. Formed in 1860, the 2nd Admin included rifle corps from the Lichfield area and was consolidated in 1880 as the 5th Corps of eight companies. The 5th became the 2nd Volunteer Battalion, North Staffordshire Regiment in 1883, and contributed to the several volunteer service companies that served with the regular troops in South Africa.

The battalion spent the First World War on the Western Front. On the 3/4 October 1918, L/Cpl. William Coltman was awarded the Victoria Cross for his part in an action that took place at Mannequin Hill, north east of Sequehart in France. (This award added to the Distinguished Conduct Medal and Bar, and the Military Medal and Bar, was to make him the most decorated NCO of the First World War.) In 1944 the battalion took part in the campaign through NW Europe.

The 6th Battalion was amalgamated in 1961 with P and R Batteries of 441 LAA Regiment, Royal Artillery (formerly the 5th Battalion) to form the 5th/6th Battalion, North Staffordshire Regiment.

7th Battalion

Formed in 1939 as a duplicate of the 6th Battalion, the 7th North Staffs served as part of the Orkneys and Shetland Island defences, before going to NW Europe in 1944.

Left
Bandmaster E. Stringer of the 5th Battalion, York and Lancaster Regiment. Mr Stringer wears his Volunteer Long Service Medal and musician's arm badge on a scarlet tunic. The badge of the Regiment, the 'Royal Tiger', commemorates its service in India between 1796–1819 and can be seen here worn on the cap and collar.
Right
2nd Volunteer Battalion, The York and Lancaster Regiment. The elaborate shoulder wings and bugle arm badge indicate that the subject of this photograph is a musician. The badge worn on the lower left arm was awarded to volunteers that had obtained 25 points and upwards in the 1st Class at 800 yards on the rifle range.

The York and Lancaster Regiment

The Hallamshire Battalion

Hallamshire is the part of the Yorkshire West Riding represented by the Parishes of Sheffield and Ecclesfield. It was in Sheffield, on 30 September 1859, that the Hallamshire Rifle Volunteer Corps was formed. It was officially known as the 2nd Yorkshire West Riding Corps, and in 1883 was redesignated as the 1st (Hallamshire) Volunteer Battalion, York and Lancaster Regiment. In 1900, 147 members of the battalion went out to South Africa and saw active service during the Boer War.

Transfer to the Territorial Force in 1908 was as the 4th (Hallamshire) Battalion, York and Lancaster Regiment. Second and third line units were formed for war service in 1914, the 1/4th and 2/4th seeing action on the Western Front, while the 3/4th remained at home as the 4th (Reserve) Battalion. While in France and Belgium, two members of the Hallamshires won the Victoria Cross.

Redesignated as the Hallamshire Battalion in 1924, the battalion served in Norway and Iceland before moving to NW Europe in 1944. The Hallamshires now are represented in the 1st and 3rd Battalions, Yorkshire Volunteers.

5th Battalion

The 2nd Volunteer Battalion, York and Lancashire Regiment provided the regiment's 5th Territorial Battalion in 1908. Dating from 1860, the battalion originated in Doncaster as the 4th Admin Battalion of Yorkshire West Riding Rifle Volunteers. The 4th Admin was consolidated in 1880 as the 8th Corps of nine companies, and redesignated as 2nd Volunteer Battalion, York and Lancs in 1883.

The battalion contributed a large number of its members to the several volunteer service companies that went out to South Africa during the Boer War. During the First World War both the 1/5th and 2/5th served on the Western Front, while the 3/5th was absorbed into the 4th (Reserve) Battalion in 1916.

In 1936 the 5th was converted and transferred as 67 AA Brigade, Royal Artillery. After serving in several gunner roles, it was absorbed into the Hallamshire Battalion, as infantry, in 1961.

6th Battalion

Formed in 1939 as a duplicate of the Hallamshire Battalion, the 6th served in France during 1940, and later in N Africa, Italy and Greece.

The Durham Light Infantry

5th Battalion

The 1st Durham Rifle Volunteer Corps was formed at Stockton-on-Tees in 1860, and in 1880 was amalgamated with other Durham corps, from Darlington, Castle Eden and Middlesbrough, to form a battalion of eight companies.

The 1st Durhams later became the 1st Volunteer Battalion of the Durham Light Infantry and as such gained the battle honour 'South Africa 1900–02' for the services of its members during the Boer War.

The 5th was extended to three battalions for war service in 1914. The 1/5th went to France as part of the 50th Division in 1915 and after seeing a great deal of action on the Western Front was reduced to a training cadre in July 1918. The 2/5th served in Salonika as a garrison battalion from October 1916, while the 3/5th formed the 5th (Reserve) Battalion.

For the Second World War, the 5th Durhams were required to serve in an anti-aircraft role, and was divided, first as 1/5th and 2/5th, and subsequently as 54th and 55th Searchlight Regiments, Royal Artillery.

6th Battalion

The 6th was formed in 1860 as one of Durhams several rifle volunteer admin battalions. Numbered as 2nd, the battalion was consolidated as the 2nd Durham Rifle Volunteer Corps in 1880. It consisted of six companies and had its head-quarters at Bishop Auckland. The 2nd Corps later became the 2nd Volunteer Battalion, Durham Light Infantry, and as such was awarded the battle honour, 'South Africa 1900–02'.

During the First World War, the 1/6th suffered heavy casualties at Ypres and as a result was temporarily amalgamated with the 8th Durhams to form 6th/8th Battalion. The 2/6th, as part of the 59th Division, served in France as a garrison guard battalion, and the 3/6th became part of the 5th (Reserve) Battalion in 1916.

In 1940, the battalion went to France with the BEF. It later fought at El Alamein and was to take part in the June 1944 assault landings in Normandy. The battalion is now represented by the 7th Light Infantry (Volunteers).

7th Battalion

During 1860, five companies of rifle volunteers were raised in Sunderland, and

Corporal J. Borthwick of the 5th Volunteer Battalion, Durham Light Infantry. Corporal Borthwick was a member of the South Shields Detachment and wears numerous badges and medals awarded in shooting competitions.

subsequently merged as the 3rd Durham Rifle Volunteer Corps. As the 3rd (Sunderland) Volunteer Battalion, Durham Light Infantry, the corps contributed a large number to the several volunteer service companies that went to serve with the regular troop in South Africa.

In 1915, the 1/7th went to France, where it became the pioneer battalion of the 50th Division, and later the 8th Division. The 2/7th remained in the UK until October 1918, when it was sent to North Russia. The 3/7th was also formed which in 1916 became part of the 5th (Reserve) Battalion. The 7th DLI was converted and transferred in 1936 as 47 AA Battalion, Royal Engineers.

8th Battalion

The 8th Durham Light Infantry was originally the 4th Durham Rifle Volunteer Corps, which had been formed in 1860 by the amalgamation of several Durham rifle companies. The 4th consisted of ten companies, many of which dated from the beginning of the Volunteer Movement in 1859.

In 1887 the 4th Durham RVC became the 4th Volunteer Battalion, Durham Light Infantry, and in 1908 its C Company transferred as the Durham University Contingent of the Officers Training Corps. The remainder of the battalion provided the 8th Durham Light Infantry which saw active service throughout France and Belgium during the First World War.

In the Second World War, the battalion served in N Africa, and in 1944 was involved in the assault landings in Normandy. The 8th DLI is now represented by part of the 7th Light Infantry (Volunteers).

9th Battalion

In 1880 the 5th Durham Rifle Volunteer Corps was formed by the amalgamation of several rifle volunteer units from the Gateshead, South Shields, Blaydon Burn and Winlaton areas. The 5th later became the 5th Volunteer Battalion, Durham Light Infantry, and in 1908 the regiment's 9th Territorial Battalion.

Members of the battalion served in South Africa during the Boer War. In 1914 three battalions were provided for war service, two members gaining the Victoria Cross while serving in France.

In the Second World War the battalion also saw service in N Africa, Sicily and NW Europe. Another Victoria Cross was awarded to a member of the 9th Durhams, Pte. Adam Wakenshaw, for his part in an action at Mersa Matruh in the Western Desert on 27 June 1942. Wakenshaw was killed that day and is buried in the El Alamein War Cemetery in Egypt.

In 1948 the battalion was converted as the 17th Battalion, Parachute Regiment. This battalion is now represented as part of the 4th (Volunteer) Battalion of the Regiment.

10th Battalion

Formed in 1939 as a duplicate of the 6th Battalion at Bishop Auckland, the battalion served in France during 1940, in Iceland, and in NW Europe from 1944.

11th Battalion

Formed as a duplicate of the 8th Battalion in 1939, the battalion fought in NW Europe during 1944, having previously served in Iceland and with the BEF in 1940.

12th Battalion

See the Tyneside Scottish, The Black Watch

13th and 18th (Home Defence) Battalions

See 30th Battalion

26th Battalion

Formed in 1915 under the title, 3rd North Coast Defence Battalion, it was redesignated later the same year as 23rd Provisional Battalion (TF). In 1917 it became the 26th Battalion Durham Light Infantry.

27th Battalion

Designated as 27th DLI in January 1917 it had originally been formed in 1915 as the 25th Provisional Battalion (TF).

30th Battalion

This battalion was formed as 41 Group National Defence Companies in 1936, and later organised as the 1/13th and 2/13th (Home Defence) Battalions of the Durham Light Infantry. For a short time in 1941 the 2/13 was known as the 18th Battalion. Later that year, however, the 18th was merged with the 13th to form the 30th Battalion.

The Highland Light Infantry (City of Glasgow Regiment)

5th (City of Glasgow) Battalion

During 1860, a number of independent rifle corps, then existing in the City of Glasgow, were merged as the 19th Lanarkshire Rifle Volunteer Corps. By the end of the year, the 19th had reached a strength of nineteen companies, and included contingents provided by Glasgow firms, the Edinburgh and Glasgow Railway, and the newspaper and printing industry. The 19th was re-numbered as 5th in 1880, and later provided the 1st Volunteer Battalion, Highland Light Infantry.

After the Boer War, the battle honour 'South Africa 1900–02' was awarded to the battalion for the service of its members. During the First World War, the 1/5th Battalion served with the 52nd Lowland Division in Gallipoli, Egypt, Palestine and on the Western Front. The 2/5th went to Ireland while the 3/5th became the 5th (Reserve) Battalion.

The 5th HLI went to France as part of the BEF in 1940, and with the 157th Infantry Brigade, fought in NW Europe throughout 1944–5.

In 1947 the 5th was amalgamated with the 6th, 10th and 11th Battalions of the Highland Light Infantry, to form the regiment's 5th/6th Battalion. Transferred to the T&AVR in 1967, it forms part of the 52nd Lowland Volunteers.

6th (City of Glasgow) Battalion

The 6th HLI was originally the 25th Lanarkshire Rifle Volunteer Corps, which had been formed in 1861 by the amalgamation of the several rifle companies that had been raised by Clyde shipbuilding and engineering yards. The 25th was re-numbered as 6th in 1880, and in 1887 became the 2nd Volunteer Battalion, Highland Light Infantry.

Members of the battalion fought in South Africa during the Boer War, and in 1914–18 service was seen in Gallipoli, Egypt, Palestine and on the Western Front. While in France, Cpl. D. Hunter won the VC. During the Second World War the battalion served in the UK and took part in the campaign in NW Europe in 1944–5.

The battalion was merged with other HLI Territorials in 1947 to form the 5th/6th Battalion.

7th (Blythswood) Battalion

The additional title 'Blythswood' was granted to the 2nd Admin Battalion of Lanarkshire Rifle Volunteers in honour of its Commanding Officer, Campbell of Blythswood. The battalion became the 31st Lanarkshire Rifle Volunteer Corps in 1865, the 8th in 1880, and the 3rd (Blythswood) Volunteer Battalion, HLI in 1887.

The battle honour 'South Africa 1900–02' was granted to the battalion for its services during the Boer War. In 1914–18, the 1/7th fought at Gallipoli, Egypt, Palestine and in France and Belgium, while the 2/7th was stationed in Ireland. The 3/7th became part of the 5th (Reserve) Battalion, HLI in 1916.

In 1938, the 7th HLI was converted and transferred to the Royal Artillery as 83rd AA Regiment.

8th (Lanark) Battalion

The 8th Battalion of Lanarkshire Rifle Volunteers, upon formation in 1860, consisted of companies situated at Lesmahagow, Lanark, Carluke and Douglas. It became the 9th Lanarkshire RVC in 1880, and later provided a volunteer battalion of the Highland Light Infantry.

During the war in South Africa, 96 members of the battalion saw active service, and earned for the 9th Lanarks the battle honour 'South Africa 1900–02'. In 1914, however, insufficient numbers volunteered for service overseas, and as a result, the battalion was later disbanded.

9th (Glasgow Highland) Battalion

This battalion was formed in 1868 as the 105th Lanarkshire Rifle Volunteer Corps by Highlanders then resident in the City of Glasgow. The corps soon consisted of twelve companies and in 1880 was re-numbered as 10th. Redesignation as the 5th (Glasgow Highland) Volunteer Battalion, Highland Light Infantry was in 1887, and the battalion sent a large number of volunteers to South Africa.

The 1/9th Battalion served in several formations on the Western Front during the First World War. The 2/9th went to Ireland with the 65th Division, while the 3/9th remained at home as part of the 5th (Reserve) Battalion. The battalion was doubled in size and divided as the 1/9th and 2/9th in 1939. Both units saw action in NW Europe during 1944–5.

In 1947 the battalion was redesignated as the Glasgow Highlanders Battalion, Highland Light Infantry and is now represented as part of the 1st Battalion, 52nd Lowland Volunteers.

10th Battalion

Formed in 1939 as a duplicate of the 5th Battalion in Glasgow, the 10th served as part of the Orkneys and Shetland Islands defences, before moving to NW Europe for the 1944–5 campaign. The 10th formed part of the 5/6th Battalion in 1947.

11th Battalion

The 11th Battalion was formed in 1939 as a duplicate of the 6th, and was converted in 1941 to 156 Regiment, Royal Armoured Corps with the 36th Army Tank Brigade. The battalion remained in the UK throughout the war, and in 1947 was merged into the 5/6th Battalion, HLI.

12th (Home Defence) Battalion

See 30th Battalion

21st Battalion

Formed in 1915 as the 9th (Scottish) Provisional Battalion (TF), it became 21st HLI in 1917 and was disbanded in 1919.

30th Battalion

Formed in 1936 as 67 Group National Defence Companies, the unit became 12th (Home Defence) Battalion, HLI in 1939, the 30th in 1941 and was disbanded in 1943.

Left
Colour Sergeant of the 105th Lanarkshire Rifle Volunteer Corps, c1870. The scarlet doublet has blue facings and is worn with a 42nd pattern tartan kilt. Black cocks' tails are worn in the glengarry. **J. B. McKay**
Right
Lance Corporal of the 6th (City of Glasgow) Battalion, Highland Light Infantry, in 1915. The kilt, of Mackenzie tartan, is seen here worn with a khaki service dress jacket.

The Seaforth Highlanders (Ross-shire Buffs, The Duke of Albany's)

4th (Ross-shire) Battalion

In 1880 the several rifle corps then in Ross-shire were merged as the 1st Ross-shire (Ross Highland) Rifle Volunteer Corps. Headquarters were located at Dingwall and the establishment authorised nine companies. The corps later became the 1st Volunteer Battalion of the Seaforth Highlanders and as such sent some 110 of its members to South Africa with the three volunteer service companies that served alongside regular troops.

The battalion transferred to the Territorial Force as the 4th (Ross-Highland) Battalion and as the 1/4th served throughout the Great War on the Western Front. One member of the battalion, Sgt. John Meikle, won the Victoria Cross for his part in an action near Marfaux, France on the 20 July 1918.

After the First World War the battalion was redesignated as 4th (Ross-shire) Battalion and in 1921 was amalgamated with the 5th Battalion to form the 4th/5th. The additional title 'Ross, Sutherland and Caithness' was later included, thus indicating the large recruiting area of the unit.

In 1939 the strength of the 4th/5th was doubled and the battalion divided as the 4th and 5th Seaforths. The 4th Battalion went to France with the BEF in 1940 and after retreating to St Valery, was captured by the Germans. The following year the 4th was absorbed into the 5th Battalion.

5th (Sutherland and Caithness Highland) Battalion

The 1st Sutherlandshire Rifle Volunteer Corps was formed in 1880 by the consolidation of the county's 1st Admin Battalion of Rifle Volunteers. The new corps consisted of ten companies, and was recruited throughout Sutherlandshire, the Orkneys, Shetlands and Caithness. The corps became a volunteer battalion of the Seaforths in 1881, and as such provided 87 of its members for service with the three volunteer companies that went out to South Africa.

The 1/5th Battalion served in France and Belgium during the First World War. During the advance on Cambrai in November 1917 a member of the battalion, L/Cpl. Robert MacBeath, succeeded in putting out of action five enemy machine guns. He captured three officers and thirty men and for his gallantry was awarded the Victoria Cross.

The battalion was amalgamated with the 4th Seaforths in 1921 and in 1939 was

Lieutenant Colonel Duncan Menzies, 1st Sutherland Rifle Volunteer Corps, c1896. Sutherland tartan is worn with a scarlet doublet and trews. The colonel's rank is indicated by the four silver feathers above the glengarry badge.

once again separated upon the expansion of the Territorial Army that year. After returning from France in 1940 the battalion absorbed those members of the 4th Battalion that were able to escape capture at St Valery. The 5th later fought at El Alamein and throughout Sicily and NW Europe.

With the reorganisations of the Territorial Army in 1947, the 5th was merged into the newly created, 11th Battalion.

6th (Morayshire) Battalion

The 1st Admin Battalion of Elgin Rifle Volunteers was formed in 1860, and included all the independent rifle corps that were formed within the county. In 1880, the battalion was consolidated as the 1st Corps of ten companies.

As the 3rd Volunteer Battalion Seaforths, the corps provided 193 of its members for service in South Africa. In 1914–18, the 1/6th served on the Western Front where Sgt. Alexander Edwards of the battalion won the Victoria Cross on 31 July/1 August 1917, north of Ypres.

At the start of the Second World War, the battalion served with the BEF. After returning from France, via Dunkirk, in 1940, the battalion travelled extensively for the remainder of the war, subsequent service being in Madagascar, India, Iraq, Iran, Sicily, Italy, Palestine and NW Europe. In 1947 the 6th Battalion became part of the regiment's newly formed 11th Battalion.

7th (Morayshire) Battalion

The battalion served throughout NW Europe during 1944–5, having been formed as a duplicate of the 6th Battalion in 1939. After the war the 7th was amalgamated with the 11th Battalion.

8th (Home Defence) Battalion

See 30th Battalion

11th Battalion

Formed in 1947 by the amalgamation of the 5th, 6th and 7th Battalions, the 11th was amalgamated with part of 540 LAA Regiment, Royal Artillery in 1961, forming in 1967 part of the 3rd (T) Bn Queens Own Highlanders, and the 51st Highland Volunteers.

30th Battalion

Formed in 1936 as 60 Group National Defence Companies, the unit became 8th (Home Defence) Battalion, Seaforths in 1939, and 30th Bn in 1941.

Senior NCOs of No 4 Company, 4th Battalion, Seaforth Highlanders, 1914–19. **J. G. Woodroff**

The Gordon Highlanders

3rd Battalion

See 4th Battalion

4th (The City of Aberdeen) Battalion

As the title implies, the 4th Gordon was recruited from the City of Aberdeen. The battalion was raised in 1860 as the 1st Aberdeenshire Rifle Volunteer Corps, and provided the 1st Volunteer Battalion of the regiment in 1881. During the war in South Africa, 128 members of the battalion served at the front, and were to distinguish themselves at Doornkop on 29 May 1900.

In the First World War, the 1/4th Battalion served on the Western Front. The 2/4th was absorbed into the 2/5th in 1915, while the 3/4th merged with other third line units of the Gordons, and became the 4th (Reserve) Battalion.

In 1939 the 4th Gordons were converted to a machine gun battalion, and as such saw action in France and Belgium with the BEF during 1940. After returning to the UK via Dunkirk, the 4th were converted to 92 Anti-Tank Regiment, Royal Artillery and remained as such in the UK for the remainder of the war.

The battalion was re-formed after the war in an infantry role and as the 4th/7th Battalion, Gordon Highlanders. In 1961 the battalion merged with the 5/6th Battalion to form the 3rd Battalion which is now represented by part of the 2nd Battalion 51st Highland Volunteers.

5th Battalion

During the regiment's territorial battalion history, there have been a number of formations that bore the numeral designation of 5th Battalion. The original battalion to be numbered as such was formed in 1908 under the designation of 5th (Buchan and Formartin) Battalion. This unit was formerly the regiment's 2nd and 3rd Volunteer Battalions, and had been previously the 2nd and 3rd Aberdeenshire Rifle Volunteer Corps. Both battalions were represented in South Africa during the Boer War.

The sub-title 'Buchan and Formartin' indicated the main recruitment area of the battalion. In 1921 the 5th was merged with the 7th Gordons, the two units having served in France and Belgium throughout the First World War, to form the 5th/7th (Buchan, Mar and Mearns) Battalion.

When the Territorial Army was expanded in 1939, the 5th/7th was separated into its former two battalions as 5th (Buchan and Formartin) and 7th (Mar and Mearns).

The 5th returned from France in 1940 and was later merged with the 9th Battalion to form the 116th Regiment, Royal Armoured Corps. The 7th then assumed the pre-1939 title 5th/7th (Buchan, Mar and Mearns) Battalion, and as such fought in Egypt, Sicily and NW Europe where it took part in the D Day landings.

In 1947 the 5th/7th was amalgamated with the 6th Gordons to form the 5th/6th (Banff, Buchan and Donside) Battalion. This was followed in 1961 by the amalgamation of the 5th/6th with the 4th/7th to form the 3rd Battalion, The Gordon Highlanders.

6th (Banff and Donside) Battalion

The battalion was formed in 1908 by the amalgamation of the 4th and 6th Volunteer Battalions of the Gordon Highlanders, which originated from a number of independent rifle companies raised in Aberdeenshire and Banffshire. Both battalions had gained the battle honour 'South Africa 1900–02' for the services of its members during the Boer War.

In the First World War, the 1/6th served in France and Belgium, and for a period was temporally amalgamated with the 7th Battalion under the title of 6th/7th Gordons. The 2/6th was merged into the 2/7th and the 3/6th became part of the 4th (Reserve) Battalion.

In 1939 the 6th (Banff and Donside) Battalion became the 6th (Banffshire) due to the Donside members being removed to form a duplicate battalion designated as 9th (Donside). The 6th went to France with the BEF in 1940, and saw subsequent service in N Africa, Italy and Palestine.

In 1947 the 6th was amalgamated with the 5th/7th Battalion to form the 5th/6th (Banff, Buchan and Donside) Battalion.

7th (Deeside Highland) Battalion

The battalion was formerly the 5th Volunteer Battalion, Gordons, and before that, the 1st Kincardineshire and Aberdeenshire Rifle Volunteer Corps. During the Boer War, 78 members of the battalion saw active service. In 1914–18, the battalion fought on the Western Front as part of the 51st Highland Division and was amalgamated with the 5th Battalion, as 5th/7th, in 1921.

In 1939 the battalion was re-formed from the 5th/7th and for a short time was known as the 7th (Mar and Mearns). It once again formed part of the 5th/7th from 1940.

8th (City of Aberdeen) Battalion

Formed in 1939 as a duplicate of the 4th Battalion in Aberdeen, the 8th was converted and transferred as 100 Anti-Tank Regiment in 1941.

9th (Donside) Battalion

The battalion was formed in 1939 as a duplicate of the 6th Battalion. In 1941 it formed part of the 116th Regiment, Royal Armoured Corps upon amalgamation with the 5th Gordons.

10th (Home Defence) Battalion

See 30th Battalion

Left
Drum-Major Goodman of the London Scottish, c1897. The uniform is Elcho grey and has a blue collar and cuffs.
Right
Gordon Highlanders Territorials, c1910. Painted by R. Caton Woodville. The scarlet doublet has yellow collar and cuffs. The tartan is Gordon pattern.

30th Battalion

Formed in 1936 as – 61 Group National Defence Companies, the unit became the 10th (Home Defence) Battalion, Gordons in 1939 and then 30th Battalion in 1941.

The Shetland Companies

Formed as three companies in 1900 and designated as the 7th Volunteer Battalion, Gordon Highlanders. The companies were located two at Lerwick and one at Scalloway, and in 1908 they were transferred to the Territorial Force as – The Shetland Companies, The Gordon Highlanders.

Members of the companies served in France with the 51st Highland Division and after heavy loses on the Somme during 1916, were absorbed into the 4th Gordons.

The London Scottish

The services of a rifle corps composed of Scotsmen living in the London area were accepted by the War Office on 2 November 1859. The corps consisted of six companies and was designated as the 15th Middlesex (London Scottish) Rifle Volunteers. The 15th was renumbered as 7th in 1880, and the following year was allotted to the Rifle Brigade as one of its volunteer battalions. In 1908, the

battalion transferred to the Territorial Force as the 14th (County of London) Battalion, The London Regiment (London Scottish).

A large number from the 'Scottish' served with the CIV in South Africa. In 1914 the battalion was the first TF battalion to go to France where it saw a great deal of action throughout the war. In June 1916, the 2/14th Battalion went to Salonika and later moved on to Palestine where two members gained the Victoria Cross.

The London Scottish became part of the Gordon Highlanders in 1916, and in 1937 were redesignated as The London Scottish, The Gordon Highlanders. In 1939 the 'Scottish' was expanded to three battalions. The 1st served in Iraq, Palestine, Egypt, Sicily and Italy; the 2nd remained in the UK and the 3rd acted in an anti-aircraft role with the title of 97th AA Regiment, Royal Artillery. While serving in Italy, Pte. George Mitchell of the 1st Battalion, gained the Victoria Cross for his part in an action at Damiano.

The London Scottish now forms part of the 51st Highland Volunteers.

Above
6th Battalion, Gordon Highlanders, 1914.
J. G. Woodroff
Below
Machine-gunners of the London Scottish, c1915.

The Queen's Own Cameron Highlanders

4th Battalion

Between 1859 and 1869, there were ten independent companies of rifle volunteers raised within the county of Inverness-shire. In 1880, the ten companies were merged as the 1st Inverness-shire Rifle Volunteer Corps. The corps later became the 1st (Inverness Highland) Volunteer Battalion of the Cameron Highlanders, and in 1908 the regiment's 4th Territorial Battalion.

During the Boer War, some 245 men from the battalion volunteered and served in South Africa. In 1915, the 1/4th Battalion went to France and after serving in several formations was absorbed into the 1st Battalion due to the heavy casualties suffered at Festubert and Loos. The 2/4th remained with the 64th Division in the UK, while the 3/4th acted as a reserve unit and was eventually absorbed into the 3rd Battalion.

The 4th Camerons was reconstituted after the First World War. In 1940 the battalion went with the BEF to France, and on the 12 June was forced to surrender to the Germans at St Valery.

The battalion was later re-formed at Inverness and in August 1940 sailed for Aruba in the Dutch West Indies for guard duties at the oil refineries. The battalion returned to the UK in 1942 and while stationed in the Shetlands assumed the title of 2nd Battalion, Cameron Highlanders. (The original 2nd Battalion of the regiment was a regular battalion and had recently been captured at Tobruk.) The battalion went on to serve in Egypt, Italy and Greece and was the only territorial battalion to be given the honour of assuming the battalion number of a regular unit.

The battalion was redesignated as 4th after the war and in 1947 was amalgamated with the 5th Camerons to form the 4th/5th Battalion. The 4th/5th provided in 1967 three companies of the 3rd (T) Bn, Queen's Own Highlanders and later companies of the 51st Highland Volunteers.

5th Battalion

Formed in 1939 as a duplicate of the 4th Battalion, the 5th Battalion was part of the 51st (Highland) Division, and saw service in Egypt, Libya, N Africa, Sicily and NW Europe. The 5th was amalgamated with the 4th Battalion, to form the 4th/5th in 1947.

6th (Home Defence) Battalion

See 30th Battalion

10th (Lovat's Scouts) Battalion

Formed September 1916 in Cairo from members of the 1/1st and 2/1st Lovat's Scouts Yeomanry, the battalion went to Salonika shortly after formation. In June 1918 it moved to France where it served on lines of communication duties.

30th Battalion

Formed in 1936 as two companies of 60 Group National Defence Companies, the units became 6th (Home Defence) Battalion, Cameron Highlanders in 1939, which was re-numbered the 30th Battalion in 1941.

The Liverpool Scottish

The Liverpool Scottish was formed in 1900 as the 8th (Scottish) Volunteer Battalion of the King's Liverpool Regiment. It was redesignated as 10th Battalion (TF) in 1908 and in 1914 moved for war duties as part of the Forth defences. The battalion went to France before the end of 1914 and while on the Western Front Capt. Noel Chavasse, RAMC, the battalion's Medical Officer, won the Victoria Cross and bar. The 2/10th Battalion was also formed and served in France. The 3/10th Battalion remained at home as a reserve unit.

In 1937 the battalion left the King's and became known as The Liverpool Scottish, The Queen's Own Cameron Highlanders. As such they formed a second battalion in 1939. The 1st Battalion served throughout the war in the UK, sending an independent platoon of volunteers to Norway in 1940, while the 2nd became 89th Anti-Tank Regiment, Royal Artillery in 1942. The 1st Battalion was stationed at Gibraltar from 1945 to 1947.

In 1967 the Liverpool Scottish became part of the 51st Highland Volunteers.

THE TERRITORIAL BATTALIONS · 213

Right
2nd Inverness-shire Rifle Volunteer Corps,
c1870. An Elcho grey doublet with green collar
and piping is worn with a kilt of Cameron of
Erracht tartan.

Left
Private Pinnington of the Liverpool Scottish in
1915. As a member of the Stretcher-Bearer
Section he wears an arm band with the initials
'S.B.' The cap badge worn is the old helmet
plate centre of the 8th Volunteer Battalion,
King's Liverpool Regiment, while the brass
shoulder title appears to have been broken and
now only consists of the top section, T/10.
Liverpool Scottish Regimental Museum

Brass shoulder title worn by the Liverpool
Scottish, c1937.

The Royal Ulster Rifles

The London Irish Rifles

Formed in 1860 as the 28th Middlesex (London Irish) Rifle Volunteer Corps by Irishmen living in the London area. From the beginning, the corps was popular, and numbered amoung its ranks the Marquises of Donegal and Conyngham, the Earls of Arran and Belmore, Lord Palmerston (who joined as a private), and W. H. Russell of the Times.

Re-numbered as 16th in 1880, the 'Irish' became a volunteer battalion of the Rifle Brigade in 1881. During the war in South Africa, the battalion sent eight officers and 200 men for active service, the volunteers seeing action with the CIV, the service companies of the Royal Irish Rifles and the Middlesex Yeomanry. One officer won the DSO while another member gained seven bars to his South Africa Medal.

The London Irish transferred to the Territorial Force in 1908 as 18th (County of London) Battalion, The London Regiment (London Irish Rifles). As part of the 47th (2nd London) Division, the battalion went to France in March 1915 and saw its first action at Festubert in May. The following September, at the battle of Loos, a rifleman, upon the order to advance, kicked a football over the top and proceeded to dribble it across 'no man's land' and up to the enemy trenches.

The 2/18th Battalion also served on the Western Front, where its first duty was to take over part of the line at Vimy Ridge. From France the battalion moved to Macedonia. It later served in Palestine where on the 23 December 1917, at Khurbet Adesah, the battalion's officers and NCOs were reduced to one subaltern and one sergeant. The 2/18th was subsequently disbanded in July 1918. The 3/18th served as a reserve battalion throughout the war.

In 1937 the London Regiment was broken up and the 'Irish' became known as The London Irish, The Royal Ulster Rifles – the connection with the regular regiment going back almost to the formation of the London Irish.

In 1939 the London Irish was organised into two battalions. The 1st left England in August 1942 and subsequently served in Iraq guarding oil installations and ammunition dumps. It later fought in Italy, where it took part in the battles for Monte Camino and Anzio. The 2nd Battalion served in N Africa and later took part in the invasion of Italy.

The two battalions were merged in 1947 and now provide part of the 4th (Volunteer) Battalion, Royal Irish Rangers, North Irish Militia.

6th Battalion

The 6th Battalion, Royal Ulster Rifles was formed in 1947 and consisted of headquarters, A and B Companies at Victoria Barracks, Belfast, C and D Companies at Ballymena and S Company at Lisburn. The battalion is now represented in both the 4th and 5th (Volunteer) Battalions of the Royal Irish Rangers.

Above
Drums and Bugles of the London Irish Rifles.
Left
Sergeant of the 28th Middlesex (London Irish) Rifle Volunteer Corps, c1870. The uniform is green with a lighter green collar and cuffs. The badge of an Irish Harp is being worn on the pouch-belt plate, the waist-belt clasp and the shako. **Major R. McDuell**

The Royal Irish Fusiliers (Princess Victoria's)

5th Battalion

The 5th Royal Irish Fusiliers (TA) was formed in 1947, and consisted of companies located at Armagh, Lurgan, Banbridge and Portadown. The battalion is now represented as part of the 4th and 5th (Volunteer) Battalions, Royal Irish Rangers.

7th Battalion

This battalion was formed as a cadre in 1969, and in 1971 was incorporated into the 5th (Volunteer) Battalion, Royal Irish Rangers.

Colour party of the 5th Battalion, Argyll and Sutherland Highlanders, having just received their Colours from the King at Windsor in June 1909.

The Argyll and Sutherland Highlanders (Princess Louise's)

5th (Renfrewshire) Battalion

The 1st Renfrewshire Rifle Volunteer Corps was formed at Greenock in 1859, and in 1880 was merged with three other Renfrewshire Corps and one from Bute, to form a battalion of nine companies. The 1st Renfrewshire later became the 1st Volunteer Battalion of the Argyll and Sutherland Highlanders, and as such was awarded the battle honour 'South Africa 1900–02' for the service of its members during the Boer War.

   In the First World War, the battalion served with the 52nd Division in Gallipoli, Egypt and Palestine. It moved to the Western Front for the last months of the war

and joined the 34th Division. The 2/5th Battalion was formed in 1914, and was later absorbed into the 2/8th Battalion. The 3/5th was amalgamated with other Argyll and Sutherland Highlanders reserve units in 1916 to form the 5th (Reserve) Battalion.

In 1921 the 5th/6th (Renfrewshire) Battalion was formed upon amalgamation. However, in 1939 the two were separated once again as 5th and 6th, and organised as machine gun units. The 5th Argylls became the 91st Anti-Tank Regiment in November 1941.

Mortar Section of the 7th Battalion, Argyll and Sutherland Highlanders. **Argyll and Sutherland Highlanders Museum**

6th (Renfrewshire) Battalion

The 2nd Renfrewshire Rifle Volunteer Corps was formed in 1880 by the amalgamation of the several independent rifle corps that constituted the 2nd Admin Battalion of Renfrewshire Rifle Volunteers. The headquarters was at Paisley and the strength of the battalion was eight companies. Also formed in 1880 was the 3rd Renfrewshire Rifle Volunteer Corps, originally being the 3rd Admin Battalion which had been created in 1860.

In 1887 the 2nd and 3rd Corps were redesignated as 2nd and 3rd Volunteer Battalions, Argyll and Sutherland Highlanders, each battalion contributing a number of its members to the several volunteer service companies that went out to South Africa in 1900. Upon transfer to the Territorial Force in 1908, the 2nd and 3rd VBs were amalgamated as the 6th (Renfrewshire) Battalion.

1st Clackmannanshire Rifle Volunteer Corps. The subject of this photograph wears the uniform in use between 1867–74 which consisted of a dark grey doublet with scarlet collar, cuffs and piping worn with Murray tartan trews. The grey caps had a red, white and green diced band.

In 1915 the 1/6th went to France and by June of the following year were serving as pioneers to the 5th Division. From France, the battalion moved to Italy, returning to the Western Front in April 1918. On 25 October 1918, Lt. William Bissett was awarded the Victoria Cross for his part in an action east of Maing. Both the 2/6th and 3/6th remained in the UK throughout the war.

The 6th was amalgamated with the 5th Argylls in 1921, to form the 5th/6th Battalion. However, in 1939 the two battalions were separated for war service. After returning from service in the BF in France in 1940, the battalion was converted and transferred as 93rd Anti-Tank Regiment, Royal Artillery.

7th Battalion

The County of Stirlingshire raised fourteen independent rifle corps between 1859–68, which in 1880 were merged as the 1st Stirlingshire Rifle Volunteer Corps. The 1st Corps, which had its headquarters at Stirling, consisted of ten companies and later became the 4th (Stirling) Volunteer Battalion, Argyll and Sutherland Highlanders.

The regiment's 7th Volunteer Battalion was recruited from both Clackmannanshire and Kinross, and also included a company from Stirlingshire. Both the 4th and 7th Volunteer Battalions contributed a number of men to the volunteer service companies formed by the Argylls for service in South Africa. In 1908, the two battalions were merged and formed the 7th Battalion, Argyll and Sutherland Highlanders.

During the First World War, the 1/7th served throughout France and Belgium, 2nd Lt. John Buchan gaining the Victoria Cross on 21 March 1918 at an action east of Marteville. The 2/7th remained in the UK, being disbanded in 1917. The 3/7th became part of the 5th (Reserve) Battalion in 1916.

In the Second World War, the 7th Argylls served with the BEF in France during 1940. It later fought in Egypt, Libya, N Africa, Sicily, Italy and NW Europe. While in Tunisia, Lt. Col. Lorne Campbell won the Victoria Cross at an action at Wadi Akarit on 6 April 1943. The battalion is now represented by part of the 51st Highland Volunteers.

8th (Argyllshire) Battalion

The 8th Argyll and Sutherland Highlanders was formerly the regiment's 5th Volunteer Battalion, and was formed from the several rifle companies that were raised in Argyllshire from 1859. Members of the battalion served with regular troops during the Boer War, their most notable action being Commando Nek on 1 October 1900.

The 1/8th served in several formations on the Western Front during the First World War. Both the 2/8th and 3/8th remained in the UK, the latter as part of the 5th (Reserve) Battalion.

The battalion served in France and Belgium in 1940, and later went on to fight in N Africa, Sicily and Italy. In 1947 it was amalgamated with the 11th Argylls and now forms part of the 3rd Battalion, 51st Highland Volunteers.

9th (Dumbartonshire) Battalion

The 1st Dumbartonshire Rifle Volunteer Corps was formed in 1859, and was later merged with other rifle corps from the county to form a battalion of twelve companies. From 1881, the 1st Dumbartons provided a volunteer battalion of the Argyll and Sutherland Highlanders, and in 1900 sent 98 of its members out for service with the regular troops in South Africa.

The 9th was organised into three battalions during the First World War, the 1/9th serving on the Western Front from 1915. One member, Lt. John Graham, gained the Victoria Cross while attached to 136 Company, Machine Gun Corps in Mesopotamia.

In 1938, the battalion was converted and transferred as 54th LAA Brigade, Royal Artillery.

10th Battalion

Formed as a duplicate of the 7th Battalion at Stirling. The battalion existed for only one year and was subsequently absorbed by its parent unit.

Pipes and Drums of the 7th Battalion, Argyll and Sutherland Highlanders, at camp in the 1960s. **Argyll and Sutherland Highlanders Museum**

11th (Argyll and Dumbarton) Battalion

Formed as a duplicate of the 8th Battalion in 1939. It remained in the UK throughout the war and was absorbed by the 8th in 1947.

12th (Home Defence) Battalion

See 30th Battalion

13th (Home Defence) Battalion

Raised in 1936 as part of the 63rd Group National Defence Companies, the unit joined the Argylls as 13th (Home Defence) Battalion in 1939 and the following year was absorbed into the 12th (HD) Battalion.

14th (Home Defence) Battalion

Formed in 1939 from the 65th and 75th Groups, National Defence Companies, the unit became the 14th (HD) Battalion. It was disbanded in 1941.

16th Battalion

Formed in 1915 as 4th (Scottish) Provisional Battalion (TF), it became 16th Argylls in 1917 and was disbanded in 1919.

30th Battalion

Formed in 1936 as part of 63 Group National Defence Companies, the unit became the 12th (Home Defence) Battalion in 1939, was absorbed the 13th (HD) Battalion in 1940 and was re-numbered as 30th Battalion in 1941. Disbandment took place in 1943.

The Rifle Brigade (Prince Consort's Own)

7th (Home Defence) Battalion

See 30th Battalion

7th and 8th Battalions, London Rifle Brigade

The London Rifle Brigade was formed as the 1st London Rifle Volunteer Corps in 1859, and within a short time consisted of fifteen companies. In 1908 the 1st Londons became the 5th (City of London) Battalion, The London Regiment (London Rifle Brigade) and as such served throughout France and Belgium during the First World War. One member of the battalion, gained the Victoria Cross south of Wieltje, St Julien Road on 13 May 1915.

In 1937 the battalion left the London Regiment and was designated as The London Rifle Brigade, The Rifle Brigade (Prince Consort's Own). The battalion was divided as 1st and 2nd LRB in 1939. The 1st became a motorised unit and in 1941 was redesignated as the 7th Battalion, Rifle Brigade. After serving in Egypt, Libya and N Africa, the 7th became a lorried infantry battalion while serving in Italy during 1944.

Formed in 1939, the 2nd LRB later became the 8th Battalion, Rifle Brigade and served in NW Europe throughout 1944–5.

The title, London Rifle Brigade, The Rifle Brigade was once again assumed in 1947, when the 7th and 8th Battalions were merged. In 1950 a new title, 'London Rifle Brigade/Rangers', was adopted upon amalgamation that year with the Rangers. This battalion is now represented by part of the 4th (Volunteer) Battalion, Royal Green Jackets.

9th and 10th Battalions, Tower Hamlets Rifles

The 2nd Tower Hamlets Rifle Volunteer Corps was formed in 1880 by the amalgamation of a number of independent rifle companies that had been formed in the area since 1859. Also formed in 1859 was the 15th Middlesex Rifle Volunteer Corps. This unit was recruited from the customs offices on the Thames and from workers in St Catherines and other London dock yards.

In 1908 the 2nd Tower Hamlets and 15th Middlesex were amalgamated under the title of 17th (County of London) Battalion, The London Regiment (Poplar and Stepney Rifles). The 1/17th served with the 47th Division in France and Belgium,

Senior NCOs of the London Rifle Brigade. The head-dress has black cocks' feathers and star plate at the front. Each man wears a silver whistle and chain attached to his dark green tunic. The star badges worn by two of the group were awarded one for each series of five years that a volunteer was returned as efficient by his corps. **J. G. Woodroff**

while the 2/17th went to France in 1916, then to Salonika and Egypt, and finally returned to France for the last months of the war.

In 1926 the battalion was redesignated as 17th London Regiment (Tower Hamlets Rifles). This was changed to Tower Hamlets Rifles, The Rifle Brigade (Prince Consort's Own) in 1937 and in 1939 the regiment was organised into three battalions for war service.

The 1st THR was designated as 9th Rifle Brigade in 1941 and as such served in Egypt and Libya. As the 10th Battalion, Rifle Brigade, the 2nd THR saw action in N Africa and Italy while the 3rd Battalion was converted as 5th Reconnaissance Corps and served in India, Iraq, Persia, Sicily, Italy, Palestine and NW Europe.

In 1947 the 9th and 10th were amalgamated and transferred to the Royal Artillery as 656 LAA Regiment.

11th (Home Defence) Battalion

See 30th Battalion

18th (London) Battalion

Formed in 1915 the battalion served as a garrison battalion in India until disbandment in February 1920.

19th (Western) Battalion

Formed in 1915 for service as a garrison battalion in Egypt and Palestine, it was disbanded in 1919.

20th (Northern) Battalion

This battalion served in Egypt and Palestine as a garrison battalion during the First World War.

21st (Midland) Battalion

Formed in 1915 for service as a garrison battalion in Egypt, it moved to India in 1918 and was disbanded in 1920.

22nd (Wessex and Welsh) Battalion

The battalion served throughout the First World War as a garrison battalion. Disbandment took place in Salonika in 1919.

23rd (North Western) Battalion

The battalion served as a garrison battalion in India until disbandment in 1920.

24th (Home Counties) Battalion

Formed in 1915, the battalion served as a garrison battalion in India from 1916 to 1920.

25th (Reserve) Battalion

Formed in August 1916, it served at Falmouth on garrison duties until the end of the war.

30th Battalion

Formed in 1936 as 23B Group National Defence Companies, the unit became 7th (Home Defence) Battalion, Rifle Brigade in 1939 and was redesignated as 11th in 1941, and as 30th Battalion in 1942.

8th London Regiment (Post Office Rifles)

The formation of a rifle corps at the General Post Office in London was sanctioned by the War Office in February 1868. Designated as the 49th Middlesex Rifle Volunteer Corps, the 49th consisted of seven companies and was recruited from the minor staff of the Post Office. At this time, senior members were already serving as part of the 21st (Civil Service) Corps.

The 49th became the 24th in 1880, and the following year joined the Rifle Brigade as one of its volunteer battalions. In 1882, a scheme was approved for the formation from within the 24th, of an Army Postal Service. The idea of the new

unit was for it to undertake all postal duties connected with an army on active service overseas.

The Army Post Office Corps was formed, and in 1882 joined the Expeditionary Force in Egypt. The 24th were subsequently awarded the battle honour 'Egypt 1882', making the Post Office Rifles the only territorial battalion to be thus honoured.

Members of the battalion also served in South Africa during the Boer War. In 1908 the 24th became the 8th (City of London) Battalion, The London Regiment and as such fought throughout France and Belgium during the First World War. In 1916 the 24th became part of the Corps of the Rifle Brigade, and in 1922 was amalgamated with the 7th London Regiment (see under Middlesex Regiment).

25th (County of London) (Cyclist) Battalion, London Regiment

The 25th London Regiment was formed in 1888 as the 26th Middlesex (Cyclist) Rifle Volunteer Corps and bore the distinction of being the first battalion to be completely composed of cyclists.

The 26th joined the Rifle Brigade as one of its volunteer battalions, and in 1908 became the 25th Battalion of the London Regiment. It served in India throughout the First World War, becoming part of the Rifle Brigade in 1916. In 1920 the Cyclists were converted to 47th Divisional Signals, Royal Corps of Signals.

The Artists Rifles

See under the Special Air Service Regiment

33rd (City of London) Battalion, The London Regiment

Formed on the 1 June 1918 at Clacton, the battalion was included as part of the Royal Fusiliers. Later the same month, the battalion absorbed members of the 7th (Service) Battalion, Rifle Brigade and was at the same time transferred. The battalion served in France with the 14th Division.

City of London Yeomanry (Rough Riders)

On 1 October 1956, the Rough Riders were incorporated in the Rifle Brigade. The regiment remained until May 1961, when upon amalgamation it formed the Inns of Court and City Yeomanry.

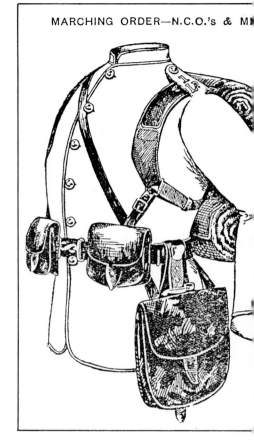

Illustrations from the 1900 Dress Regulations for the London Rifle Brigade.

Members of the 26th Middlesex (Cyclist) Rifle Volunteer Corps showing one of the functions in which they and their machines were used.

MARCHING ORDER—N.C.O.'s & MEN.

TUNIC—RANK & FILE.

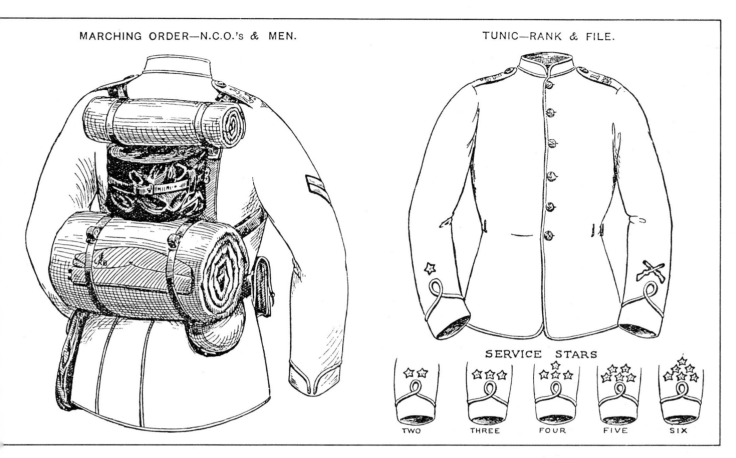

SERVICE STARS

TWO   THREE   FOUR   FIVE   SIX

15

The Honourable Artillery Company

The Honourable Artillery Company which had been given its charter by King Henry VIII in 1537. In 1871 it was divided into two branches, artillery and infantry. By early 1900, the latter section of the regiment comprised four companies, and that year sponsored a section of mounted infantrymen for the City Imperial Volunteers.

When the Territorial Force was formed in 1908, the HAC was directed to transfer as the 26th Battalion of the London Regiment. This new arrangement was not found satisfactory, and the order was ignored and subsequently rescinded.

During the First World War, the 1/1st Battalion, HAC served with several formations on the Western Front, two of its members gaining the Victoria Cross during the action on 28–29 April 1917 near Gavrelle in France. The 2/1st Battalion landed at Havre in October 1916 and fought as part of the 7th Division throughout France and Belgium until November 1917 when it transferred to the Italian Front. The 3/1st was formed in 1914 and served as a reserve battalion.

In 1939, the HAC infantry battalion, was organised as – 162 (HAC) Officer Cadet Training Unit. Re-formation as infantry took place in 1947.

Left
Colour Party of the Honourable Artillery Company, 1890s. The uniforms
are scarlet and styled on those of the Grenadier Guards.
Right
Members of the HAC in a front line trench at St Eloi in April 1915.
Imperial War Museum

The Monmouthshire Regiment

The Monmouthshire Regiment was formed in 1908 from the volunteers affiliated to the South Wales Borderers.

1st (Rifle) Battalion

The 1st Admin Battalion of Monmouthshire Rifle Volunteers was formed in 1860, and was to include the 1st, 3rd, 4th, 10th and 11th Corps of the county.

In 1880, the battalion was consolidated as 1st Corps, comprising seven companies with headquarters at Newport. The 1st later became the 2nd Volunteer Battalion of the South Wales Borderers and as such received the battle honour 'South Africa 1900–02' for its services during the Boer War.

In February 1915, the 1/1st Battalion went to France, where it later joined the 46th Division as its pioneer battalion. The 2/1st remained in the UK until disbandment in March 1918. The 3/1st became the 1st (Reserve) Battalion.

The battalion was converted to an air defence role in 1930, and the following year was transferred to the Royal Artillery as 68th Searchlight Regiment.

2nd Battalion

The 2nd Monmouthshire Rifle Volunteer Corps was formed at Pontypool in December 1859. It was redesignated as 3rd Volunteer Battalion, South Wales Borderers in 1885 and by 1900 consisted of ten companies.

The battalion contributed a large number from its ranks for service in South Africa. In 1914–18, the 1/2nd served in France as pioneers, while the 2/2nd and 3/2nd remained in the UK.

During the 1944–5 war, the 2nd Monmouths fought in NW Europe as part of the 53rd Infantry Division. In 1947 the battalion was amalgamated with the 4th Monmouths and is now represented as part of the 3rd (Volunteer) Battalion, Royal Regiment of Wales.

3rd (Brecknockshire and Monmouthshire) Battalion

In 1880 the 3rd Monmouthshire Rifle Volunteer Corps was formed by the amalgamation of the several corps that had previously constituted the 2nd Admin Battalion of Monmouthshire Rifle Volunteers. By 1900 the corps, which had

Bandsmen of the 4th Volunteer Battalion, The South Wales Borderers. The ornate musician's shoulder wings are seen here in scarlet and trimmed with white lace embroidered with scarlet crowns, and edged with a scarlet and white fringe. The tunic is scarlet and also carries green bugle cords.

become the 4th Volunteer Battalion, South Wales Borders in 1885, consisted of ten companies, from which a number of volunteers served in South Africa.

Upon transfer to the Territorial force in 1908, the 4th Volunteer Battalion became the 3rd Battalion, Monmouthshire Regiment. It served in the First World War as a pioneer battalion with the 49th Division, and in 1922 was amalgamated with the Brecknockshire Battalion, South Wales Borderers as the 3rd (Brecknockshire and Monmouthshire) Battalion.

The recruiting area of the battalion embraced both counties until 1939, when the Brecknockshire portion was separated to form The Brecknockshire Battalion. The Monmouthshire section of the battalion served throughout NW Europe during 1944–5 while the Brecknockshire Battalion served in the UK.

In 1947 both the Monmouth and Brecknock Battalions were converted and transferred as 637 and 638 LAA Regiments, Royal Artillery.

BOW STREET CAMP. 1910

1st MONMOUTHSHIRE

4th Battalion

The battalion was formed in 1916 as 48th Provisional Battalion (TF) from members of the three battalions that were unfit or unwilling to serve overseas. Redesignated the 4th Monmouths in 1917, the battalion was eventually disbanded in 1919.

In 1939 a new 4th Battalion was formed, this time as a duplicate of the 2nd Battalion. The 4th remained in the UK throughout the war, and in 1947 was amalgamated with its parent unit.

The Brecknockshire Battalion

See 3rd Battalion

1st Battalion, The Monmouthshire Regiment at Bow Street Camp in 1910. The green uniforms have black facings.

The Cambridgeshire Regiment

1st Battalion

The Cambridgeshire Regiment was previously the 3rd Volunteer Battalion of the Suffolk Regiment, and before that, the 1st Cambridgeshire Rifle Volunteer Corps. Formed in 1880, the battalion was created by the consolidation of the county's 1st Admin Battalion of Rifle Volunteers. At that time, the 1st Admin Battalion included in addition to those Cambridgeshire corps that were formed outside the University, one company from Essex and one from Huntingdonshire.

As the 3rd (Cambridgeshire) Volunteer Battalion, Suffolk Regiment, the battalion sent a contingent of 46 men to South Africa in 1900. In 1908 the battalion became the Cambridgeshire Regiment and although nominally an independent unit, remained a part of the Suffolk Regiment.

The 1/1st Battalion went to France in 1915 and by the end of the year were serving as a training battalion with the 3rd Army School at Flixecourt. The battalion was later to see action on the Somme and at Ypres as part of the 39th Division. The 2/1st Battalion remained in the UK throughout the war. The 3/1st was later merged with the 4th (Reserve) Battalion, Suffolk Regiment to form the Cambridgeshire and Suffolk Reserve Battalion. The 4/1st was also formed which served in the UK until disbandment in 1917.

In 1942 the 1st Battalion served in Malaya and while taking part in the Battle for Singapore Island, was captured by the Japanese.

The battalion was re-formed after the war and in 1947 was transferred to the Royal Artillery as 629 LAA Regiment. It subsequently served in several gunner roles, including as a Para Light Regiment, until October 1956, when it was reconstituted as the 1st Battalion Cambridgeshire Regiment.

In 1961, the battalion was amalgamated with the Suffolk Regiment (TA) to form the Suffolk and Cambridgeshire Regiment. This regiment is now represented as part of the 6th (Volunteer) Battalion, Royal Anglian Regiment.

Cambridgeshire Regiment, c1910. The scarlet tunic has a blue collar and white piping. Both the cap and collar bear the Regimental badge – the Castle of Cambridge superimposed with the Arms of Ely. The version worn on the blue cap also carried a scroll inscribed 'SOUTH AFRICA 1900–01'.

2nd Battalion

The 2nd Cambridgeshires were formed for war service in 1939. They later went to Malaya and were subsequently captured by the Japanese in February 1942.

The London Regiment

The London Regiment existed between 1908 and 1937, and was formed from the various volunteer battalions that existed within the Greater London area. The regiment contained 26 battalions, numbered 1 to 28. The numbers 26 and 27 were intended for the Honourable Artillery Company and the Inns of Court Regiment, who were not satisfied with their positions in the new formation, and chose to ignore them.

The 1st to 8th Battalions were recruited from within the City of London, while the 9th to 28th were spread around the county. A further six battalions were raised during the First World War, numbered 29th to 34th.

Pipers of the 14th (County of London) Battalion, The London Regiment (London Scottish).

10th (County of London) Battalion, The London Regiment (Paddington Rifles), 1910.

With its 26 peace time battalions, the London Regiment was the largest infantry regiment in the army. Battalions were independent of each other and wore their own cap badge. For the first eight years of its existence, the regiment was not connected or attached to any regular regiment.

Until 1916, each battalion was numbered and designated, e.g. 1st (City of London) or 9th (County of London) Battalion, The London Regiment. Battalions were also permitted additional suffixed titles e.g. – (London Irish Rifles).

In 1916, each battalion of the London Regiment became part of a regular regiment, in most instances those that they had served under as volunteers prior to 1908. At this time the original designation of each unit was retained. In 1922, the remaining battalions were given the status of separate regiments, and assumed designations e.g., 1st City of London Regiment (Royal Fusiliers).

Two members of the 2/10th (County of London) Battalion, The London Regiment (Hackney) with captured German machine gun near Sailly Laurette, 8 August 1918.
Imperial War Museum

HM King George VI inspecting a battalion of the London Regiment at the People's Palace, Mile End Road.

The London Regiments finally ceased to exist in 1937, when those units that had not already been reorganised into other roles, were transferred, either as anti-aircraft units of the Royal Artillery, Royal Engineers, or numbered battalions of their regular regiments.

1st Battalion	See 8th Battalion, Royal Fusiliers.
2nd Battalion	See 9th Battalion, Royal Fusiliers.
3rd Battalion	See 10th Battalion, Royal Fusiliers.
4th Battalion	See Royal Fusiliers.
5th Battalion	See 7th and 8th Battalions, Rifle Brigade.
6th Battalion	See City of London Rifles, King's Royal Rifle Corps.
7th Battalion	See Middlesex Regiment.
8th Battalion	See Rifle Brigade.
9th Battalion	See 7th and 8th Battalions, King's Royal Rifle Corps.
10th Battalion (Paddington)	Formed in 1860 at Paddington as the 36th Middlesex Rifle Volunteer Corps, it was re-numbered as 18th in 1880, and the following year was allotted to the Rifle Brigade as one of its volunteer battalions. The battalion became the 10th (County of London) Battalion, London Regiment in 1908 and was disbanded four years later.
10th Battalion (Hackney)	See 5th Battalion, Royal Berkshire Regiment.
11th Battalion	See The Finsbury Rifle, The King's Royal Rifle Corps.
12th Battalion	See 9th and 10th Battalions, The King's Royal Rifle Corps.
13th Battalion	See Princess Louise's Kensington Regiment, The Middlesex Regiment.
14th Battalion	See The London Scottish, The Gordon Highlanders.
15th Battalion	See 11th and 12th Battalions, The King's Royal Rifle Corps.
16th Battalion	See 11th and 12th Battalions, The King's Royal Rifle Corps.
17th Battalion	See 9th and 10th Battalions, Rifle Brigade.
18th Battalion	See The London Irish Rifles, The Royal Ulster Rifles.
19th Battalion	See The Middlesex Regiment.
20th Battalion	See The Queen's Own Royal West Kent Regiment.
21st Battalion	See First Surrey Rifles, The East Surrey Regiment.
22nd Battalion	See 6th Battalion, Queen's Royal West Surrey Regiment.
23rd Battalion	See 7th Battalion, East Surrey Regiment.
24th Battalion	See 7th Battalion, Queen's Royal West Surrey Regiment.
25th Battalion	See Rifle Brigade.
28th Battalion	See 21st Special Air Service Regiment.

FESTIVAL OF EMPIRE KING AND QUEEN SOUTH LONDON

King George V and Queen Mary passing members of the 13th (County of London) Battalion, The London Regiment (Kensington).

29th (City of London) Battalion

Formed in 1916 as 100 and 102 Provisional Battalions (TF), the battalion became 29th London Regiment after amalgamation in 1917, and was disbanded in 1919.

30th (City of London) Battalion

Formed in 1916 as 101 Provisional Battalion (TF), the battalion became 30th London Regiment in 1917 and was disbanded in 1919.

31st (County of London) Battalion

Formed in 1916 as 105 and 107 Provisional Battalions (TF), the battalions amalgamated in 1917 as 31st London Regiment. It was disbanded in the following September.

32nd (County of London) Battalion

Formed in 1916 as 106 and 108 Provisional Battalions (TF), the battalions amalgamated in 1917 as 32nd London Regiment. It was disbanded in 1918.

33rd (City of London) Battalion

See The Rifle Brigade

34th (County of London) Battalion

See the King's Royal Rifle Corps

Above
Drums and Bugles of the 30th (City of London) Battalion, The London
Regiment at Colchester in 1917. **D. Millbery**
Centre
Machine-Gun Section of the 24th (County of London) Battalion, The
London Regiment.
Below
Senior NCOs of the 12th (County of London) Battalion, The London
Regiment (The Rangers).

The Inns of Court Regiment

The Inns of Court had provided a volunteer unit in the early 1800s. At a review of the regiment in 1803, George III, on being told that it consisted entirely of lawyers, dubbed them 'The Devil's Own', a nickname carried to this day and represented in the badges.

The regiment was re-formed at Lincoln's Inn on the 15 February 1860 and again consisted of members of the legal profession belonging to the four Inns. The new unit was designated as the 23rd Middlesex Rifle Volunteer Corps. It was re-numbered as 14th in 1880 and the following year, became a volunteer battalion of the Rifle Brigade.

In 1908 the regiment transferred to the Territorial Force as The Inns of Court Officers Training Corps, undertaking the role of producing officers for the Special Reserve and Territorial Force. At this time the regiment was made up of one squadron of cavalry and three companies of infantry.

During the First World War, between 11,000 and 12,000 men that had served with the Inns of Court received commissions. In 1940 the regiment transferred to the Royal Armoured Corps, as an armoured car unit.

Above
Band of the Inns of Court OTC.
Below
The Bugle-Major and band boys of the 1st Volunteer Battalion, The Bedfordshire Regiment, c1904. The Bugle-Major's rank badges of four inverted chevrons, surmounted by a bugle, can be clearly seen being worn on both arms. The flat head-dress worn is the 'Brodrick' and was introduced to the Army in 1902.

The Hertfordshire Regiment

On 1908, the two volunteer battalions (1st and 2nd) of the Bedfordshire Regiment, then recruited throughout Hertfordshire, were amalgamated as the Hertfordshire Battalion of the Bedfordshire Regiment. Both battalions had originated in 1859, and were formerly the 1st and 2nd Hertfordshire Rifle Volunteer Corps. Each battalion provided contingents for service in South Africa during the Boer War.

The Hertfordshire Battalion was redesignated as a regiment in 1909, and in 1914 was organised into four battalions. The 1/1st Battalion served on the Western Front, while the remaining three remained at home as training and reserve units.

The regiment was increased once again in 1939, this time to two battalions. The 1st Battalion spent a number of months during 1943–4, as part of the garrison at Gibraltar, before moving to Italy and Palestine. The 2nd Battalion remained in the UK until 1944 when as part of 9 Beach Group, it took part in the D Day assault landings at Ver Sur Mer in Normandy.

The two battalions were amalgamated in 1947, and in 1961 formed part of the Bedfordshire and Hertfordshire Regiment (TA). This regiment is now represented in the TA as part of 5th (Volunteer) Battalion, Royal Anglian Regiment.

The Herefordshire Light Infantry

The 1st Admin Battalion of Herefordshire and Radnorshire Rifle Volunteers was formed in 1861, and contained the several rifle companies that were formed by both counties. Amalgamated as 1st Herefordshire Rifle Volunteer Corps in 1880, the battalion became a volunteer battalion of the King's Shropshire Light Infantry in 1881. In 1908, it formed the Herefordshire Battalion of the KSLI, but by the following year, had been redesignated 1st Battalion, The Herefordshire Regiment.

The 1/1st Battalion went to Gallipoli with the 53rd (Welsh) Division in 1915. It later moved to Egypt and then on to France for the last months of the war. The 2/1st and 3/1st remained in the UK as training and reserve units.

Increased to two battalions in 1939, the 1st Herefords served throughout NW Europe during 1944–5. The 2nd Battalion remained at home as part of the 38th Infantry Division.

The Herefordshire Regiment was designated 'Light Infantry' in 1947 and now forms part of the 5th Light Infantry (Volunteers).

Above
Herefordshire Rifle Volunteers at camp in the
1870s. **G. Archer Parfitt**
Below
Sergeant Corey of the 1st Herefordshire Rifle
Volunteer Corps, c1893. Numerous medals
and badges awarded for good shooting are seen
here worn on the left arm.

The Cyclist Battalions

The Essex and Suffolk Cyclist Battalion

See 6th Battalion Suffolk and 8th Battalion Essex Regiments

The Northern Cyclist Battalion

Formed in 1908 at Sunderland as the 8th (Cyclist) Battalion, Northumberland Fusiliers, the battalion became the Northern Cyclist Battalion in 1910 and served as three battalions throughout the UK during the First World War. The battalion was re-formed in 1920 as 3rd (later 55th) Medium Brigade, Royal Garrison Artillery.

The Highland Cyclist Battalion

In 1880, the components of the 2nd Perthshire Admin Battalion of Rifle Volunteers were amalgamated as the 2nd Perthshire Corps consisting of eight companies and headquarters at Birnam.

Redesignated as the 5th (Perthshire Highland) Volunteer Battalion, The Black Watch in 1887, the battalion contributed a number of its members to the several volunteer service companies of the Black Watch that went out to South Africa.

Upon transfer to the Territorial Force, the 5th Volunteer Battalion became the 8th (Cyclist) Battalion, Black Watch. This was changed, however, to the Highland Cyclist Battalion in 1909.

The battalion formed three battalions for home service during the First World War, and in 1920, was converted as part of the Highland Divisional Signals.

The Kent Cyclist Battalion

Formed in 1908 at Tonbridge as the 6th (Cyclist) Battalion, The Queen's Own Royal West Kent Regiment, the battalion was redesignated as the Kent Cyclist Battalion in 1910 and in 1916 went to India. Two additional battalions were formed during the war which remained at home in reserves.

In 1920, the battalion was converted as part of the Royal Artillery.

The Huntingdonshire Cyclist Battalion

See 5th Battalion, Northamptonshire Regiment

The Parachute Regiment

10th (County of London) Battalion

Formed 1947 at Carlton, the battalion is now represented by the 10th (Volunteer) Battalion.

11th Battalion

Formed in 1947 by the amalgamation of the 1/8th and 2/8th Battalions of the Middlesex Regiment, the battalion resumed its Middlesex title as 8th Battalion in 1956.

12th (Yorkshire) Battalion

Formed in 1939 as the 2nd East Riding of Yorkshire Yeomanry, it was redesignated as 10th Battalion, Green Howards in 1940, and transferred to the Parachute Regiment as 12th (Yorkshire) Battalion in 1943. The battalion took part in the Normandy Assault Landings on the 6 June 1944.

When the TA was re-organised in 1947, the 12th Battalion continued service. However, it was considered by the War Office to be a new unit.

The 12th/13th (Yorkshire and Lancashire) Battalion, Parachute Regiment was formed upon amalgamation in 1956 and is now represented by the 4th (Volunteer) Battalion.

13th (Lancashire) Battalion

Raised in 1939 as the 2/4th Battalion, South Lancashire Regiment, it was transferred to the Parachute Regiment as 13th Battalion in 1943, and as such took part in the Assault Landings in Normandy on the 6 June 1944.

The battalion returned in 1947 to the South Lancashire Regiment as 2/4th, and later became 644 LAA/SL Regiment, Royal Artillery.

A new 13th (Lancashire) Battalion was raised at Liverpool in 1947, and formed the 12th/13th (Yorkshire and Lancashire) Battalion upon amalgamation in 1956.

14th Battalion

Formed in 1947 by the transfer of the 5th Battalion, Royal Hampshire Regiment, the battalion returned to its original regiment in 1956.

Above
Presentation of new colours to the 15th (Scottish Volunteer) Battalion, The Parachute Regiment, in 1982. **15 Parachute Regiment**

Below
Colours of the 5th (Volunteer) Battalion, Royal Regiment of Fusiliers passing 10th Battalion, The Parachute Regiment at the Duke of York's Headquarters, Chelsea in 1978. **5th (V) Bn, Royal Regiment of Fusiliers**

15th (Scottish Volunteer) Battalion, The Parachute Regiment in the late 1970s.
15 Parachute Regiment

15th (Scottish) Battalion

Formed at Glasgow in 1947, the battalion is now represented by the 15th (Scottish Volunteer) Battalion.

16th (Welsh) Battalion

Formed 1947, the battalion became the 6th Battalion of the Welsh Regiment in 1956.

17th Battalion (9th Durham Light Infantry)

Formed in 1948 by the transfer of the 9th Battalion, DLI, the battalion is now represented by part of the 4th (Volunteer) Battalion.

18th Battalion

Formed in 1947 by the transfer of the 8th Battalion, Royal Warwickshire Regiment, it returned to its original regiment in 1956.

16th (Lincoln) Independent Parachute Company

This unit was formed in 1950.

Members of 15th (Scottish Volunteer) Battalion, The Parachute Regiment, on exercise with American troops in Southern Germany in the late 1970s.
15 Parachute Regiment

The Special Air Service Regiment

21st (Artists) (Volunteers)

On 25 May 1860, a corps of rifle volunteers was formed and numbered as the 38th Middlesex. The corps included, painters, sculptors, musicians, architects, actors, and other members of artistic occupations.

Re-numbered 20th in 1880, the corps became the 28th (County of London) Battalion, The London Regiment (Artists Rifles), upon transfer to the Territorial Force. During the First World War, the 1/28th and 2/28th Battalions were merged and in addition to active service with the 63rd Division, operated as an officers' training unit, in France. Throughout the war, some 10,256 officers were commissioned after training with the 'Artists'. The 3/28th Battalion, which was formed in 1914, later assumed the title 2/28th, and in 1916 it became the 15th Cadet Battalion, OTC.

The 'Artists' became part of the Rifle Brigade in 1929, assuming the title The Artists Rifles, The Rifle Brigade in 1937. During the Second World War, the battalion served as 163 Officer Cadet Training Unit.

In 1947, the regiment transferred to the Army Air Corps as 21st Battalion (Artists Rifles) Special Air Service. It became part of the SAS Regiment in 1950 and now serves under the title 21st Special Air Service Regiment (Artists) (Volunteers).

23rd Special Air Service Regiment (Volunteers)

Formed in N Africa as No 2 SAS Regiment in 1943, it became part of the Territorial Army in 1947 and designated as 23rd SAS Regiment. Battalion headquarters is in Birmingham.

Above left
Lance Corporal of the Artists Rifles, c1915. Three overseas service chevrons are worn on the lower right arm. **D. Millbery**

Above right
20th Middlesex Rifle Volunteer Corps, c1880. Each man wears riding boots and spurs. The standing figure displays a badge of crossed whips, indicating that his duties include the handling of horsed transport.
Major R. McDuell

Right
Grey helmet of the 38th Middlesex RVC in 1879. Seen in the centre of the 'Maltese Cross' helmet plate is the regimental badge of Mars, God of War, and Minerva, Goddess of the Arts.

Expansion Programme for the Territorial Army 1986–90

The formation of six new battalions of infantry for the Territorial Army was announced in 1984. In the main, each battalion will contain a nucleus provided by existing TA companies. The remainder, it is hoped, will be found from new recruits drawn in by a one and a half million pound campaign that began in September 1985. The proposed titles and organisation of the new units are as follows:

8th (Volunteer) Battalion The Queen's Fusiliers (City of London)

Comprising a new HQ and A Company together with the present B Coy, 6/7th (Volunteer) Bn The Queen's Regt at Edgware and C Coy, 5th (Volunteer) Bn The Royal Regiment of Fusiliers at Balham.

1st Battalion The Yorkshire and Cleveland Volunteers

Comprising new A, C and D Coys, together with HQ at York, now the battalion HQ of the 1st Bn Yorkshire Volunteers, and the present B Coy, 1st Bn Yorkshire Volunteers at Middlesbrough.

3rd Battalion The Devon and Cornwall Rifle Volunteers

A new HQ will be formed at Plymouth and will take under command the present C and D Coys, 6th Bn The Light Infantry (Volunteers) at Cambourne and Truro respectively, and E Coy, 1st Bn The Wessex Regiment (Rifle Volunteers) at Exeter.

3rd (Volunteer) Battalion The Cheshire Regiment

Comprising a new HQ at Runcorn A and B and D Coys, together with the present A Coy, 1st Bn The Mercian Volunteers at Stockport and C Coy, 2nd Bn the Mercian Volunteers at Ellesmere Port.

8th Battalion The Light Infantry (Volunteers)

The battalion HQ will be at Wakefield and will take under command the present A and B Coys, 5th Bn The Light Infantry (Volunteers) at Wakefield and Pontefract together with a new C Coy at Batley and D Coy.

5th (Volunteer) Battalion The Royal Green Jackets

Consisting of a new battalion HQ at Oxford and the present A and D Coys of the 4th (Volunteer) Bn Royal Green Jackets at Oxford and Aylesbury as A and B Coys. Other companies will be newly raised.

Select Bibliography

OFFICIAL PUBLICATIONS.
Army Council Instructions.
Army Lists.
Army Orders.

Revised Titles and Designations of Major Units of the Territorial Army, War Office, 1951.
Territorial Force Regulations.
Territorial Army Regulations.
Territorial Year Book, London, Hodder & Stoughton, 1909.
Volunteer Force Regulations.

GENERAL WORKS.
Bulletins of the Military Historical Society (Various editions).
Regimental and Unit Histories (Various).
Register of the Victoria Cross, Cheltenham, This England, 1981.

BECKE, Major A. F., *Order of Battle of Divisions,* London, HMSO, 1935–44.
BECKETT, I. F. W., *Riflemen Form,* Aldershot, Ogilby Trusts, 1982.
EDWARDS, Major T. J., *Regimental Badges,* Aldershot, Gale & Polden, 1951–68 (5 editions).
EDWARDS, Major, T. J., *Regimental Badges,* London, Charles Knight, 1974.
FREDERICK, J. B. M., *Lineage Book of the British Army,* New York, Hope Farm Press, 1969.
GAILEY, GILLESPIE, HASSETT, *An Account of the Territorials in Northern Ireland 1947–78, TAVR Association of Northern Ireland, 1979.*
GAYLOR, John, *Military Badge Collecting,* London, Seeley Service, 1971.
GRIERSON, Lieut.-General Sir James Moncrieff, *Records of the Scottish Volunteer Force 1859–1908,* Edinburgh and London, William Blackwood & Sons, 1909.
JAMES, Brigadier E. A., *Historical Records of the British Infantry Regiments in the Great War,* London, Samson, 1976.
JOSLEN, Lieut.-Colonel H. F., *Orders of Battle 1939–45,* London, HMSO, 1960.
RICHARDS, W., *His Majesty's Territorial Army,* London, Virtue & Co., 1910–11.
WESTLAKE, R. A., *The Rifle Volunteers,* Chippenham, Picton Publishing, 1982.
YOUNG, Brigadier P., *A Dictionary of Battles 1816–1976,* New York, Mayflower Books, 1977

Acknowledgements

I would like to thank the following museums and individuals for their help in providing information and photographs for this book: National Army Museum, Imperial War Museum, 5th (V) Bn. Royal Regiment of Fusiliers, Green Howards, Argyll and Sutherland Highlanders, 15th (Scottish Volunteer) Battalion, Parachute Regiment, King's Own Royal Border Regiment, Lancashire Fusiliers, King's Own Scottish Borderers, Leeds Rifles, Liverpool Scottish, Somerset Light Infantry, York Castle, Harringey Archives Committee. Lt. Col. D. J. Bottomley MBE, Lt. Col. G. P. Wood MC, Lt. Col. R. K. May, Lt. Col. D. C. Ward, Lt. Col. R. G. Woodhouse, Major J. McQ. Hallam, Major R. Wilson, Major R. McDuell, Capt. A. Grant, K. Goodson, G. Archer Parfitt, D. J. Barnes, P. Bronson, D. Millbery, R. J. Marrion, S. Kretschmer, A. H. Mayle, J. B. McKay, W. Younghusband, D. Reeves, B. Boon, E. Dickinson.

Regimental and Unit Index

For numbered volunteer and territorial battalions see under parent regiment.
Illustrations are indicated within brackets.

General Index

References to active service in the following theatres of war throughout the Battalions section have been omitted: France, Belgium, N W Europe, Africa, India, Egypt, Palestine, Gallipoli, Italy, Sicily.